Courtesy of The Port of New York Authority

THE CONSTITUTION OF THE UNITED STATES

ITS SOURCES AND ITS APPLICATION

BY

THOMAS JAMES NORTON

COMMITTEE FOR CONSTITUTIONAL GOVERNMENT, INC.

117 Liberty Street

New York 6, New York

First Printing January 1941
Second Printing March 1941
Third Printing August 1941
Fourth Printing September 1941
Fifth Printing August 1942
Sixth Printing March 1943
Seventh Printing March 1943
Eighth Printing June 1943
Ninth Printing September 1944
Tenth Printing November 1945
Eleventh Printing April 1946
Twelfth Printing September 1947
Thirteenth Printing April 1949
Fourteenth Printing March 1951
Fifteenth Printing March 1952
Sixteenth Printing February 1956
Seventeenth Printing April 1960
Eighteenth Printing October 1960
Nineteenth Printing September 1961
Twentieth Printing January 1962
Twenty-first Printing April 1962
Twenty-second Printing October 1962
Twenty-third Printing November 1962

COMMITTEE FOR CONSTITUTIONAL GOVERNMENT, INC.
117 Liberty Street, New York 6, New York

Our Constitution — Civil Bible of America

Menaced by collectivist trends, we must seek revival of our strength in the spiritual foundations which are the bedrock of our republic. Democracy is the outgrowth of the religious conviction of the sacredness of every human life. On the religious side, its highest embodiment is the Bible; on the political, the Constitution. As has been said so well, "The Constitution is the civil bible of Americans." Next to the Bible, the best book on the Constitution should be in every home, school, library and parish hall.

HERBERT C. HOOVER

JAMES M. COX

ALFRED E. SMITH

JOHN W. DAVIS

ALFRED M. LANDON

MRS. WILLIAM H. TAFT

MRS. CALVIN COOLIDGE

MRS. BENJAMIN HARRISON

MRS. THEODORE ROOSEVELT

MRS. THOMAS J. PRESTON, JR.
(MRS. GROVER CLEVELAND)

"This government, the offspring of our own choice, uninfluenced and unawed, adopted upon full investigation and mature deliberation, completely free in its principles, in the distribution of its powers uniting securely with energy, and containing within itself a provision for its own amendment, has a just claim to your confidence and support."

GEORGE WASHINGTON, "Farewell Address."

"For I think it an undeniable position that a competent knowledge of the laws of that society in which we live is the proper accomplishment of every gentleman and scholar, an highly useful, I had almost said essential, part of liberal and polite education."

WILLIAM BLACKSTONE.

"Civil governments, in their first institution, are voluntary associations for mutual defense. To obtain the desired end it is absolutely necessary that each individual should conceive himself obliged to submit his private opinion and actions to the judgment of the greater number of his associates."

GIBBONS "Decline and Fall of the Roman Empire." Vol. I, ch. IX.

PREFACE

To Special Edition

IN this era of world-wide social and political change, it behooves us, as never before, to know the fundamentals of our Constitution which, in times of stress as well as in peace, has provided the American people with a more enduring and practical government, and a greater degree of prosperity than any other people have ever had.

The Constitution is of particular importance to men and women in the armed services of the United States. Whereas sworn allegiance to the Constitution is not formally required of private citizens, every one who served in our military and naval forces in World War II took an oath of direct or indirect adherence to that document. Every commissioned officer, like every elected or appointed official of the United States Government, swore " true faith and allegiance " to the Constitution and pledged to "support and defend" it "against all enemies, foreign and domestic." And the oath of enlistment of all non-commissioned personnel pledges obedience to "the orders of the officers appointed over me . . ." namely, those who had sworn allegiance to the Constitution.

But the importance of the Constitution to those who served in World War II does not end with oaths of allegiance. War veterans have preferment by law over non-veterans in civil service. A record of war service is often a helpful qualification of candidates for elective offices. A big proportion of members of Congress are veterans of World War I. In the hands of the 13,000,000—roughly one-tenth of our entire total national population—who served this country in World War II rests in large part the future destinies of our country. America will be safe as long as these service men and women are familiar with the Constitution they swore to support and defend "against all enemies."

The purpose of this book is to make accessible to every citizen such knowledge of the Constitution of the United States as will serve him well, in peace or war. But the means of acquiring the information essential to stalwart citizenship never has been available in practical and simple form to the mass of the people.

"Almost every provision in that instrument," said a great jurist, "has a history that must be understood before the brief and sententious language employed can be comprehended in the relations its authors intended."

The simple plan of this book is to explain the Constitution by a note to every line or clause that has a story or drama from history back of it, or that has contributed during the 156 years of our life under this document to the welfare of mankind. This method leaves the text of the Constitution and the Amendments in unbroken connection, so that the whole great design is plainly seen as the explanation appears immediately under the part to be explained. In addition to showing the historic sources of particular provisions of the Constitution examples are also given of the application of the clauses in great matters which have arisen during our nation's life.

One who reads closely the full explanation in the text will discover that each clause or word in the Constitution was carefully designed to protect the individual—his life, his liberty and his property. By a few, the erroneous belief has been spread that the Constitution is a barrier in the way of American progress. Actually, the Constitution is a coat of mail which man himself fashioned for his own protection, and which he has changed from time to time that the protection might be the more complete—protection against the abuse of power by his servants in the legislature or Congress, whom he may dismiss at election time or by impeachment, and against whose invasion of his rights he can appeal to the courts; against his executive officers, whom he may dismiss by impeachment or by ballot; against his judges, whom he may remove for lack of "good behavior." His government is not his master, as the king or the dictator has always been, but his servant.

"In questions of power, then," wrote Jefferson, "let no more be heard of confidence in man, but bind him down from mischief by the chains of the Constitution."

The founders of the Republic feared abuse of power by political parties as much as they did abuses by kings. "Wherever there is an interest and power to do wrong," wrote Madison to Jefferson in 1788, "wrong will generally be done, and not less readily by a powerful and interested party than by a powerful and interested prince."

Our Constitution has exerted wide influence upon other nations. Canada, Mexico, the five republics of Central America, nine South American republics, the Commonwealth of Australia and the Union of South Africa have adopted constitutions patterned to a greater or less degree after ours. France, Belgium, and Switzerland have embodied in their constitutions many provisions first employed in ours. So also the German Constitution following World War I. So also, we hope, other countries following the war just ended at the cost of sacrifice and devotion by millions who are proud of the title American.

In the twenty-three years since the first edition of this book, many countries of the world have undergone political changes of a revolutionary character. Even as this revised edition goes to press, peoples in many foreign lands are choosing not only new leaders but new forms of government. For example, the French are now preparing a new constitution to supplant the one in force since 1875. Although recently brought up to date by the author, references in the text to constitutions in other countries may need to be read in the light of this morning's newspapers.

It will be seen that the underlying principles of our Constitution were not formulated in a day. When our forefathers declared their independence some of the colonists had lived under written charters from the English Crown for one hundred sixty-nine years, or thirteen years longer than we have lived (1945) under the present Constitution. During that long period many of the Colonies were practically self-governed. The English historian Lecky ("England in the Eighteenth Century") says that all of them enjoyed greater privileges in this respect than did the English people themselves. Many leading principles of the Constitution were adaptations of what the colonists had worked out in experience while they were subjects of the English government. After the Declaration of Independence the thirteen States framed constitutions of their own from which many important provisions were borrowed by the Constitutional Convention and made a part of our fundamental law. Many other provisions of our Constitution merely re-state ancient principles of English law which had served the cause of freedom for generations. Our Constitution was "far brought from out the storied past."

In the Constitutional Convention there were men of extraordinary ability and experience, like Washington, Franklin, and Hamilton. There were men who had studied law at the Inner Temple in London, who had been educated in the University of Edinburgh, who had been graduated from American colleges, who had been governors of States, chief justices of supreme courts, and men who had achieved distinction at the bar and in business life. Of the fifty-five members of the Constitutional Convention, thirty-one were lawyers. Blackstone's Commentaries were taught by Chancellor Wythe in William and Mary College before the Declaration of Independence. John Marshall, Thomas Jefferson, and James Monroe were among his pupils.

The task of the Constitutional Convention was not to construct a government from the foundation up. There had already been firmly set by experience thirteen basestones in the form of State republican governments. Upon these, and for the benefit of their population as a whole, the National structure was placed. This super-government was to deal with foreign nations, and also to administer at home all matters of National (as distinguished from State or local) character. The National government was to be supreme in its domain, and the State governments were to be sovereign in all affairs not National or foreign. As will be seen, this duality, while conducing to a happy balancing of governmental powers, has at the same time been the strongest force in political and material advancement. For the Nation has learned from the States, as they have learned from one another and from the Nation.

In many ways the competition of the States has been vitalizing and progressive. It is a question whether a vast republic not having such political subdivisions could long stand.

It is not generally mentioned that our present fundamental law is the second written form of government of the United States. The first was called the Articles of Confederation. The Articles went into effect as a government of "the United States of America" in 1781. In 1777, less than a year after the Declaration of Independence, the Articles which had been drafted were adopted by the Convention chosen by the Continental Congress to frame them.

But, owing mostly to disputes regarding western lands (the royal grants to the Colonies reaching westward indefinitely), the last State did not give its ratification until 1781. The Articles were so inadequate that within four years plans originated at Mount Vernon to remodel them. Washington and a company of statesmen recommended the calling of a convention the next year (1786) at Annapolis. Five States only sent representatives and, therefore, the Convention adjourned to the next year at Philadelphia. All the States except Rhode Island were then present by representatives. Washington, a delegate from Virginia, was chosen to preside. "Let us raise a standard to which the wise and honest can repair," he said; "the event is in the hand of God." The Convention, which had been called to remodel the Articles of Confederation, cast them aside and drafted an entirely new instrument.

I believe that this is the greatest and simplest one-volume text on the most successful government free men have ever established. I am proud to urge its earnest study by my fellow-Americans.

SAMUEL B. PETTENGILL

SOUTH BEND, INDIANA
November, 1945

CONTENTS

Articles XIII–XV, Known as the Civil War Amendments

Contents

SOURCES OF ILLUSTRATIONS

Charles Phelps Cushing: Page 8, opposite pages 30, 50, page 130, opposite page 140, pages 154, 155, opposite pages 170, 171, 202, 203, 220, 221, 258, 259.

Acme Photos: Opposite page 51, pages 71, 98, opposite pages 114, 115, 141.

Culver Service: Opposite page 31, page 193.

H. E. Homan: Page 270.

CONSTITUTION OF THE UNITED STATES OF AMERICA

ADOPTED JULY 2, 1788

IN EFFECT MARCH 4, 1789

THE PREAMBLE

WE THE PEOPLE of the United States,[1]

[1] It is important to notice that this is a government of the people, not of the States. Under the Articles of Confederation, in effect as our first form of government from 1781 to 1789, the States as political entities, and not the people, entered into "a firm league of friendship", each State retaining "its sovereignty, freedom and independence." The new Constitution brought in a new Nation, deriving its "just powers from the consent of the governed."

"The people, the highest authority known to our system," said President Monroe, "from whom all our institutions spring and on whom they depend, formed it."

"Its language, 'We the people,' is the institution of one great consolidated National government of the people of all the States, instead of a government by compact with the States for its agents," exclaimed Patrick Henry in the Virginia ratifying convention while leading opposition to its adoption. "The people gave the [Constitutional] Convention no power to use their name." Some States restricted the authority of their delegates to revising the Articles of Confederation. It was claimed that the casting aside of the Articles of Confederation (which could be altered or amended only by the concurrence of every State) for a constitution to become effective when adopted by nine of the thirteen States was revolutionary. Revision only was uppermost in the minds of many. On February 21, 1787, the Congress existing under the Articles called a convention "for the sole and express purpose of revising the Articles of Confederation and reporting to Congress and the several legislatures such alterations and provisions therein as shall, when agreed to in Congress and confirmed by the States, render the federal Constitution adequate to the exigencies of government and the preservation of the Union." But it was the belief of the Constitutional Convention that as the new instrument was to go to the people for ratification or rejection, the objections stated by Henry and others were really unimportant.

in Order to form a more perfect Union,[2]

[2] Meaning "a more perfect union" than had been achieved by the Articles of Confederation.

"In the efficacy and permanency of your Union," wrote Washington in his Farewell Address, "a government for the whole is indispensable. . . . Sensible of this momentous truth you have improved upon your first essay [the Articles of Confederation] by the adoption of a Constitution of government better calculated than your former for an intimate Union and for the efficacious management of your common concerns."

The Union, made "more perfect" by the Constitution, was nevertheless in later times said to be dissoluble at the pleasure of any State that might desire to secede. In his Farewell Address (1796) Washington had called upon the people "indignantly" to frown "upon the first dawning of every attempt to alienate any portion of our country from the rest or to enfeeble the sacred ties which now link together the various parts." To put the question beyond controversy it required a four-year Civil War, after the secession of the southern States, beginning with that of South Carolina in December, 1860, following the election of Abraham Lincoln to the Presidency in the preceding month.

In a great debate in the Senate between Daniel Webster of Massachusetts and John C. Calhoun of South Carolina, the former contended that the National Government, through its Supreme Court, is the ultimate expounder of its own powers, while the latter stood for what was known as the doctrine of States' Rights and argued for the right of the individual State, under its reserved sovereignty (Note 163), to determine such questions for itself, as South Carolina had done (1832) by an ordinance declaring null a tariff law of Congress. Secession, he said, was the State's remedy of last resort. Of Calhoun's theory, and of the historic facts with which it assumed to deal, President Lincoln said, in a message (July 4, 1861) to a special session of Congress called to prepare for the Civil War:

"The States have their status in the Union, and they have no other legal status. If they break from this, they can only do so against law and by revolution. The Union, and not themselves separately, procured their independence and their liberty. By conquest or purchase the Union gave each of them whatever of independence and liberty it has. The Union is older than any of the States, and, in fact, it created them as States."

The citizen was not, under the theory of States' Rights, in contact with the National Government. He owed allegiance to his State, and the State, in turn, dealt with the Nation. After the Civil War the Fourteenth Amendment set that theory aside by declaring: "All persons born or naturalized in the United States, and subject to the jurisdiction thereof, are citizens of the United States and of the State wherein they reside." Every citizen now owes an allegiance to the Nation as well as to the State.

It is interesting to notice with what singular clearness James Wilson of Pennsylvania, a scholar from Edinburgh, laid down in the Constitutional Convention the doctrine which was, eighty years later, removed from debate by the Fourteenth Amendment (Note 171), the question under discussion being whether the State or the people should be represented in the Senate:

"A citizen of America is a citizen of the general government, and is a citizen of the particular State in which he may reside. . . . In forming the general government we must forego our local habits and attachments, lay aside our State connections, and act for the general good of the whole. The general government is not an assemblage of States, but of individuals."

Profiting by the experience of our country, the United States of Brazil, which was established in 1890, after the overthrow of a monarchy, carefully provided, in a constitution closely copying the fundamentals of ours, for a "perpetual and *indissoluble* union between former provinces into the United States of Brazil." And in 1900, when the various provinces of Australia were united as the Commonwealth of Australia, the Constitution, also closely following ours and adopting our terms, "State," "House of Representatives," and "Senate", provided for an "*indissoluble* Federal Commonwealth."

establish Justice, insure domestic Tranquillity, provide for the common defence,[3]

[3] Under the Articles of Confederation the expenses of the common defence were to "be defrayed out of a common treasury" supplied "by the authority and direction of the legislatures of the several States." The Nation itself had no power of self-defence in the raising of money and in some other important respects. It turned out in practice that some of the States signally failed in emergencies to make their contributions to the "common treas-

ury." Indeed, only New York and Pennsylvania paid their full proportion of the costs of the Revolution. One State, which had suffered none from the ravages of war, contributed nothing. But (to illustrate the difference between a league of States and a Nation) when the United States entered the World War in 1917 the Congress promptly exerted its power under the Constitution and raised by the issue of Liberty Bonds, by income taxes, and by other means all the money that it needed for "the common defence." The States as such were not concerned except in providing militia, a subject to be noticed later. So it had been in the War of 1812, in the Mexican War, in the Civil War, and in the War with Spain. The Articles of Confederation were wholly deficient in this most important of all respects, in the power of "common defence."

promote the general Welfare, and secure the Blessings[4] of Liberty to ourselves and our Posterity, do ordain and establish this CONSTITUTION for the United States of America.

[4] Comment has been made that God is not mentioned in our Constitution. In the Declaration of Independence "firm reliance on the protection of Divine Providence" is expressed, and in the Articles of Confederation it is mentioned that "it has pleased the Great Governor of the world to incline the hearts of the legislatures we respectively represent in Congress to approve of and to authorize us to ratify the said Articles of Confederation and perpetual union."

The Commonwealth of Australia put in the preamble of the Constitution which it submitted to the English Parliament for approval (1900) that "Whereas, the people of New South Wales, Victoria, South Australia, Queensland, and Tasmania, humbly relying on the blessings of Almighty God, have agreed to unite," etc.

A very interesting discussion of the proposition that "this is a religious people" is contained in a decision of the Supreme Court of the United States (1892) holding that the Alien Contract Labor Law of 1885 (prohibiting the bringing in of "foreigners and aliens under contract or agreement to perform labor in the United States"), while applying to an alien brought in to perform "labor or *service* of *any* kind", did not relate in purpose — although it did in language — to a minister of the Gospel who had been employed to come from England to accept service in a New York church. In applying the rule of statutory interpretation, that the intent of the legislature must be followed, the court said that "no purpose of action against religion could be imputed to any legislation" when the language did not clearly state it, for the reason that from the commission given by Ferdinand and Isabella to Columbus down through all the charters to the colonies, as well as in the Declaration of Independence and in the constitutions of all the States, there is to be found a "profound reverence for religion and an assumption that its influence in all human affairs is essential to the well-being of the United States."

ARTICLE I

Section 1. All legislative Powers herein granted shall be vested in a Congress of the United States, which shall consist of a Senate and House of Representatives.[5]

[5] "The whole system of the National Government," said President Monroe, speaking of the powers given by the Constitution to Congress, "may be said to rest essentially on the powers granted to this branch. They mark the limit within which, with few exceptions, all the branches must move in the discharge of their respective functions."

In the Colonial Declaration of Rights of October 14, 1774, it was said to be indispensably necessary to good government that "the constituent branches of the legislature be independent of each other."

It was in the reign of Edward III (1341) that the Parliament of England divided into two Houses.

The Congress which had existed under the Articles of Confederation consisted of only one House, which was made up of "delegates . . . appointed in such manner as the legislature of each State shall direct", who might be replaced by others at any time within the year for which they were chosen. A Congress consisting of two Houses makes the first fundamental difference between the new Constitution and the Articles of Confederation. In the Constitutional Convention the first resolution adopted declared for a Congress of two Houses.

Section 2. The House of Representatives shall be composed of Members chosen every second Year [6]

[6] As already noted, the Congressmen under the former government were chosen for one year and were changeable in the meantime at the pleasure of the State.

"All legislative Powers . . . shall be vested in a Congress. ."

By an act of the English Parliament in 1694 the term of a member of the House of Commons was fixed at three years. In 1716 the Septennial Act was passed extending the term to seven years. Because it extended the term of the members who passed it instead of applying to future Parliaments, and because it was intended to keep a party longer in power than the time for which the members were elected by the people, some authorities considered it illegal. The Parliament Act of 1911 reduced the term from seven years to five.

Congress, unlike Parliament, is, by virtue of this clause, without power to fix its term.

In France the term of a member of the House of Deputies is four years. A member of the House of Commons in Canada sits for five years, and the term in the Australian House of Representatives is three years.

by the People [7] of the several States

[7] Emphasis should be here laid upon the fact that ours is the only government in the world in which all the chief constitutional officers of the Executive and Legislative Departments are elected by the votes of the people. It stands unprecedented and unparalleled as a "government of the people, by the people, for the people." Even in the countries which have closely patterned their governments on our Constitution, the election of officials is not so general. Thus in Canada, in Australia, and in South Africa the Governor General is appointed by the English sovereign. In the Republic of France the President is chosen by the Senate and the Chamber of Deputies sitting together as the National Assembly. In Brazil the senators are chosen by the legislature (as ours once were) instead of being elected by the people.

and the Electors in each State shall have the Qualifications requisite for Electors of the most numerous Branch of the State Legislature.[8]

⁸ The property qualifications of the voters in the different States, as well as other requirements, were so various that it was concluded to let the practice in each State determine who should be qualified to vote for a candidate for a seat in the National House of Representatives. "To have reduced the different qualifications in the different States to one uniform rule," wrote Hamilton in the "Federalist", "would probably have been as dissatisfactory to some of the States as it would have been difficult to the Convention."

No Person shall be a Representative who shall not have attained to the Age of twenty-five Years, and been seven Years a Citizen of the United States, and who shall not, when elected, be an Inhabitant ⁹ of that State in which he shall be chosen.

⁹ A member of the English House of Commons need not be an inhabitant or even a resident of the district of his constituency.

This limitation had no reference to sex; and therefore it was permissible for a congressional district in a State to elect a woman to a seat in Congress. The first woman thus to be distinguished was Miss Jeannette Rankin of Montana, who was elected to the National House of Representatives in 1916, four years before the adoption of the Nineteenth Amendment (Note 187) gave suffrage to women under both State citizenship (where the State had not already granted it) and National citizenship.

Representatives and direct Taxes ¹⁰ shall be apportioned among the several States which may be included within this Union, according to their respective Numbers,

¹⁰ Confusion and contention springing from this language brought about the adoption in 1913 of the Sixteenth Amendment (Note 182), which gives Congress power "to lay and collect taxes on incomes, from whatever source derived,

without apportionment among the several States, and without regard to any census or enumeration."

Although in the Constitutional Convention there was some question of the meaning of direct taxes, Congress early placed an interpretation upon the term by an act (July 14, 1798) "to lay and collect a direct tax within the United States."

This act had been preceded five days by an act "to provide for the valuation of Lands and Dwelling-houses, and the enumeration of slaves within the United States."

A tax of two mills was by the laws mentioned laid on buildings worth from one hundred dollars to five hundred dollars; and this was graduated up as high as ten mills on houses valued at thirty thousand dollars or more. A tax of fifty cents was laid on each slave.

In 1880, in upholding the Income Tax laws of 1864–1865, the Supreme Court pointed out that whenever the Government had imposed a direct tax it had never applied it except to real estate and slaves.

The Income Tax Law of 1894 imposed (with other taxes) a tax on the rent or income from land. But the tax on the income from land was not apportioned among or allotted to the States according to population, as other direct taxes always had been. In 1895, the question having been raised by numerous taxpayers, the Supreme Court held that the tax upon the income from land was in reality a tax on the land itself and therefore a direct tax which should have been apportioned in accordance with the command of the Constitution. It was held on rehearing that as in English history, and also in Canadian cases arising under a constitution with a provision like that in ours, an income tax had been treated as a direct tax, it was therefore necessary to apportion the income tax as to incomes from personal property as well as to incomes from land. Fourteen years thereafter the Sixteenth Amendment was proposed by Congress to permit the taxation of income from whatever source derived without apportionment according to the population as ascertained by the census. The Amendment had been pending for over three and one half years when it received the ratification of the requisite number of States to make it a part of the Constitution.

which shall be determined by adding to the whole Number of free Persons, including those bound to Service for a Term of Years, and excluding Indians not taxed, three fifths of all other Persons.[11]

[11] Referring to slaves. The word slave or slavery does not appear in our Constitution until we reach the Thirteenth Amendment, adopted (1865) after the Civil War. This is the first of the three "compromises of the Constitution" (Notes 61 and 121), which have been called the beginning of the Civil War that burst in fury three quarters of a century after. Although slaves were not citizens or voters, the number of them was considered in laying direct taxes and in ascertaining how many members a State should have in the House of Representatives. The fraction "three fifths" had been agreed upon in Congress three years before, when the question was whether, in the levy of direct taxes, slave-holding States would be undertaxed (as Northern men contended) by not counting the slaves as population or overtaxed (as the South claimed) by counting them. The compromise then made as to taxation was employed as to representation in the House. While these compromises were under discussion at Philadelphia the last Congress under the Articles of Confederation, sitting at New York, passed the ordinance creating the Northwest Territory (later Ohio, Indiana, Illinois, Michigan, and Wisconsin) and forbidding that slavery ever exist within its limits. Fiske (" Critical Period in American History ") says that in 1787 slavery was a cloud no larger than a man's hand. The institution had been

dying slowly for fifty years. It had become extinct in Massachusetts and in nearly all other northern States, and it had just been prohibited by Congress in the National domain. In Virginia and Maryland there was a strong party of abolition and the movement had also gained some strength in North Carolina. It was only in the rice swamps of the far South that slave labor was wanted. The slave States, for receiving a disproportionate representation in the House of Representatives on account of their slave population, gave their support in the Convention to the Constitution; and when the abolition of the slave trade was postponed by one clause for twenty years (Note 61) the South agreed in return to the commerce clause (Note 45) providing for absolutely free trade between the States. In the Constitutional Convention George Mason of Virginia and other southern delegates spoke severely against slavery.

Virginia contributed to the Union a large part of the Northwest Territory, and delegates from Virginia in Congress under the Articles of Confederation aided in drafting the ordinance which forever prohibited slavery in that domain. The ordinance received the votes of delegates from Virginia, Georgia, South Carolina, and North Carolina, as well as those from Delaware, New Jersey, New York, and Massachusetts.

But the invention of the cotton gin, which could clean as much cotton as two hundred slaves, and the coming in of spinning machinery, changed the course of events.

The actual Enumeration shall be made within three Years after the first Meeting of the Congress of the United States, and within every subsequent Term of ten Years, in such Manner as they shall by Law direct.[12]

[12] Under acts of Congress a complete census has been taken every ten years, the last in 1940. The census of

1790 showed a total population of ˙3,929,326, of which 679,681 were slaves. The population of the United States in 1940 was 131, 409, 881.

The Number of Representatives shall not exceed one for every thirty Thousand,[13] but each State shall have at Least one Representative;

[13] The number of people entitling a State to have a representative in the lower House of Congress has been changed from time to time after the decennial census. In 1921 each State had one member of the House of Representatives for every 211,877. After the census of 1920 a bill to increase the number of members of the House of Representatives from 435 to 483 was defeated, and in 1921 another bill failed to pass which proposed to increase the number of members to 450.

and until such enumeration shall be made, the State of New Hampshire shall be entitled to chuse three, Massachusetts eight, Rhode-Island and Providence Plantations one, Connecticut five, New-York six, New Jersey four, Pennsylvania eight, Delaware one, Maryland six, Virginia ten, North Carolina five, South Carolina five, and Georgia three.[14]

[14] That would have made a House of sixty-five members. But Rhode Island and North Carolina did not ratify the Constitution until after the new government had gone into effect. In 1940 the House had a membership of 435.

When vacancies happen in the Representation from any State, the Executive Authority thereof shall issue Writs of Election to fill such Vacancies.[15]

[15] It often happens that the governor of a State must call a special election for choosing a member of the House of Representatives to take the place of one who resigned or died.

The House of Representatives shall chuse their Speaker [16] **and other Officers;**

[16] So in England, in Canada, in Australia, and in South Africa the presiding officer of the House is elected by the members, and also in the Argentine Republic and in Brazil. In England the Speaker of the House of Commons is to a degree nonpartisan, usually holding office through successive administrations.

and shall have the sole Power of Impeachment. [17]

[17] The House formulates the charge against the official and reduces it to writing. Then the Senate sits as a court (with the Chief Justice of the United States presiding when the accused is the President) and hears the witnesses and pronounces judgment. It is to be said with pride that there have been but few impeachments in our history. One judge of a United States Court was impeached, tried and removed for drunkenness, another for disloyalty during the Civil War, and a third for conduct not becoming to a judge. A member of President Grant's Cabinet was impeached by the House of Representatives, but as he resigned the Senate did not convict him.

The great impeachment was that of President Andrew Johnson, which the House of Representatives brought on February 24, 1868. The President and the Congress had been in passionate conflict over the reconstruction of the southern States which had seceded from the Union and which had been overcome in the Civil War. It was the belief of the President that he, as commander in chief of the victorious army and navy (Note 85) and possessed under the Constitution of the pardoning power (Note 87), which he had exercised toward those lately in hostile arms, should supervise and control the return of the southern States, which had never been legally out of the Union. He claimed to be carrying out the plan of

Lincoln.   But Congress, insisting that it had the authority, and that as many of the southern States had enacted vagrancy laws and other statutes designed to put the liberated Negro practically in his former state of bondage, it became its duty to effectuate the decision reached by war, passed two Reconstruction Acts over the President's veto.   The President denounced the acts as not only unconstitutional but as also indefensibly harsh, especially as they affected a great number of people in the southern States who had been loyal to the Union.   In 1867 Congress passed over the President's veto the Tenure of Office Act, which forbade him to remove his appointees to office without the consent of the Senate, which is required by the Constitution to approve (Note 89) the appointments. That Act of Congress was in disregard of an early congressional interpretation of the Constitutional clause cited and of the practice which had been sanctioned through the administration of sixteen Presidents.   President Johnson transgressed the Act by removing Edwin M. Stanton, Secretary of War, who was openly hostile to the reconstruction policy of his chief.   For this the House of Representatives voted articles of impeachment, and from March 5, 1868, to May 16 the Senate sat as a trial court, Chief Justice Salmon P. Chase presiding.   The managers of the impeachment failed to secure the two-thirds vote necessary under the Constitution to convict (Note 24).

In messages to Congress President Grant and President Hayes requested the repeal of the Tenure of Office Act. It remained upon the statute book until Cleveland's administration, when (1886) that Executive sternly refused to give to the Senate his reasons for removing an official whose appointment the Senate had of course confirmed.   He said that it was his duty to maintain the Chief Magistracy "unimpaired in all its dignity and vigor"; and he denied "that the Senate has the right in any case to review the act of the Executive in removing or suspending a public officer." Later (1887) the Tenure of Office Act, which had been the basis of the impeachment of President Johnson, was repealed by Congress.

A humorous writer of the day who was opposed to the theories of President Johnson, as expressed in a series of speeches by the Executive, said that the President was trying "to arouse the people to the danger of *concentrating* power in the hands of Congress instead of *diffusing* it through one man."

Section 3. The Senate of the United States shall be composed of two Senators from each State, [18]

[18] It has already been remarked that the Congress under the Articles of Confederation consisted of only one House. The provision for two senators from each State, regardless of size or population, while population was to determine the number of members in the House of Representatives, was agreed to so that the smaller States might not be overborne in both Houses of Congress by the votes of the larger States. Besides, it was desired that the States as political organizations be represented in Congress. So at loggerheads over this were the large States and the small States that more than once the Constitutional Convention was at the point of breaking up. Benjamin Franklin was so affected by the disagreement that he suggested that the meetings be opened with prayer. Lord Bryce says that the Americans invented this plan of having one House represent the people directly on the basis of population, and the other (the Senate) represent the States on the basis of State equality as autonomous communities. He believes that it was this device which made federation possible in the United States. The device has been adopted in many other countries.

In 1890 the United States of Brazil followed our example and provided in its Constitution for the equality of the States in the Senate, while the number of members in the

Chamber of Deputies is determined by population.   Brazil
has three senators from each State chosen by the State
legislature (as ours were chosen before the adoption
of the Seventeenth Amendment in 1913) for a term of
nine years, one third of the number going out of office
every three years, instead of every two years, as our
senators go out.

The Constitution of Canada (North America Act of
the British Parliament of 1867) contains provisions for
keeping the provinces in a definite (though not equal) relationship in the Senate.

In the Commonwealth of Australia the Constitution
(1900) provides for not less than six senators from each of
the five States, whose term is six years.   One half of the
senators go out every three years.   Parliament may increase the number of senators from each State, but it cannot impair the relationship of the States in the Senate.

**chosen by the Legislature thereof,[19] for six Years;
and each Senator shall have one Vote.**

[19] Election of senators by the legislatures of the States
was superseded by direct election by the people upon the
adoption (May 31, 1913) of the Seventeenth Amendment,
which should be here referred to (Note 183) and read.

In the Constitutional Convention it was determined
to have the States as political bodies represented in the
Senate, the people themselves being represented in the
other House.   As the State itself was to be represented in
Congress, it was concluded that the State government
(the legislature) could best choose its spokesmen.   A plan
to have senators elected by the House of Representatives
was rejected because it "would create a dependence contrary to the end proposed."   A plan to have senators
appointed by the President was opposed as "a stride
towards monarchy."   There were strong advocates of the
popular election which the Seventeenth Amendment long

after brought about, such as James Wilson of Pennsylvania, who became a Justice of the Supreme Court of the United States.

Immediately after they shall be assembled in Consequence of the first Election, they shall be divided as equally as may be into three Classes. The Seats of the Senators of the first Class shall be vacated at the Expiration of the second Year, of the second Class at the Expiration of the fourth Year, and of the third Class at the Expiration of the sixth Year, so that one-third may be chosen every second Year; [20]

[20] As has been seen, Brazil and Australia have similar provisions for making the Senate a perpetual body, so that it cannot be made up (as the House may be) entirely of inexperienced members.

and if Vacancies happen by Resignation, or otherwise, during the Recess of the Legislature of any State, the Executive thereof may make temporary Appointments until the next Meeting of the Legislature, [21] **which shall then fill such Vacancies.**

[21] Now, under the Seventeenth Amendment, appointments are made until an election by the people can be held.

No Person shall be a Senator who shall not have attained to the Age of thirty Years, and been nine Years a Citizen of the United States, and who shall not, when elected, be an Inhabitant of that State [22] **for which he shall be chosen.**

[22] See Note 9.

The Vice President of the United States shall be President of the Senate, but shall have no Vote, unless they be equally divided. [23]

[23] A search of the records in 1942 showed that in the course of our history the Vice President had cast the deciding vote in the Senate 188 times, often with respect to the most momentous matters.

In Washington's administration the vote of Vice President Adams more than once saved the policy of neutrality. On April 22, 1793, President Washington proclaimed, notwithstanding a strong public sentiment for France because of its help to us during the Revolution, that as a state of war existed between France on the one hand, and Great Britain, the United Netherlands, Austria, Prussia, and Sardinia, on the other, he thought it fitting to declare the disposition of the United States "to adopt and pursue a conduct friendly and impartial toward the belligerent powers" and to exhort and warn citizens carefully to avoid all acts which might in any manner tend to contravene such disposition. It was further stated that any citizen violating the proclamation "will not receive the protection of the United States." Thus was established a policy which has ever since been pursued. The deciding vote of Vice President Hobart on February 14, 1899, ratified our treaty with Spain after the war. But of course one vote cast in conformity with the Constitution as fully expressed the people's will as though they all had voted so.

In Brazil the Vice President is, like ours, President of the Senate and in case of a tie casts the deciding vote.

Under the Constitution of Canada the Speaker of the Senate is appointed by the Governor General instead of being elected, and a tie vote in the Senate is recorded as a negative and the measure or motion is lost, while in the Canadian House of Commons, which elects its presiding officer, the Speaker casts the deciding vote in case of a tie.

In the Australian Senate the members elect from their number a president, who votes with the others, and therefore a tie is recorded as a negative.

When President Harding took office (1921) he gave Vice President Coolidge a seat at the Cabinet table. Theretofore the Vice President had been practically apart from the executive affairs of the Nation. Of course much of his time is devoted to the Legislative Department as the constitutional presiding officer of the Senate.

The Senate shall chuse their other Officers, and also a President pro tempore, in the absence of the Vice President, or when he shall exercise the Office of President of the United States.

The Senate shall have the sole Power to try all Impeachments. When sitting for that Purpose, they shall be on Oath or Affirmation. When the President of the United States is tried, the Chief Justice shall preside: And no Person shall be convicted without the Concurrence of two thirds of the Members present.

[24] The "concurrence of two thirds of the members present" in an impeachment trial may produce widely varying numerical results. To illustrate : in 1922 the Senate has ninety-six members, of whom forty-nine (a majority) are a quorum for doing business. If the whole membership should be present the two thirds necessary to impeach would be sixty-four. But if only the quorum of forty-nine should be present, the accused might be convicted by two thirds of that number, or by thirty-three.

Judgment in Cases of Impeachment shall not extend further than to removal from Office, and disqualification to hold and enjoy any Office of honor, Trust, or Profit under the United States: [25]

[25] This means that none of the imprisonments, confiscations of property, or degradations of name and family, common under European law, should be known to our

system of government. Any law of Congress prescribing punishments upon impeachment beyond those named the courts would be in duty bound to declare void and for that reason to decline to give it effect.

but the Party convicted shall nevertheless be liable and subject to Indictment, Trial, Judgment and Punishment, according to Law.[26]

[26a] That is, if one be impeached and removed from an office of honor, trust, or profit because of theft or other crime, he will, notwithstanding the judgment in impeachment, be liable to punishment for such theft or other crime.

Section 4. The Times, Places, and Manner of holding Elections for Senators and Representatives, shall be prescribed in each State by the Legislature thereof; but the Congress may at any time by Law make or alter such Regulations, except as to the Places of chusing Senators. [26a]

[26a] This provision respecting the time and manner of holding elections was not touched by Congress until 1842, when it was enacted that members of the House of Representatives should be elected by districts. Until that time they had been elected by "general ticket", each voter in a State voting for as many candidates as the State was entitled to; but that method gave undue preponderance of power to the political party having a majority of votes in the State, when it might not have a majority in each district.

In 1872, to cure various evils, Congress required all elections for the House to be held on the Tuesday after the first Monday in November, beginning in 1876.

To prevent the failure of the election of a senator by the legislature, where one House voted for one candidate

and the other for another and they refused to reconcile
their differences, Congress directed the two bodies to meet
in joint session on a fixed day and required their meeting
every day thereafter.

Congress also fixed the day for the voting in all States
for President and Vice President, the first Tuesday after
the first Monday in November.

In 1921 the Supreme Court of the United States passed
upon the Corrupt Practices Act of Congress of June 25,
1910, which forbids a candidate for a seat in the House of
Representatives or for a seat in the Senate to contribute
or expend "in procuring his nomination and election any
sum, in the aggregate, in excess of the amount which he may
lawfully give, contribute, expend or promise, under the
laws of the State in which he resides." The defendant was
charged with having made use of more money than the law
of his State permitted, not in an effort to control a nominating convention or a general election, but in the primary
election which has in some of the States superseded the
nominating convention. The decision was that the Act
of Congress could not constitutionally include the primary
election. The selection of a party candidate who will
later run for election "is in no real sense", said the Court,
"part of the manner of holding the election." However
the candidate may be offered — by convention, by primary,
by petition, or voluntarily — that "does not directly
affect", said the Court, "the manner of holding the
election." The "manner of holding elections for Senators" is the only subject, the Supreme Court held, that the
Constitution empowers Congress to regulate.

That holding overruled (1941) in a case from a State
where there was only one party, making nomination equivalent to election. "The elections for the new Parliament
which met in 1768," says Green's "English People",
Section 1501, "were more corrupt than any that had as yet
been witnessed; and even the stoutest opponents of

reform shrank aghast from the open bribery of constituencies and the prodigal barter of seats."

The Congress shall assemble at least once in every Year,[27] and such Meeting shall be on the first Monday in December, unless they shall by Law appoint a different Day.

[27] This rendered impossible such conflicts as existed in England when the King convened and dissolved Parliament at pleasure; and when, in retaliation, Parliament resolved that it could be dismissed only by its own action. During those troublous times the Short Parliament sat three weeks and the Long Parliament over nineteen years.

Charles I ruled England eleven years (1629–1640) without calling a Parliament. He obtained money for his needs by so-called loans from wealthy barons, by taxes upon ships, which were called tonnage, by many kinds of fines for trumped-up offenses, and by reviving monopolies which Elizabeth and other Tudor sovereigns had employed. The hopes of the country were finally raised by the sitting of the so-called Short Parliament, which was abruptly dismissed by the King at the end of three weeks because it would not vote money to carry on a war against the Scots. With England in defection and the Scots invading the North, Charles was driven (1640) "with wrath and shame in his heart" to "summon again the Houses to Westminster." This was the Long Parliament, which lasted for nearly twenty years. This Parliament having determined upon perpetuating itself, Cromwell and his soldiers dissolved it. "But you mistake, sir," said John Bradshaw, "if you think the Parliament dismissed. No power on earth can dissolve the Parliament but itself, be sure of that!" Subsequently it was revived and again expelled. In 1640 it called the election of a new Parliament and then dissolved itself.

As far back as the reign of Edward III (1327–1377) it had been enacted that Parliament "should be held every year or oftener if need be"; but Hallam ("Constitutional History of England") says that this enactment had been respected in no age. A complaint in the Declaration of Independence was that King George III "has dissolved representative houses repeatedly for opposing with manly firmness his invasion of the rights of the people; he has refused for a long time after such dissolution to cause others to be elected."

In 1933 the Twentieth Amendment to the Constitution changed the day of the first assembly of Congress to January 3, two months after the November elections. Increased facility in traveling cut down the time necessary for newly elected representatives to reach Washington (Note 188).

The Canadian Constitution requires a session of Parliament every year, and it forbids that twelve months intervene between sessions, and the like provision is in the Australian Constitution and in the Constitution of South Africa.

The Constitution of France requires the Chamber of Deputies and the Senate to convene at least once each year for at least five months, and the sessions of the Houses must begin and end together.

In Froissart's time (1396) it was the custom (Chronicles, Ch. 174) for the English Parliament to sit in the King's palace at Westminster for forty days; but as Richard II was going to Calais to marry Isabella of France, he attended only five days and that ended the session.

Until May, 1789, the month after Washington entered upon his duties as President, the States General of France had not been convened by the King for 175 years. Upon coming together they immediately precipitated the Revolution.

Enough has been stated to make plain what lies back of this clause for orderly and stable government.

Section 5. Each House shall be the Judge of the Elections, Returns and Qualifications of its own Members,[28]

[28] The English Parliament always claimed this right. After the World War a member of our House of Representatives was denied his seat on the ground that he had been disloyal to the Republic. Hallam gives as the first instance of record the expulsion from the House of Commons in 1581 of Arthur Hall, a burgess from Grantham. In addition to being expelled he was fined five hundred marks and then sent to the Tower, where it was the intention of the Commons to leave him, but the dissolution of Parliament by the King ended its jurisdiction over him and he was released.

and a Majority of each shall constitute a Quorum to do Business; but a smaller Number may adjourn from day to day, and may be authorized to compel the Attendance of absent Members, in such Manner, and under such Penalties as each House may provide.

Each House may determine the Rules of its Proceedings, punish its Members for disorderly Behavior and, with the Concurrence of two thirds, expel a Member.[29]

[29] But that power cannot be extended to outside matters. Thus in 1876 the House of Representatives appointed a committee to inquire into the insolvency of a firm with which the Secretary of the Navy had deposited money of the government. A witness who was called by the committee declined to give names requested or to produce papers. Repeating his refusal when brought to the bar of the House, he was adjudged in contempt and was committed to the common jail, from which he was released by *habeas corpus* after forty-five days. He thereupon

brought an action for money damages against the Speaker of the House and others on the ground of false imprisonment, and Congress paid by appropriation the judgment which he recovered. When the case reached the Supreme Court of the United States it was held that the House does not possess under the Constitution any general power to punish for contempt. While it may punish its own members and pass upon questions of election and some others, the Court said, it was without authority to imprison as it did. Because the United States was a creditor of a man whose business methods were questioned, said the Court, that did not warrant the House of Representatives in subjecting him to the unlimited scrutiny or investigation of a Congressional committee; and the recourse of the government was, like that of any other creditor, an action in a court of law for the recovery of its money. Thus we see how needful to the citizen, even in a republic, are definite constitutional safeguards, and how effectively they are worked out under our system.

As late as 1916 the liberty of the citizen was again threatened in a like manner. The House of Representatives issued a warrant for the arrest of a United States attorney in New York for making statements which were considered "defamatory and insulting" and as tending "to bring the House into public contempt and ridicule." After he had been taken into custody by the sergeant at arms of the House he sought release by a writ of *habeas corpus*, which the trial court denied. The Supreme Court reversed that holding. It referred to the provisions in the early constitutions of the States which were intended "to destroy the admixture of judicial and legislative power" which had been possessed by the Houses of Parliament in England. That blending of power does not exist under our Constitution. For redress on account of slanderous or libelous accusations a member of the House must, like other citizens, resort to a court of law.

Each House shall keep a Journal of its Proceedings, and from time to time publish the same, excepting such Parts as may in their Judgment require Secrecy;[30] and the Yeas and Nays of the Members of either House on any question shall, at the Desire of one fifth of those Present, be entered on the Journal.

[30] Every word uttered in the House and in the Senate (except in executive sessions) is taken down stenographically and appears in print the next morning as the *Congressional Record*. Each House keeps a journal.

Neither House, during the Session of Congress, shall, without the Consent of the other, adjourn for more than three days, nor to any other Place than that in which the two Houses shall be sitting.[31]

[31] The reign of Charles II of England (1660–1685) was hardly more remarkable, says Hallam, for the vigilance of the House of Commons against the arbitrary use of authority by the King than for the warfare which it waged against the House of Lords whenever it saw, or thought it saw, a usurpation by that body. In one instance it became necessary for the King to resort to successive adjournments for fifteen months to stop a quarrel between the Houses. A few years later the strife again appeared and the King made peace once more. The provision in our Constitution requires the House of Representatives and the Senate to sit at the same place and to work together. As the Constitution defines quite clearly the powers and duties of each House, the disputes about authority which are blots on English history never occur in the United States. If either House could adjourn at pleasure it might completely obstruct public business and practically destroy a session of Congress. The two Houses must agree upon adjournment, and if they cannot agree the President

may (Note 94) adjourn them. But except in case of the inability of the Houses to agree, the President has no control over the adjourning of Congress.

The Congress of one House under the Articles of Confederation was authorized to adjourn to any time (not beyond six months) and to any place in the United States.

In Canada and Australia the Governors General are empowered by the Constitutions to prorogue (postpone or dissolve) the legislative body or Parliament. In Chile both Houses (Deputies and Senate) must convene and adjourn at the same time. In France the President may adjourn the Chamber of Deputies and the Senate (which must meet at least once each year and continue in session for at least five months), but not for a longer time than one month and not more than twice during one session. In France a meeting of one House when the other is not in session is illegal, except when the Senate sits as a court.

Section 6. The Senators and Representatives shall receive a Compensation for their Services, to be ascertained by Law,[32]

[32] That is, a bill must be passed by themselves and signed by the President, fixing their salaries.

and paid out of the Treasury of the United States.[33]

[33] This was another American innovation. In the Parliament of England members had not been paid. The distinction of the office was considered enough. The practice excluded the poor citizen. But members are paid in Parliament now.

As far back as the reign of Henry III (1265) the shires and boroughs paid the expenses of the persons summoned by the King to his Court of Parliament. In the reign of Edward II (1322) the salary of a knight was fixed at four shillings a day, and that of a citizen or burgher at two shillings a day; but the tax rate for payment ran against the constituents. In the course of time the practice of allowing any compensation passed away. As the Reform Bill of 1832 left the working classes almost altogether without the privilege of voting, a programme was drawn up for numerous reforms, which was named "The Charter", and the movement was called Chartism. One of the things demanded was pay for the members of Parliament. In 1893 and again in 1895 the House of Commons voted by a small majority for an adequate allowance; but in 1906, by a vote of more than three to one, a definite salary of three hundred pounds was fixed. In Canada the members of both Houses receive $2500 a year, with a deduction of $15 for each day absent. In Australia each member receives six hundred pounds a year. In South Africa each member receives four hundred pounds a year, less three pounds for each day's nonattendance. In Argentine each member receives 1060 pounds a year; and in France fifteen thousand francs.

The Articles of Confederation required (Art. V, sec. 3) each State to maintain its delegates to Congress.

In 1789 the compensation of our senators and representatives was fixed at $6 for each day's attendance; in 1815 at $1500 a year; in 1817 at $8 a day; in 1855 at $3000 a year; in 1865 at $5000; in 1871 at $7500; in 1874 it was made $5000; in 1907, $7500; and in 1925, $10,000.

Madison thought it an "indecent thing" that congressmen should be empowered by the Constitution to fix their salaries. After the advance in 1815 many of the members of the House were defeated for reëlection. The advance of March 3, 1873, affecting the President, the Congress, the Cabinet, the Supreme Court, and some other departments, made on the last day of Grant's first term and operating retroactively during "the term for which he shall have been elected", was denounced by the country as a "salary grab." On January 20, 1874, it was repealed as to all "except the President of the United States and the

Washington, presiding over the Constitutional Convention, urged
"a standard to which the wise and honest can repair"

Constitutional Convention, in session from May, 1787, until September 17, spent 86 working days on its task

Justices of the Supreme Court", whose salaries the Constitution (Notes 82 and 98) forbids Congress to reduce.

They shall in all Cases, except Treason, Felony, and Breach of the Peace, be privileged from Arrest during their Attendance at the Session of their respective Houses, and in going to and returning from the same; [33a]

[33a] This privilege, which is given for the despatch of public business, does not extend to the member's family. Once in England the privilege covered the family, the domestics, and the property of the member, in consequence of which creditors and others seeking redress were helpless. In the reign of George III an act of Parliament abolished the privilege as to domestic servants, lands, and goods. The charters of the colonies did not mention the privilege. It first appears in this country in the Constitution of Massachusetts of 1780.

The privilege from arrest, except for treason, felony, or breach of the peace, was granted (Art. V) by the Articles of Confederation to members of Congress.

and for any Speech or Debate in either House, they shall not be questioned [34] in any other Place.

[34] The privilege of having debates unquestioned was denied to members of Parliament in the reign of Elizabeth when they began to speak their minds freely, and they were punished by that ruler and her two successors, but the privilege was soon afterwards firmly established. Hallam says that the single false step by Charles I which made compromise impossible and civil war certain was his attempt to seize five members (Pym, Hollis, Hampden, Haselrig, and Strode) within the walls of the House.

Hampden and his associates were accused of high treason (against the sovereign or the government, as distinguished from other treasons, of which there were then many).

Followed by a body of armed men the King left his palace
(1642) at Whitehall, after having told the Queen (Henri-
etta, daughter of Henry IV of France, and accused of having incited Charles to the rash action) that he would return "master of my Kingdom", and proceeded to the House
of Commons.   Apprised of his approach, the House ordered
the accused members to withdraw.   The King entered
and told the Speaker that he needed the chair.   Calling
for the members wanted and hearing no response, "I see
my birds are flown," he said.   He went out in defeat, pro-
testing that he had not intended to use force.   As he returned he heard everywhere in the streets the cry of "privilege."   Macaulay says ("History of England", Vol. 1,
p. 107) that at the very moment when the subjects of
Charles I were returning to him with feelings of affection
after a long estrangement "he had aimed a deadly blow
at all their dearest rights, at the privileges of Parliament,
at the very principle of trial by jury."

The Articles of Confederation provided (Art. V) that
"freedom of speech and debate in the legislature shall
not be impeached or questioned in any court or place out
of Congress."

The privilege for "any speech or debate" was held by
the Supreme Court of the United States to cover a resolution offered by a member of Congress.

**No Senator or Representative shall, during the
Time for which he was elected, be appointed to any
civil Office under the Authority of the United States,
which shall have been created, or the Emoluments
whereof shall have been encreased during such
time;** [35]

[35] After a senator's term began Congress increased
(1889) the emoluments of our Minister to Mexico.   Before
the expiration of his senatorial term the President appointed

him Minister to that country. The Attorney-General ruled that under this provision he was not eligible.

President-elect Taft selected Senator Knox to be Secretary of State in his cabinet. Then it was found that during the senatorial term of Knox the emoluments of the secretaryship had been increased 'by Congress, which rendered him ineligible. Congress thereupon qualified him by reducing the emoluments of the office to what they were before.

One may conceive of great abuses which might arise did this prohibition not exist. Of course, after the term of a senator or a representative has expired, he may accept the office created during his term or the office the emoluments of which were increased while he was in Congress.

and no Person holding any Office under the United States, shall be a Member of either House during his Continuance in Office.[36]

[36] But few provisions in the Constitution were more earnestly debated in the Constitutional Convention.

Hallam says that it appears possible that persons in office formed at all times a very considerable portion of the House of Commons in the time (1485–1603) of the Tudors. In the reign of Henry VIII (1509–1547) most of the members of the House of Commons held offices for the appointments to which they were indebted to the King. Parliament, being thus interested, passed an act "releasing the King's highness from all and every sum of money" which the Parliaments or his subjects had given to him "by way of trust or loan." As mentioned elsewhere, the practice of "borrowing" from the rich subjects was a common practice of the kings of those times, but it was stopped with the dethronement of James II and the accepting by William and Mary of the Declaration of Rights in 1689.

Scores of other historical facts might be given to illustrate the meaning lying back of the simple language of this clause. If Congress were to become partly filled with appointees of the President to other offices under the United States, or by holders through election of other offices, the independence of the Legislative Department which the Constitution undertook to safeguard would soon be undermined.

The Constitution of Georgia of 1777 declared that "no person shall hold more than one office of profit under this State at the same time." The Constitution of Maryland had a similar provision.

It was forbidden by the Articles of Confederation (Art. V) that any delegate in Congress hold "any office under the United States for which he, or any other for his benefit, receives any salary, fees, or emolument of any kind."

So this clause, like many another in the Constitution, took rise from colonial experience.

Section 7. All bills for raising Revenue shall originate in the House of Representatives; [37] but the Senate may propose or concur with Amendments as on other bills.

[37] That is, money bills must originate in the body then elected directly by the people. Senators have been so elected (Note 183) since 1913. One of the almost irrepressible conflicts between the King of England and the Houses of Parliament was respecting the power of raising money for the support of the King and the conduct of the government.

In a Congress (called the Stamp-Act Congress) composed of delegates from the Colonies a Declaration of Rights was promulgated in New York on October 19, 1765, which said:

"That it is inseparably essential to the freedom of a people and the undoubted right of Englishmen that no taxes be imposed on them but with their own consent, given personally or by their representatives; that the people of these Colonies are not, and from their local circumstances cannot be, represented in the House of Commons in Great Britain; that the only representatives of the people of these Colonies are persons chosen therein by themselves, and that no taxes ever have been or can be constitutionally imposed on them but by their respective legislatures; that all supplies to the Crown being free gifts of the people, it is unreasonable and inconsistent with the principles and spirit of the British constitution for the people of Great Britain to grant to His Majesty the property of the Colonists."

In the Declaration of Rights of October 14, 1774, the delegates from the several Colonies in Colonial Congress assembled protested against acts of Parliament passed in the fourth, fifth, sixth, seventh, and eighth years of George III, "which imposed duties for the purpose of raising revenue in America", and they condemned them as measures "which demonstrate a system formed to enslave America."

In the early times in England the House of Lords and the House of Commons made separate grants of supply to the King for the maintenance of the government and himself. Later, as the Commons' proportion of the taxes was greater, that House made the grant with the assent of the Lords. In the reign of Henry VIII they joined in the grants. But in the last Parliament of Charles I the grant recited that it was made by the Commons. Since then that House originates money bills.

The Kings of England always found need for more money than they got from Parliament. Some of the early kings, Henry III (1216–1272) and Edward I (1272–1307), for example, introduced the scheme of granting to their military tenants the privilege of knighthood; but those who wished to decline the honor (costly to maintain) could excuse their absence by a moderate fine. Once in the reign of Elizabeth (1558–1603) and often in the time of James I (1603–1625) this ancient method of raising money without the aid of Parliament was employed.

Another lucrative plan of those two monarchs was to grant exclusive or monopolistic privileges. A monopolist in the making of soap, for example, agreed to pay the King eight pounds in money ($40) on every ton of soap made, in addition to ten thousand pounds ($50,000) for the charter or grant of the monopoly. Almost every necessity was under monopoly, but in 1639 the grants were revoked because of public displeasure. Enormous revenues flowed to the monarch from such sources.

Another device of resourceful royalty was to borrow heavily from wealthy nobles and never (or seldom) pay. It was not often that a wealthy man had the temerity to refuse. Elizabeth always discharged such obligations. In the reign of James I a forced loan of this kind was frustrated by the declaration of the House of Commons that no one be bound against his will to lend money to the King. While such practices were believed to be in violation of Magna Charta (1215), signed by King John, Parliament made the matter certain by requiring James' successor, Charles I, to assent (1628) to the Petition of Right wherein it was said that "no man shall be compelled to make or yield any gift, loan, benevolence to or such like charge without common consent by Act of Parliament; that none be called upon to make answer for refusal so to do." And in 1689 William and Mary accepted the Declaration of Rights, which prohibited the levying of money for the use of the sovereign without the grant of Parliament. Could the King raise money (which provides armies and navies) without the consent of Parliament there might soon be no Parliament. A dispute between Charles I and Parliament involving this money question and some others was carried into civil war and the sovereign's head was severed by the executioner.

Mentioning that in Tudor and Stuart times "the crown was always tending to bankruptcy and always requiring help of Parliament", an English writer (Jenks' "Constitutional Experiments of the Commonwealth", p. 39) states: "It might almost be said that the development of the English Constitution is due to the fall in the value of money. It is certain that many of the constitutional crises of English history were brought about by that fact." It has been stated that the value of money in the time of Elizabeth, whose reign ended in 1603, was about twelve times what it is to-day.

The foregoing references to historic facts show why the framers of the Constitution so carefully entrusted the raising and expending of the public treasure to the representatives elected by the direct vote of the people. But under our clearly defined powers of government conflicts like those of English history have hardly threatened; and as senators also are now elected, discord is very improbable.

A "bill for raising revenue" is one for levying taxes in the strict sense of the word and not one which incidentally brings in money. Thus a currency act of Congress which, to meet expenses, put a tax on notes of banking associations in circulation was held by the Supreme Court not to be a revenue bill which should have originated in the House of Representatives.

Under the Canadian Constitution bills for raising revenue originate in the House of Commons, but not before recommendation by the Governor General. The Australian Constitution forbids that the Senate either originate or amend money bills.

In Brazil the Chamber of Deputies (elected by the people) originates all bills for raising revenue, and so does the House of Deputies in Chile.

The Constitution of France permits the Senate to originate all but revenue bills, which must first pass the Chamber of Deputies.

Every Bill which shall have passed the House of Representatives and the Senate, shall, before it become a Law, be presented to the President of the United States; If he approve he shall sign it, but if not he shall return it, with his Objections to that House in which it shall have originated, who shall enter the Objections at large on their Journal, and proceed to reconsider it.   If after such Reconsideration two thirds of that House shall agree to pass the Bill, it shall be sent, together with the Objections, to the other House, by which it shall likewise be reconsidered, and if approved by two thirds of that House, it shall become a Law.   But in all such Cases the Votes of both Houses shall be determined by yeas and Nays, and the Names of the Persons voting for and against the Bill shall be entered on the Journal of each House respectively.   If any Bill shall not be returned by the President within ten Days (Sundays excepted) after it shall have been presented to him, the Same shall be a Law, in like Manner as if he had signed it, unless the Congress by their Adjournment prevent its Return, in which Case it shall not be a Law.[38]

[38] That paragraph was designed to prevent any question as to how and by whom a bill may be passed into a law.

Could the House of Commons enact a law without the concurrence of the Lords?   Could it do so without the signature of the King?   Could both Houses ignore the King and make a law?   Could the King prevent at will the taking effect of a bill passed by Parliament?   Those were questions which had often stirred England deeply.

A bill returned by the President "with his objections" to the House in which it originated is said to have been vetoed, but the word "veto" does not appear in the Constitution. In most of the colonies the governors had the power to veto legislation and their misuse of it was one of the grievances causing the Revolution. Massachusetts was the first of the original States to grant (1780) the veto power to the governor. This power in the executive officer is carried down in our country to the mayors of cities, who are generally authorized to veto ordinances. It is the popular belief that the interposition of the veto is a salutary (and indispensable) check upon hasty or otherwise objectionable legislation.

Many bills passed by the two Houses of Congress have been vetoed by the President because he regarded them as contrary to some provision of the Constitution, or at variance with the policy or promise of his political party, or against sound financial principles, or as inopportune or injudicious. Although the language of the Constitution — "if he approve it he shall sign it, but if not he shall return it with his objections" — places no limitation upon the veto power, it has been contended that the President really has authority to veto only bills which he considers obnoxious to some Constitutional provision. Others have argued that the power should be exercised only to prevent encroachments by Congress upon the domain of the Executive. But Madison's writings show that the veto was to be "a check to the instability in legislation, which had been found the besetting infirmity of popular governments, and been sufficiently exemplified among ourselves in the legislatures of the States." Jefferson said that the veto was to protect from invasion by Congress (1) "the rights of the Executive", (2) those of the Judiciary, and (3) those of "the States and State Legislatures." The first bill (of two) vetoed by Washington (April, 1792) was for apportioning members of the House of Representatives (Note 10) according to population. He believed that the apportionment proposed was unfair. When the bill was returned to the House of Representatives with his objections, "a few of the hottest friends of the bill expressed passion," wrote Jefferson, "but the majority were satisfied, and both in and out of doors it gave pleasure to have at length an instance of the negative being exercised." Adams, Jefferson, John Quincy Adams, Van Buren, William Henry Harrison, Taylor, Fillmore, and Garfield never vetoed a bill passed by Congress. Including regular and pocket vetoes, Washington vetoed 2; Madison, 7; Monroe, 1; Jackson, 12; Tyler, 10; Polk, 3; Pierce, 9; Buchanan, 7; Lincoln, 6; Johnson, 28; Grant, 92; Hayes, 13; Arthur, 12; Cleveland (first term), 414; Benjamin Harrison, 44; Cleveland (second term), 170; McKinley, 42; Roosevelt, T., 82; Taft, 39; Wilson, 44; Harding, 6; Coolidge, 50; Hoover, 37; Roosevelt, F. D., (to Jan. 1 '45), 612.

Except in times of unusual feeling, or when a bill of extraordinary importance has been involved, Congress has but seldom repassed a measure over the veto by the President. Much deference is shown by the Legislative Department of the government to the opinion of the Executive Department, to which the Constitution commits a share of the law-making power.

But many vetoed bills have been repassed by Congress and have so become laws despite the veto. Many others Congress has tried to repass and failed because it could not muster a two-thirds vote in each House — not two thirds of the membership of each House, the Supreme Court held (1919) where that claim was made by a citizen affected by a law, but two thirds of the members present, assuming the presence of a quorum or majority necessary to do business. The Reconstruction acts and many others affecting the return of the southern States after the Civil War were quickly passed over the veto of President Johnson as though Congress found pleasure in domination. Generally, however, the power of veto in the President has been a positive quantity in legislation. "A power of this nature in the Executive," wrote Alexander Hamilton in "The Federalist " (No. LXXIII), "will often have a silent and unperceived, though forcible, operation." That statement has been amply justified by experience.

The sovereigns of England, says Bagehot, "must sign their own death warrant if the two Houses send it to them." The King still has legally the veto power, but he has not exercised it since the accession of the House of Hanover (George I, 1714).

The colonists had often felt the evils of slow, uncertain, or capricious legislation. "He [George III] has refused," says the Declaration of Independence, "his assent to laws the most wholesome and necessary for the public good. He has forbidden his governors to pass laws of immediate and pressing importance unless suspended in their operations, till his assent should be obtained. . . . He has refused to pass other laws for the accommodation of large districts of people. . . . He has obstructed the administration of justice by refusing his assent to laws for establishing judiciary powers."

Therefore the Constitutional Convention formulated a method which at once checks haste or unwisdom in the Legislative Department and obstructiveness in the Executive.

Our Constitutional provision has been adopted substantially by many nations. The Constitution of Chile (1833, which has been frequently amended) provides that the President must return the vetoed bill within two weeks; and that the two Houses of Congress may repass it by a two-thirds vote. Under the Constitution of Canada (1867) the English sovereign may veto ("disallow") within two years an act of the Dominion Parliament, even though the Governor General has approved it and it has gone into effect.

The Australian Constitution provides for disallowance or veto by the sovereign within one year of a bill approved by the Governor General. But both in Canada and

Australia the Governor General may veto the bill or with-hold assent for the sovereign's pleasure. But of course in Australia and Canada there is no way to overcome the obstruction of a veto.

The foregoing references to other constitutions are made to illustrate how widely extended has been the influence of this provision of our Constitution for careful and orderly legislation.

Every Order, Resolution, or Vote to which the Con-currence of the Senate and House of Representatives may be necessary (except on a question of Adjourn-ment) shall be presented to the President of the United States; and, before the Same shall take Effect, shall be approved by him, or, being disap-proved by him, shall be repassed by two thirds of the Senate and House of Representatives, according to the Rules and Limitations prescribed in the Case of a Bill.[39]

[39] That is designed to prevent Congress from ignoring or evading the constitutional prerogative of the President and in disregard of him enacting laws under the guise of orders or resolutions. The historic tendency of one depart-ment of government to usurp the functions or prerogatives of another was clearly understood by the authors of the Constitution.

But a resolution proposing an amendment to the Consti-tution of the United States (Note 129) is not, the Supreme Court has held, an act of legislation, and therefore it need not be submitted to the President for signature.

Although the signature of the President is not necessary to a congressional resolution proposing an amendment, President Lincoln signed the joint resolution "inadver-tently", as it was said, proposing the Thirteenth Amend-ment. The resolution proposing the Fourteenth Amendment was not submitted to President Johnson, who protested on that account, and who said that an Amendment should not be submitted to a State legislature or State convention which had not been chosen by the people since the proposal to amend was made.

Section 8. The Congress shall have Power [40]

[40] By this section the sovereign people, in whom resides all authority, conferred upon Congress exclusive power to deal with twenty subjects properly within the sphere of National authority; and they concluded by authorizing it to make all laws necessary to effectuate those powers. Under the Articles of Confederation the State, which "retains its sovereignty, freedom, and independence", exercised too many such powers. In trade and commerce, and in other ways, the States treated one another as foreign countries, imposing duties and other taxes and enacting much selfish legislation. After 132 years of experience it would be difficult to improve upon the following enumeration of National powers. Every constitution that has been drawn since, those of France, Switzerland, Chile, Brazil, Argentine, New Zealand, Canada, Australia, South Africa, and others, have followed quite closely this chart of legislative National powers. It will be at once interesting and useful to study it in detail.

To lay and collect Taxes, Duties, Imposts and Excises, [41]

[41] Reference has been made (Note 10) to the failure in operation of the "common treasury" created by the Articles of Confederation, which was to be "supplied by the several States." Often a State failed to provide its supply and of course the National Government was thereby hampered and sometimes crippled. Now the Nation would raise necessary money itself. In the Constitutional Convention there was question of the meaning of "duties", "imposts"

and "excises." The comprehensive word "taxes" would have been enough. By the use of that language the purpose was manifested to authorize the Nation to raise needed money by any of the known methods of taxation — "a power of vast extent", wrote President Monroe, "not granted by the Confederation, the grant of which formed one of the principal inducements to the adoption of this Constitution."

In the enumeration of National powers the first named in the original draft and in the suggestions brought before the Constitutional Convention was the power to lay taxes and raise money. "Money is one of the essential agencies of Government," wrote Hamilton. "Without it no Government can exist, and without the power to raise it, it cannot be had."

While the direct break with England was caused by taxation, by the Stamp Act of Parliament (1765), which required the use in the Colonies of paper bearing costly stamps for notes, bonds, deeds, wills, and other documents, the frame of mind to revolt had been developed in the colonists by over a century of oppressive legislation. Colonial commerce had been hindered by the Navigation acts of 1660 and 1663, requiring that buying and selling be done in England and that goods be moved in English ships; by the Act of 1732, prohibiting trade in woolens among the Colonies, a trade which was growing rapidly; by the Molasses Act of 1733, placing a duty or tax on all rum, molasses, and sugar imported into any English colony, a heavy blow to a great trade with Spanish possessions; by the Act of 1750, prohibiting the sending of pig iron to England and forbidding the manufacture of certain iron articles at home, a manufacture which had already become important; by the Sugar Act of 1764, restricting trading with the West Indies in lumber, food stuffs, and some other articles; and by an act in the same year legalizing writs of assistance, by which revenue officers of the Crown (seeking to prevent smuggling in violation of the restrictive laws) made searches and seizures and were empowered to call citizens to their aid. When, therefore, the English Government attempted by the Stamp Act to impose upon the Colonies a part of the tax burden of the French and Indian War (the name of the American section of a world-wide engagement between England and France), after they had spent eleven million dollars and given up thirty thousand lives, the step was denounced in a Colonial Declaration of Rights (1765) by a Continental Congress as part of a policy "to enslave America." That declaration said that as the colonists were not represented in Parliament, and by reason of distance could not be, no tax by Parliament could be imposed upon them. That could be done only by their elected representatives in the colonial assemblies or legislatures.

to pay the Debts and provide for the common Defence and general Welfare of the United States; [42]

[42] Answering fierce objections that "general Welfare" left Congress without restraint in taxing and spending, Madison wrote in the Federalist that only as to subjects covered by grants of power in this section — none being for aid to individuals — could Congress spend. Yet the Social Security Act of 1935, taxing employers and employees to provide funds for old-age pensions, was upheld under this Clause by the Supreme Court.

President Monroe vetoed a bill for the improvement of the Cumberland Road because he did not believe the work to come within this clause. President Jackson for the like reason, vetoed every bill for public improvements that was not clearly for National welfare, as distinguished from local or State advantage. "We are in no danger," said he, "from violations of the Constitution from which encroachments are made upon the personal rights of the citizen. . . . But against the dangers of unconstitutional acts which, instead of menacing the vengeance of offended authority, proffer local advantages and bring in their train the patronage of the government, we are, I fear, not so safe."

River and harbor bills were vetoed by Presidents Tyler, Polk, Pierce, Grant, Arthur, and Cleveland. A bill appropriating $19,000,000 was passed over President Arthur's veto in 1882, and a bill which President Cleveland vetoed in 1896, appropriating $80,000,000, was repassed by Congress. The Presidents regarded the appropriations as largely for local rather than National purposes, and therefore, as President Arthur put it, "beyond the powers given by the Constitution to Congress and the President." Declaring that when the citizens of one State found that money of all the people was being appropriated for local improvements in another State they naturally "seek to indemnify themselves . . . by securing appropriations for similar improvements", he concluded:

"Thus as the bill becomes more objectionable, it secures more support."

President Cleveland deplored "the unhappy decadence among our people of genuine love and affection for our Government as the embodiment of the highest and best aspirations of humanity, and not as the giver of gifts."

It is a question under discussion to-day whether the desire of communities and States to share in congressional appropriations from the National treasury has not operated to extend unconstitutionally National power and weaken correspondingly the constitutional authority of the States.

On this subject President Harding said in 1921:

"Just government is merely the guarantee to the people of the right and opportunity to support themselves. The one outstanding danger of to-day is the tendency to turn to Washington for the things which are the tasks or the duties of the forty-eight commonwealths."

but all Duties, Imposts and Excises shall be uniform throughout the United States; [43]

[43] This prevents preference to one State or locality to the prejudice of another. Otherwise, such oppressive inequalities might exist as to affect the pursuits and employments of the people. The agriculture of one State or section might be heavily burdened to the upbuilding of that in another. So of commerce. So of manufacture. The rivalries of States under the Articles of Confederation had taught a lesson.

To borrow Money on the credit of the United States;[44]

[44] In addition to raising funds by the various forms of taxation shown in the preceding paragraph, Congress is authorized, when the present resources of the Nation are insufficient, to borrow on its credit — that is, to raise money upon the resources and paying power of future years. Even if sufficient funds could be raised at once for a war or other great emergency, it would not be fair to lay the burden wholly upon the present generation. Therefore Congress raises part of needed funds by heavy income taxes, by stamp taxes on many kinds of sales and other transactions, and by various sorts of special taxes devised for the emergency and removed when it has passed. But it transfers a part of the burden to future generations by the issue of bonds, which are like the promissory note of a person, a simple statement that at a time named the United States will pay to the bearer a specified amount of money, with interest paid twice a year in the meanwhile. The people at large buy those bonds as an investment, but the taxes out of which the Nation finally pays the holder of the bond or note are collected in later years and generally from a later generation.

The last of the Civil War debt was retired in 1934. As of June 30, 1919 the Treasurer of the United States reported the estimated gross cost of World War I as $30,177,000,000

The debt for World War II is placed at around $275,000,-000,000.

The Articles of Confederation forbade Congress to borrow money or "emit bills" unless "nine States assent to the same." It was too often impossible to secure the support of that many. Hence this National power in our Constitution, which is entirely independent of State will.

In the Constitutional Convention the words "or emit bills," following the word "money" in the foregoing clause, were stricken out. Bills of credit or paper money had been the bane of the Confederation and the States. Madison raised the question whether it would not be enough to forbid that such bills be made a legal tender, that is, equivalent to gold or silver coin. He thought that would check the paper-money evil. Seventy-five years thereafter (February, 1862) the question stirred the country when Congress issued $150,000,000 of paper money known (because of the color) as "greenbacks," which were made "a legal tender in payment of all debts, public and private, within the United States." A woman who had before the passage of this Act become bound to pay a stated number of *dollars* in what was at that time the money of the United States tendered "greenbacks" (worth less than coin), which were refused. When the case reached the Supreme Court of the United States, Salmon P. Chase, who as Secretary of the Treasury in Lincoln's Cabinet had advocated the law, had been made Chief Justice. In an opinion written by him (upon fuller study, as he explained) the Act (and one of 1863) was held (1869) beyond the constitutional power of Congress, the chief ground being that the power of Congress could not be implied, and that the acts of Congress could not apply to debts contracted before their passage. Soon after the Greenback Case was decided, the Supreme Court was enlarged (Note 97) from seven judges to nine. In 1872 two similar cases were disposed of by the Court, one involving a debt contracted before the acts of Congress and one an obligation arising subsequently thereto. The Supreme Court overruled its decision in the first case and held that the war powers granted to Congress (Notes 55 and 56) by the Constitution warranted the legislation.

Next the question came up whether Congress could issue legal tender paper in time of peace, as well as in time of war. In 1878 it passed such an act. The other cases had been rested by the Supreme Court on the war power of Congress. It was believed by many that the Supreme Court could go no further. But in the last Legal Tender Case (1884) it held that, whether in peace or war, when the exigency is so great, owing to "unusual and pressing demands on the resources of the government, or of the inadequacy of the supply of gold and silver", that it is expedient to resort to such means, the question of exigency is political and not judicial, and therefore to be determined, not by the courts, but by Congress. The Court said that "the power to make the notes of the Government a legal tender in payment of private debts" is "one of the powers belonging to sovereignty in other civilized nations." Therefore, as the power is not withheld from Congress by the Constitution, the existence of it is necessarily implied. This legal tender paper, after being in use seventeen years, during which it was below the value of gold coin (it requiring at one time $2.85 of paper money to equal one dollar in gold), was redeemed, beginning January 1, 1879, under "an Act to provide for the resumption of specie payments" passed in 1875 and directing the Secretary of the Treasury to "redeem, in coin, the United States legal-tender notes then outstanding on their presentation for redemption." Prices and wages had been so high during the time of paper money that the Greenback Party was organized in 1874 to oppose the resumption of specie payments.

In 1921 the Supreme Court, following the foregoing case, upheld an act of Congress creating a Federal Land Bank in each of the twelve districts into which it divided the United States. In addition to providing "capital for agricultural development" the plan was "to create government depositaries and financial agents for the United States." The latter undertaking was clearly within National power.

The foregoing history is detailed as one of almost countless illustrations of the expansiveness of our Constitution and of the practical construction which the Supreme Court has employed to fit it to "new occasions" and "new duties."

Notwithstanding the redemption in specie of the paper money of the Civil War, the Act of Congress of February 25, 1862, as revised down to March 3, 1863, is still effective, declaring that "United States notes shall be lawful money, and a legal tender in payment of all debts, public and private, within the United States, except for duties on imports and interest on the public debt."

To regulate Commerce with foreign Nations, and among the several States, and with the Indian tribes;[45]

[45] This is called the commerce clause, second in importance to no other provision in the Constitution. The delegates to the Constitutional Convention from the southern States voted for it in return for the first clause of Section 9 (Note 61), which the delegates from the North accepted in the belief that slavery was already going out and would soon be extinct.

This clause put an end to the taxes, duties, and other burdens which the States had imposed under the Articles of Confederation upon one another's trade and activities. A writer on the Constitution, who served as Justice of the Supreme Court and therefore had an unusual opportunity to observe, expressed the opinion that were it not for the commerce clause the States would long since have wrecked the Union.

The commerce clause has been a barrier to the activ-

"Congress shall have Power . . . to regulate Commerce with foreign Nations and among the several States"

"Congress shall have Power . . . to provide and maintain a Navy"

ities of States in more than two thousand cases that have reached the courts of last resort in the several States and the Supreme Court of the United States. Tax laws, license laws, and regulative laws of infinite variety enacted by State legislatures have been held invalid under this clause as interfering with the free flow of interstate commerce. And so of State statutes intended to promote local prosperity, as an act prohibiting pipe-line companies from transporting except between points within the State.

After the Constitution was adopted and while it was before the conventions of the States for ratification Washington wrote to Lafayette that his own State had recently tried to pass "some of the most extravagant and preposterous edicts on the subject of trade" that had ever been written. Under the Articles of Confederation Rhode Island met all its expenses out of the duties which it levied at one port on the commerce entering from other States. Necessaries paid oppressive duties before entering New York City. Examples of this kind are too many to be enumerated.

But with years and experience the belief has grown that while the citizen of the State may naturally favor development at home, the same person as a citizen of the Nation must take into account the welfare of all the States. The advancement of a State is a National as well as a local benefit, and the advantages of that advancement should not accrue to the State alone.

The commerce clause is said to have been suggested by James Monroe of Virginia, afterwards President, who believed National regulation "necessary to preserve the Union; without it, it will infallibly crumble to pieces." As a member from 1783 to 1786 of the Congress under the Articles of Confederation, he endeavored to secure for Congress the power to regulate commerce and thereby remove what he considered the chief defect in the existing government.

Commerce, said the Supreme Court, in an early case, "comprehends traffic, trade, navigation, communication, the transit of persons and the transmission of messages by telegraph — indeed, every species of commercial intercourse."

In 1887 Congress, in pursuance of this clause, passed the Act to Regulate Commerce, commonly called the Interstate Commerce Law. It has been frequently amended and improved as experience has suggested. Railway lines, steamship lines, express companies, oil-pipe lines, telegraph lines and telephone lines, and wireless transmission of messages are brought within the control of the Interstate Commerce Commission, a tribunal now (1940) grown from three to eleven members, created by the Act with power to prescribe what charges the public shall pay and with authority otherwise to regulate the business practices of railway companies and others engaged in interstate commerce.

In 1890 Congress enacted under this clause the Sherman Anti-Trust Law, providing heavy penalties for the offence of conspiring or combining to prevent competition among merchants and others moving commodities in interstate commerce. That was supplemented by the Clayton Law of October 15, 1914; and on September 26, 1914, the Federal Trade Commission Law, to prevent "unfair methods of competition in interstate commerce", was passed.

In 1933 the National Industrial Recovery Act was passed to regulate commerce under this Clause by removing obstructions to its free flow, and by providing for organization of industry for cooperative action among trade groups. A "national emergency productive of unemployment and disorganization of industry" was declared to exist. The President was authorized to approve "codes of fair competition" upon the application of "one or more trade or industrial groups". When a code was approved by him, disregard of it was punishable by a fine of $500 for each day of non-observance. For violation of the Code of

Fair Competition for the Poultry Industry slaughterers of poultry for New York City were convicted and fined. The Act of Congress was held unconstitutional by the Supreme Court (1) as a delegation of legislative power "to trade or industrial groups", and (2) as a regulation of transactions "not directly affecting interstate commerce".

In 1937 the National Labor Relations Act of 1935 was sustained by the Supreme Court as valid regulation under the Commerce Clause. It recited that the denial by employers of the right of workers to organize and bargain collectively led to strikes and other forms of unrest necessarily obstructing interstate commerce. Congress therefore asserted the power to remove those conditions through orders of the National Labor Relations Board.

Australia was quick to put a commerce clause in its Constitution (1900) and thus end as to the new States of the Commonwealth the burdens and exactions which as provinces they had imposed upon one another. Brazil had made (1890) its federal government supreme over commerce, as Canada had done twenty-three years before. In short, it may be said that all important constitutions have followed ours by introducing a clause to prevent the States from interfering with commerce.

To establish an uniform Rule of Naturalization,[46]

[46] A complaint against George III in the Declaration of Independence was that "he has endeavored to prevent the population of these States, for that purpose obstructing the laws for the naturalization of foreigners, and refusing to pass others to encourage their migration hither." On the day of the signing of the Declaration of Independence the Continental Congress passed a resolution that "all persons abiding in any of the United Colonies and deriving protection from the laws of the same owe allegiance to said laws, and are members of such Colonies." That resolution governed until the Articles of Confederation went into effect

on March 2, 1781, the fourth of the Articles providing that "the free inhabitants of each of these States — paupers, vagabonds, and fugitives from justice excepted — shall be entitled to all the privileges and immunities of the free citizens in the several States." That enabled the States to affect citizenship in one another and much confusion resulted. Hence the provision in the Constitution for National and uniform control.

In Washington's first message to Congress (or, rather, first annual address, for his message was oral) he recommended "that the terms on which foreigners may be admitted to the rights of citizens should be speedily ascertained by a uniform rule of naturalization." That Congress passed a law and there have been many supplemental enactments and revisions since. It was then assumed by the Government of the United States that the citizen of one country could cast off allegiance at pleasure and declare fealty to another government; but most European governments did not permit this, although some did. Thus, in "Burnet's History of His Own Times" he says that James II of England asked the States of Holland to surrender him to face a charge of treason, but that he, "being a subject of Holland (for I was naturalized), claimed their protection." Our War of 1812 with England was caused in part by its claim that, notwithstanding naturalization in the United States, it could take English-born seamen from our ships to serve in its defence against Napoleon. The American doctrine, laid down by Daniel Webster, Secretary of State to Presidents Harrison, Tyler, and Fillmore, was that the flag of the ship protects the crew and determines their nationality. Great Britain had always claimed the right to raise both land and naval forces by compulsion. Men were seized wherever found and often their relatives never knew what had become of them. Although the Treaty of Ghent, which closed the War of 1812, left this question unmentioned, the English Government never again seized men; but it insisted upon the right forcibly to visit and search our ships in time of peace until President Buchanan sent (1858) our navy to the Gulf of Mexico to stop it. In the proclamation issued by George III in 1807, two years after the great naval battle of Trafalgar, in which the English fleet under Nelson overcame Napoleon I on the sea, all men born under the English flag were called home from all lands and they were warned that no foreign letters of naturalization could in any manner divest natural-born citizens of allegiance to the English Government or release them from duty. It was not until the thirty-third year of the reign of Queen Victoria (1870) that England came to the American viewpoint respecting this subject, when the British Government entered into a treaty with the United States providing that naturalized subjects in each country should be treated in all respects as natives. In pursuance of the treaty a Naturalization Act was passed in that year by Parliament under which aliens who became naturalized were authorized to hold property (except British ships) as if they were natural-born subjects, after a residence of five years, or after service to the Crown. The Act authorized a subject of the British Government to expatriate himself by becoming naturalized in a foreign country. Down to that time the rule of English law was that no one could renounce the country or allegiance in which he was born.

A legal change of citizenship probably arose with the Romans. Roman citizenship was at first confined to the city. Gradually it was extended until it included Italy. From that it was widened to favored provinces. Gibbon mentions in his "Decline and Fall of the Roman Empire" (Vol. I, ch. VI) that the Emperor Caracalla (A.D. 222–235), "communicated to all the free inhabitants of the Empire the name and privileges of Roman citizens." The provincial considered it a great distinction to have the protection of Roman citizenship. In a dramatic scene in the New

Testament (Acts XXII, 24–28) St. Paul claims the protection of the Roman citizenship in which he was born.

Under our laws an alien of the age of eighteen may declare his intention to become a citizen of the United States. This declaration must be made at least two years before he becomes a citizen. Not more than seven years thereafter he must file a petition for naturalization, signed by him, and containing full particulars of his personal history. He must state that he is not a disbeliever in or opposed to organized government, that he is not a member of or affiliated with any organization so opposed, and that he is not a polygamist. In this petition he must repeat his first declaration that it is his intention to become a citizen, to reside permanently in the United States, and to renounce absolutely all allegiance or fidelity to any other government.

In addition to naturalization under the "uniform rule" of the Act of Congress, aliens have been made citizens by treaties, as was done in 1848 by the treaty of Guadaloupe Hidalgo for all those in the territory acquired from Mexico; and when Texas was admitted to the Union by joint resolution of Congress its inhabitants were thereby naturalized.

Where a naturalized citizen returns to his native country within five years, or goes to any other country for permanent residence, that is taken as *prima facie* evidence of his lack of intention to become a citizen, and his certificate will be therefore cancelled. This provision was enacted by Congress, following messages of President Grant showing that aliens had taken our certificates of naturalization and then returned to their native country or gone to some other country and made use of the certificates to protect them against military service and in other ways.

While our States have no jurisdiction over naturalization as it affects citizenship alone, most of them have legislative enactments touching the status of the alien in the ownership of land, or in the right to inherit property or to transmit it to his heirs. In some States aliens may hold and transmit property as if they were native citizens. In other States aliens may hold land only for a limited time, when they must dispose of it. The regulations of the various States are numerous. In some States the alien who has declared his intention to become a citizen is permitted to vote for candidates for minor offices. Since the World War this privilege has been revoked in at least one State.

In the first Act of Congress (1790) under this clause " a free white person " was declared eligible to naturalization. Except for a short time the quoted words have remained in the law. Confusion came because different courts understood the words differently, some as including Caucasians, and others as embracing Aryans. The Supreme Court held (1923) that " white person " describes, not an Aryan or a Caucasian (names of doubtful scientific value), but an immigrant of the stock of Europe.

Under an act of Congress passed in 1906 providing for the cancellation of a certificate of naturalization on the ground of fraud in its procurement many certificates were revoked during the World War because the sympathy shown by the naturalized persons for the nations at war with the United States proved that when they renounced allegiance to their former governments and swore that they would defend the United States they acted fraudulently.

and uniform Laws on the subject of Bankruptcies throughout the United States; [47]

[47] The Articles of Confederation did not deal with the bankrupt. The word originally applied to one who defrauded his creditors. Now it means one who is unable, for any reason, to pay them.

From time to time Congress has enacted bankruptcy laws. In 1800, in 1841, and in 1867, bankruptcy acts were passed which were of short duration.

On July 1, 1898, a bankruptcy law was enacted which

(with amendments) has been in effect ever since.   While an act of Congress is in effect the law of a State on bankruptcy is necessarily suspended because the Constitution makes the National law uniform "throughout the United States."

One becomes a voluntary bankrupt by filing a petition in a United States District Court and turning over all of his possessions (except exempted property, like the homestead, or the tools of a workman) for division among his creditors.   If no fraud appear he will be released from his debts, except those to a municipality, except as to credits which he secured on fraudulent pretenses, except alimony, and except one or two other obligations.   A creditor may file a petition against a debtor and place him in involuntary bankruptcy when he believes that a debtor is making away with property or favoring other creditors, and for some other reasons; and then the court takes immediate possession of the debtor's assets and protects them for the benefit of all creditors.   The law therefore operates to the advantage of both the debtor and the creditor.

The bankruptcy or insolvency law of a State cannot, the Supreme Court held (1819), discharge a debtor in that State from his previously incurred liability to pay, as the Constitution forbids (Note 71) the State to impair the obligation of a contract.   The State law under consideration in that case was designed not only to liberate the debtor from prison, but also to discharge him from all contractual liability. Later the court held (1827) that such a State law does not impair the obligation of future contracts.   In such circumstances the creditor contracts with full knowledge of the possibility of the debtor's insolvency.   And as the law of a State can have no extraterritorial effect (that is, cannot operate directly in another State), the discharge of a debtor by the insolvency law of his own State does not, it has been held (1891), release him (even as to future contracts) from an obligation to a creditor who is a citizen of another State and who has not submitted himself to the jurisdiction of the courts of the State in which the insolvency law was passed and applied.

Much difference of opinion prevails as to the value or the justice of the National Bankrupty Act, some believing it to be not only a shield but also an inducement to dishonest men. The provision in the Constitution undoubtedly came from the rigor with which unfortunate debtors were once treated and were dealt with down to the time of its adoption. In President Jackson's annual message of 1829, and again in his message of 1831, he recommended the discharge from imprisonment of debtors to the Government where no fraud had been practiced in incurring the debts. "The continuance of the liability after the means to discharge it have been exhausted," said he, "can only serve to dispirit the debtor. . . . The personal liberty of the citizen seems too sacred to be held, as in many cases it now is, at the will of the creditor to whom he is willing to surrender all the means he has of discharging his debt." While the Constitution of Pennsylvania of 1776 was about the first to open the prison doors of debtors, it was not until 1827 that a general agitation was begun in this country to abolish imprisonment for debt. Such imprisonment is forbidden in many States except in cases of fraud.

An act of Congress of 1839 (with revisions) forbids imprisonment by a Federal Court where imprisonment for debt has been abolished by the law of the State in which the Federal Court is sitting. It had been held by the Supreme Court of the United States (1823) that a debtor who had been discharged under a law of New York (1819) abolishing imprisonment for debt was not entitled to release from imprisonment on a judgment rendered against him in favor of the United States.

One Hebrew law (Deuteronomy XV) requires that "every creditor shall release that which he hath lent unto his neighbor" in the general release which was commanded "at the end of every seven years." But historians point out that the Hebrew laws of leniency were frequently if not generally disregarded. Thus Jesus spoke (Matthew XVIII, 23–25) of the king's servant who owed a heavy debt and who was ordered "to be sold, and his wife, and children, and all that he had, and payment to be made." Two sons of a widow were released from bondage for a small debt by a miracle performed by Elisha.

Gibbon says ("Decline and Fall of the Roman Empire", Vol. IV, p. 505) that under the Roman law of the 500's a debtor might either be sold to slavery or put to death In "Little Dorrit" the harsh treatment of the debtor in England down to late years is portrayed by Dickens. "When the fortress [Bastile] was taken," says Dicey, "there were not ten prisoners within its walls; at that very moment hundreds of debtors languished in English gaols."

It was the unhappy lot of the debtor in England that impelled James Oglethorpe, who as a member of Parliament had served on a committee to investigate conditions in prison, to found (1733) in the reign of George II the Colony of Georgia for the relief of such unfortunates.

At the time our Constitutional Convention was sitting the Congress acting under the Articles of Confederation erected the Northwest Territory (now Ohio, Indiana, Illinois, Wisconsin, and Michigan) and in the ordinance or act provided for imprisonment for debt. The first Congress under the new Constitution confirmed the ordinance.

To coin Money, regulate the Value thereof, and of foreign Coin,[48]

[48] Because this clause of the Constitution gives Congress jurisdiction over coinage and the value of coins, and because Section 10 of the same Article forbids the State to "make anything but gold and silver coin a tender in payment of debts", it was argued in the *Legal Tender Cases*, arising out of legislation during the Civil War, that it was the purpose of the people in their Constitution to put an end

to the misuses and abuses of paper money as they had known them. But it was answered that the prohibition of the making of "anything but gold and silver coin a tender in the payments of debts" stands in the Constitution, not against the Nation, but against the State. The Supreme Court held that the necessities of the Nation, which are to be determined by Congress, must control (Note 44).

Under authority from Congress the President reduced (1934) the standard gold dollar from 25.8 grains to 15.238, or from 100¢ to 59.1¢. An act (1933) had "declared to be against public policy" every provision "contained in . . . any obligation which purports to give the obligee the right to require payment in gold . . . or in any amount of money measured thereby." The act repealed legislation making Liberty Bonds payable in gold of the standard when issued. In the Gold Clause Cases (1935) the Supreme Court held (1) gold contracts between individuals void as against public interest; and (2) while the United States could not repudiate its gold contracts, plaintiff would suffer no damage from payment in paper because he would have to surrender gold under a call of Government which had already taken the American's gold possessions. A National Debt of over 30 billion, and State debts aggregating over 7.5, all promised in gold, thus became payable in dollars devalued to 59.1¢ each.

and fix the Standard of Weights and Measures; [49]

[49] The Articles of Confederation (Art. IX, sec. 4) gave to its Congress "the sole and exclusive right and power of . . . fixing the standard of weights and measures throughout the United States", so this provision in the new Constitution is substantially like that in the Articles. Uniformity here is almost if not quite as important as it is with respect to money. Because of systematic frauds

practiced, Chapter 35 of Magna Charta (1215) defined liquid measures, measures of cloth, and weights.

In his first annual address to Congress, January 8, 1790, Washington said that "uniformity . . . is an object of great importance and will, I am persuaded, be duly attended to."

Congress never has fixed a complete standard of weights and measures. It has adopted the wine gallon of 231 cubic inches as the standard of liquid measure. The English or Winchester bushel has always been in use. The standard size or capacity of the barrel for apples and other dry commodities has been prescribed by Congress, as well as the size of the basket for fruits and vegetables. Electrical units have been defined. The gold dollar of 25.8 grains, nine-tenths fine, was standard until 1934 (Note 48). In 1866 Congress permitted, without requiring, the use of the metric system in the United States and declared that no contract or other writing should be held invalid when expressed in terms of that system. Later (1881) it authorized the Secretary of the Treasury to deliver to the governor of each State, for the use of agricultural colleges, a complete set of all weights and measures adopted as standard. The Postmaster General has authority to supply to the post offices postal balances denominated in grams of the metric system. In 1901 Congress established the Bureau of Standards. It has custody of the standards, and its duties are to compare standards in use, and to construct and test standards, as well as to make a general study of the subject.

To provide for the Punishment of counterfeiting the Securities and current Coin of the United States; [50]

[50] Had this power not been expressly conferred upon Congress it would be implied from the preceding power "to coin money and regulate the value thereof", if not from the inherent power of any government to protect its sovereignty

and itself. The power was not conferred by the Articles of Confederation. It has been held that "the securities" which may not be counterfeited include treasury notes of the United States, its certificates of indebtedness (like silver certificates), its bonds, and the bills or paper money issued by National banks.

In 1920 a Federal court held that war savings stamps come within this language and that the alteration of them would be punishable under the provisions of the penal code enacted by Congress in pursuance of this clause.

To establish Post Offices and post Roads; [51]

[51] In its relation to the intellectual, social, and material advancement of the people this provision goes alongside of the commerce clause for importance. The Post Office Department deals more directly with the individual than any other activity of the government.

In the Articles of Confederation provision was made (Art. IX, sec. 4) for "establishing and regulating post offices from one State to another throughout all the United States, and exacting such postage on the papers passing through the same as may be requisite to defray the expenses of the said office."

The scope of the Constitution is wider, including post roads as well as post offices.

Postal service was given in the Colonies as far back as 1639. An act of Parliament of 1710 authorized a deputy postmaster general for America at New York. Benjamin Franklin took the office in 1753 and made a success of it. When the government under the Constitution began in 1789 there were about seventy-five post offices in the thirteen States. In 1846 a postal treaty was negotiated with England. Postage stamps were introduced in 1846, stamped envelopes in 1852, the registered letter in 1855, free delivery and the traveling post office in 1863, the money order in

1864, postal cards in 1872, rural delivery in 1896, postal savings depositories in 1910, and the parcel post in 1912 — in all these matters Congress exercising power under this clause.

The government is not required to furnish postal facilities for every purpose, the Supreme Court has held, and therefore an act (1868) forbidding the mailing of matter relating to lotteries was sustained (1877) under this clause. So of the Act of 1873 excluding obscene and like matter. The Supreme Court held further (1892) that the Amendment (1890) to the law excluding from the mails newspapers and periodicals containing advertisements of lotteries did not abridge the freedom of the press (Note 142). The circulation of newspapers as such was not prohibited. The newspapers could enter the mails by omitting the advertisements. The Court said that Congress could not be "compelled arbitrarily to assist in the dissemination of matters condemned by its judgment." Of course, the Post Office Department cannot open mail to find whether it is objectionable except in conformity with the clause (Note 146) regarding search.

On March 20, 1908, President Roosevelt wrote the Attorney-General in denunciation of anarchistic publications, declaring them to be the enemies of mankind and asking for an act of Congress excluding them from the mails :

"The Immigration Law now prohibits the entry into the United States of any person who entertains or advocates the views expressed in this newspaper. It is, of course, inexcusable to permit those already here to promulgate such views. . . . No law should require the Postmaster General to become an accessory to murder by circulating literature of this kind."

To promote the Progress of Science and useful Arts, by securing for limited Times to Authors and Inventors the exclusive Right to their respective Writings and Discoveries; [52]

[52] These subjects were not mentioned in the Articles of Confederation. Nor were they in the first draft of this Constitution. Copyrights had been granted by some of the States, and this probably suggested to Mr. Madison and Mr. Pinckney the motions which resulted in this clause. In 1782 Noah Webster began an effort with the States to secure copyrights of two elementary works on English. The legislature of Connecticut granted his request in 1784 by passing probably the first copyright law in the United States. New York and Massachusetts followed. In 1783 Congress had recommended such action by the States. Thus the ground had been well prepared before the Constitutional Convention assembled (1787) and the proposal was quickly accepted. A copyright law, entitled "An Act for the Improvement of Learning", was passed (1790) by the first Congress under the Constitution and many revisions have since been made. The present copyright law gives to the originator the exclusive right to make, publish, or sell books, maps, charts, pictures, prints, statues, models, and some other things for a term of twenty-eight years, with the privilege of renewal to him or to certain of his dependents for another term of twenty-eight years. The copyright extends to the publication and sale of popular songs and the use of them upon the stage and in the phonograph ; and it covers also moving-picture films. Thus the short statement of a principle in the Constitution is given in the course of time the widest practical application — to things which the mind in 1789 could not have conceived. One infringing the right is subject to penalty and is also liable for damages done to the holder of the copyright.

By the common law of England (which was adopted in America) an author was protected from the publication of his manuscript by another. But after he himself had published he lost his property and any one else might publish. However, by copyright he is protected from publication by others for the full statutory term.

An act of Parliament in 1710 (as later amended) gave to the English author the sole right to print and vend his writings, thus adding to the common-law protection.

The benefit of our copyright laws was at first given to citizens only, but now it extends to citizens of countries which make reciprocal arrangements for the protection in those countries of American authors.

The law of copyrights in the United States was largely formulated by decisions of Judge Story (later a Justice of the Supreme Court of the United States), sitting in the United States Circuit Court at Boston, between 1830 and 1845.

A patent law, "An Act to Promote the Progress of Useful Arts", also was passed by the first Congress. The patent law as we know it really dates from 1836, when the Acts of Congress were fully revised. From 1835 to 1845 Judge Story laid in numerous decisions the foundations of patent law as Lord Mansfield created the commercial law of England. Not until 1845 did patent cases appear commonly in the Supreme Court of the United States. An early and famous one, decided by Chief Justice Taney (1842), had to do with the landside of a common plow. In 1853 Samuel F. B. Morse was held by the Supreme Court, in a case arising in Kentucky, to have been the first inventor of the magnetic telegraph capable of recording signs at a distance. He applied for a patent on September 28, 1837. Davy secured a patent in England in 1838 and Wheatstone secured one in 1840.

The tide of emigration into western territory brought up patent cases respecting reaping machines, grain elevators, plows, and other inventions springing from agricultural life. In 1853 the great case of Seymour *v.* McCormick, involving an infringement of the rights of Cyrus H. McCormick, the inventor of the reaping machine, patented in 1834, was passed upon. In the trial court at Cincinnati, Abraham Lincoln was associated with Edwin M. Stanton, later to be selected by Lincoln as Secretary of War.

Between 1850 and 1860 litigation arose concerning the invention of the breech-loading firearm, Elias Howe's sewing machine, and many other useful devices.

To this provision of the Constitution is due, undoubtedly, the supremacy of the United States in all fields of electrical and mechanical invention. In no other country has the use of machinery gone so far or done so much for human comfort and advancement. In every quarter of the earth some American machine has lessened toil or given pleasure. The monopoly offered to the inventing genius stimulated him to seek the great rewards given for a useful device.

While the purpose of the constitutional provision and the Acts of Congress passed from time to time to give it effect is that the genius of the inventor shall be recompensed by a monopoly of the manufacture and sale of his invention, the Supreme Court has held (1918) that "the exclusive right to make, use and vend the invention or discovery ceases when the right to vend has been once exercised." Having once sold the article, he can no longer control the price. Therefore, a notice placed by the patentee upon his invention that it was "licensed by us for sale and use at a price of not less than $1", and that any violation of the condition would be an infringement of his patent right, was held beyond the protection and purpose of the patent laws; and accordingly a merchant who purchased the article in trade could resell it at less than a dollar.

In the *Trade Mark Cases* (1879) it was held that the grant of power to Congress by this clause of the Constitution did not authorize it to give exclusive rights in the use of registered trade-marks. A trade-mark is not an invention, nor is it the work of an author. However, the courts exercise their equity powers to prevent by injunction the unfair use of a mark or name (or something deceptionally resembling it) under which another has built up a trade or patronage; and at the same time the public is protected from the imposition upon it of an article different from the one which it thinks it is buying. During the fierce competition of recent years and the litigation growing out of it there has been built up in the form of decisions of the courts a vast body of what is called the law of unfair trade.

To constitute Tribunals inferior to the supreme Court; [53]

[53] This provision is repeated in Article III (Note 97), dealing with the Judicial Department of the Government. Section 1 of that Article vests the judicial power in a Supreme Court, "and in such inferior courts as Congress may from time to time ordain and establish."

"Without such inferior courts in every State," said President Monroe, "it would be difficult and might even be impossible to carry into effect the laws of the general government."

There are in the United States (including Hawaii, Puerto Rico, and Alaska) 83 district or trial courts. In many places a district is divided. There are 144 divisions, so it may be said that in reality the number of courts is above one hundred. Appeals lie from those courts in some cases directly to the Supreme Court of the United States, but in a large number of instances appeal is taken to the Circuit Court of Appeals, a tribunal of three judges created in 1891 for the relief of the Supreme Court, the decision of which is final in many cases. The United States and its possessions are divided into nine circuits, and one of the justices of the Supreme Court is, under an act of Congress, allotted by the Chief Justice to each circuit, where he sits as presiding judge whenever he attends (which is not often) a session of the court. There is a Court of Claims at Washington, established in 1855, in which the Government consents to be sued. In 1909 Congress established a Court of Customs Appeals with jurisdiction over import duties. In China and some other countries we have consular courts.

To define and punish Piracies and Felonies committed on the high Seas, and Offenses against the Law of Nations; [54]

[54] It is fitting that matters touching the law of nations should be under the power of the Nation rather than under those of the States. Otherwise, a State dealing with a foreign nation might embroil all the States. The Articles of Confederation (Art. IX) gave to "the United States in Congress assembled" the "sole and exclusive right and power of . . . appointing courts for the trial of piracies and felonies committed on the high seas." But "to define and punish" was not contained in the Articles. The high seas are the public seas over which all vessels have the right to travel, like a highroad or highway. They include the uninclosed waters of the ocean and those on the coast outside of the low-water mark. Piracies (robberies) and felonies (offences punished by imprisonment or death) as they were known in 1787 have disappeared from the sea. Piracy was a profitable business then, as it had been from time immemorial. Captain Kidd and many others became noted at it. By the Treaty of Ryswick (1697) England, France, Spain, and Holland bound themselves to make common cause against piracy. Algiers covered the sea with pirates and in Washington's administration the safety of American commerce was purchased by the payment of tribute to pirates. At the close of the War of 1812 the United States sent Commodore Decatur with a fleet of nine ships to punish the Barbary pirates. He captured their chief vessels, entered the Bay of Algiers, and dictated a treaty to the humbled Dey. He then sailed to Tunis and Tripoli, where he took pledges of good conduct. Since then this clause of our Constitution has been practically obsolete, except as to offences against international law.

To declare War, grant Letters of Marque and Reprisal, and make Rules concerning Captures on Land and Water; [55]

[55] The Articles of Confederation conferred upon Congress the "sole and exclusive right and power of determining on peace and war." But the United States could not engage in war "unless nine States assent to the same." More definite and full language is used in the Constitution. All those powers are attributes of nationality and would exist without mention in the Constitution. But it was desirable to make definite the department of the government in which they should reside. In the Constitutional Convention some thought the President should have the powers; others favored bestowing them upon the Senate as representing the States; but the prevailing opinion was that the grave acts of declaring and conducting war should be performed by the whole Congress. In 1812 Congress passed an act declaring war on Great Britain because of hostile acts done by that country. In 1846 a resolution of Congress declared that a state of war already existed with Mexico owing to hostile acts of that nation. In 1898 Congress declared war upon Spain. In 1917 a resolution of war was passed by Congress as a result of the sinking by Germany of the *Lusitania* and other merchant ships with the loss of American lives, and of other violations of international law with respect to the United States.

In 1941, Japan attacked at Pearl Harbor. Congress immediately declared that a state of war existed between the United States and Japan, Germany and Italy. The United States emerged as the only great nation in the modern world that never lost a war. This proud record again demonstrates the strength of free institutions. When their representatives vote for war, the people respond.

The important lesson to be learned here is that in the United States one man (or one coterie) cannot declare war.

"Congress shall have Power . . . to declare War . . . to raise and support Armies . . ." Here Woodrow Wilson asks Congress for war on Germany

That can be done only by the two Houses of Congress (531 members), elected by the direct vote of the people. Action is not likely to be hurried or unjust.

"The genius and character of our institutions are peaceful," said the Supreme Court of the United States (1849), "and the power to declare war was not conferred upon Congress for the purposes of aggression or aggrandizement, but to enable the general government to vindicate by arms, if it should become necessary, its own rights and the rights of its citizens."

In the foregoing case the question was whether the city of Tampico, Mexico, while in the military possession of the United States in 1847, ceased to be a foreign country so that customs duties could not be laid on imports from it. The answer was No. While the United States may acquire territory, it can do so only through the treaty-making or the legislative power—the victories of the President as Commander in Chief "do not enlarge the boundaries of this Union, nor extend the operation of our institutions and laws beyond the limits before assigned to them by the legislative power."

Half a century later a somewhat similar question arose after the war with Spain. Puerto Rico and the Philippines were ceded by that Government to the United States. Did the acquisition change the status of the islands so that they ceased to be "foreign countries" within the meaning of the tariff laws under which duties had been paid by their citizens on their exports to this country? Next, how were they affected by the clause of the Constitution (Note 63) requiring that "all duties, imposts, and excises shall be uniform throughout the United States"? In a series of decisions in what were called the *Insular Cases*, extending from 1901 to 1905, the doctrine was established that it is for Congress first to determine when acquired territory is in a condition to become in legal completeness a part of the United States. Territory comes into the United States through the door of congressional legislation and preparation. Until brought in by Congress new territory, while it has ceased to be a foreign country, does not become a part of the United States to the extent that its people have all the constitutional guaranties of civil and political rights.

Letters of marque and reprisal, authorized by the Articles of Confederation and by this clause, are authority issued by a government to its citizens to fit out ships (privateers) to capture the ships or property of another nation with which it is at war. Once every armed vessel was required to carry a letter of marque as evidence that it was not a pirate.

In a later section (Note 70) the State is forbidden to issue letters of marque and reprisal. By the Declaration of Paris (1856), to which the United States declined to assent because private property was not to be exempt from capture at sea, privateering was abolished by a convention of European powers.

To raise and support Armies, but no Appropriation of Money to that Use shall be for a longer Term than two Years; [56]

[56] To raise and support armies is a power implied from the grant of the preceding one "to declare war." But to leave no question as to what department of the government would do it, the power was expressly conferred upon Congress; for otherwise the President as Commander in Chief (Note 85) might assume to raise armies after Congress had made the declaration of war. The President cannot raise an army, nor can Congress maintain one by an appropriation for a longer term than two years. England, which suffered much from <u>Kings</u> and Parliaments that raised armies, resorted from 1689 (the year of the Bill of Rights) to 1879 to the device of the Mutiny Act. That Act, passed each year, began by reciting that the Bill of Rights made illegal a standing army except by consent of Parliament, and then it expressed the opinion that certain forces would be neces-

sary for the coming year and accordingly made an appropriation of money. In addition it made regulations separate from the civil law for the discipline of the forces and for the prevention and punishment of mutiny. In 1879 a revision of the Mutiny Act was called the Army Discipline and Regulation Act, which also was passed each year. It is now called the Army (Annual) Act.

By raising ship money through a system of taxation of his own, instead of asking Parliament for an appropriation, Charles I was able to construct and man a powerful navy; but in the Civil War which followed his course he was defeated by the Parliamentary party and then beheaded.

While the new Constitution was undergoing the ordeal of ratification by State conventions, Alexander Hamilton said in " The Federalist ":

"The legislature of the United States will be *obliged* by this provision, once at least in every two years, to deliberate upon the propriety of keeping a military force on foot; to come to a new resolution on the point; and to declare their sense of the matter by a formal vote in the face of their constituents. They are not *at liberty* to vest in the Executive Department permanent funds for the support of an army, if they were even incautious enough to be willing to repose in it so improper a confidence."

As the President cannot raise an army, and as Congress can maintain one for only two years (the length of a term of Congress), the possibility of collusion between them is very remote. Anything indicating collusion would be dealt with by the voters, who can retire every member of the House of Representatives and one third of the Senate every two years and put in those who would respect the popular will. In the Constitutional Convention there was much opposition to a standing army; but it was felt that that danger would be averted by placing the support of it in Congress, and then restricting the power of Congress to make appropriations.

The Articles of Confederation were weak as to raising and supporting armies. First, while "the United States in Congress assembled" had the "sole and exclusive right and power of determining on peace and war" (Art. IX), it was declared in the same article (Sec. 6) that the government "shall never engage in war . . . unless nine States assent to the same." Second, "all charges of war . . . shall be defrayed out of a common treasury" (Art. VIII) to "be supplied by the several States." There was an almost total lack of the concerted powers which are necessary to that swift and decisive action often required in National emergencies.

The Constitution corrected those faults. Thus in 1917 Congress by resolution announced that because of the acts of Germany a state of war existed with that nation; and then, without any reference to the States, it passed in rapid succession acts laying on all the people (not of the States. but of the Nation) many kinds of emergency taxes, laws providing for the issuing of liberty bonds, for the conscription of men for the army and the navy, for the building of ships, for the making of munitions, and for all the other purposes of war. During World War I many of the States enacted laws in aid of the National endeavor.

The army of Europe which our fathers feared was developed through centuries of plunder by adventurous or predatory rulers, one of the inducements to hireling service in the rank and file being a share of the pillage. But the armies which have been raised in the United States have been of entirely different origin and training. They have come from homes, from generations of home-keeping and right-respecting people, and they have been anxious to return home. Within a few months after the Grand Review of the Union armies in Washington after the Civil War, over a million veterans, fully equipped, had dissolved, as it were, and disappeared in the civilian life whence they came. And after World War I 4,800,000 men, of whom

2,084,000 had gone to France and 1,300,000 had seen active service at the front, hurried gladly to their homes and left off even the military titles which they had won. However, it is well to have written in the Constitution the limitations regarding an army.

To provide and maintain a Navy;

To make Rules for the Government and Regulation of the land and naval Forces;

To provide for calling forth the Militia to execute the Laws of the Union, suppress Insurrections and repel Invasions; [57]

[57] A militia was provided for in the Articles of Confederation (Art. VI, sec. 4), each State being required to keep up a body of disciplined men "sufficiently armed and accoutred." The State was forbidden to keep "any body of forces" in time of peace, unless Congress should deem it necessary as a garrison.

Under our Constitution each State maintains a militia, some of the States having bodies of the highest class in discipline and equipment. By act of Congress the methods of training are uniform, so that when bodies from different States are brought together they work as one.

The Nation may call out the militia of the State for three purposes only: (1) to execute the laws of the Union (the Constitution, the Acts of Congress, and the treaties); (2) to suppress insurrections (the open and active opposition of a number of persons to the execution of law); and (3) to repel invasions, that is, the entrance of an enemy for war. Congress has authorized the President to make those calls.

It is noticeable that the militia is not in the power of the President, and that the authority of Congress over it is limited to three purposes. Here, again, both the President and the Congress are prevented from achieving an armed dictatorship.

To provide for organizing, arming, and disciplining the Militia, and for governing such Part of them as may be employed in the Service of the United States, reserving to the States respectively, the Appointment of the Officers, and the Authority of training the Militia according to the discipline prescribed by Congress; [58]

[58] Under this clause Congress has from the beginning provided for the training and the maintenance of the militia. The National Defence Act of 1916 revised and extended preceding legislation. There are a National Guard, a Naval and an Unorganized Militia. For the purpose of maintaining appropriate organizations and to assist in instruction and training the President is authorized to assign the National Guard of the State to divisions, brigades, and other tactical units and to detail officers from either the National Guard or the regular Army to command such units.

The watchfulness of the people over State authority and their fear of the encroachment of National power are exhibited again in the provision that the militia must be officered by appointees of the State. Of such a military body the State would have no fear. Besides, officials of the State would be better informed as to who would be competent as officers. It was once a threatening question whether militia in the service of the United States could be commanded by any but militia officers and the President; but any officer under the commander in chief (the President) outranking the militia officer may command.

The Articles of Confederation provided (Art. IX, sec. 4) that the Nation should appoint "all officers of the land forces in the service of the United States, excepting regimental officers." The clause in our Constitution was probably intended to restate that idea.

Hamilton said that the powers granted in this clause are naturally incident to the "common defence" of the Nation.

To exercise exclusive Legislation in all Cases whatsoever, over such District (not exceeding ten Miles square) as may, by Cession of particular States, and the Acceptance of Congress, become the Seat of the Government of the United States,[59] and to exercise like Authority over all Places purchased by the Consent of the Legislature of the State in which the Same shall be, for the Erection of Forts, Magazines, Arsenals, dock-Yards, and other needful Buildings;

[59] This refers to the coming District of Columbia, where a city was to rise and be called Washington. In 1788–1789 Maryland ceded to the Nation sixty square miles east of the Potomac and Virginia thirty square miles west. The cession by Virginia was returned in 1846. The District is governed directly by Congress.

In 1793 Washington laid the corner stone of the Capitol. The building of the White House had been begun the year before. In 1800 President Adams transferred the seat of government from Philadelphia to Washington.

Where the Nation establishes a fort, a magazine, an arsenal, a post office, or a dockyard in a State, the Nation assumes control over the land to the exclusion of State authority.

This clause may have had its origin in an unhappy experience of Congress, which indignantly left Philadelphia and sat at Princeton because Pennsylvania had been unable or unwilling to protect it near the close of the Revolution from mistreatment by a body of mutineers of the Continental Army. It was determined that the National Government should be upon its own premises and within its own control. Further, it was felt that the capital should not be also the capital of a State, or a large commercial city.

The choice of a site for the National capital resulted from a compromise effected by Secretary of State Jefferson and

Secretary of the Treasury Hamilton. Congress was at deadlock respecting a bill for the assumption of State debts, States like Virginia, which had kept their debts well up, opposing the assumption of the debts of those badly delinquent. Nor could Congress come to an understanding as to where the capital of the United States should be. Jefferson undertook to influence votes enough to pass the Assumption Bill if Hamilton would procure votes enough to establish the capital somewhere on the Potomac River. The stipulation was carried out.

To prevent encroachments upon the State it is required that "the consent of the legislature" be given to the purchase by the Nation of grounds for forts, magazines, arsenals and other buildings.

— And

To make all Laws which shall be necessary and proper for carrying into Execution the foregoing Powers, and all other Powers vested by this Constitution in the Government of the United States, or in any Department or Officer thereof.[60]

[60] This clause has been aptly described as "the most solid and excellent work done by the [Constitutional] Convention." It made a Constitution adaptable to unforeseen conditions and serviceable for all time. For example, it enabled Congress to pass many laws under the commerce clause for the control of the steamboat when it came, of the railway, of the telegraph, of the telephone, of the airplane, all undreamed of when the clause was written. After granting to Congress power in twenty particular instances the people say in this clause that Congress may pass all additional laws that time and circumstances may make necessary or proper to give full execution and efficiency to each or all of the twenty grants of power. Experience under the Articles of Confederation had made this clause so plainly

desirable that hardly any contention was raised by it in the Constitutional Convention. It neither grants a new power nor enlarges any of the others. Under the ordinary rules of interpretation what is stated in this clause would be implied had the language been omitted. But it was deemed necessary to express it clearly — to put it beyond question that such restrictions as that of the Articles of Confederation (Art. II), that each State should retain the powers "not by this Confederation *expressly* delegated to the United States in Congress assembled", should not embarrass the new Nation. It has been said that the grant of power to do what may be necessary is express and not implied. However, it is the custom to speak of a power necessarily flowing from the previous grant of another power as an implied power.

The question of implied powers, in a large aspect, first arose in Jefferson's administration (1803) over the purchase of Louisiana from France. Jefferson was a "strict constructionist" — nothing was constitutional in his view if it was not clearly written in the fundamental law. But the Constitution does not expressly authorize the purchase of territory. He was, therefore, between a theory of constitutional law and a great necessity of governmental administration. In a message to Congress he referred to the control of the Mississippi by France and mentioned the recent "suspension of our right to deposit at the port of New Orleans." He at first felt an amendment to the Constitution necessary to the exercise of such power, but "if our friends think differently", he added, "certainly I shall acquiesce with satisfaction." But the Senate confirmed the treaty (Note 88) of purchase and the House of Representatives originated the money bill (Note 37) necessary to carry it out without so much as even proposing an amendment. The very first clause granting power to Congress authorizes it to "provide for the common defence and general welfare of the United States." That is precisely what was held in mind by Jefferson and Congress when the purchase of Louisiana was made, and the control of the Mississippi River acquired. The Constitution therefore gave the power to purchase.

Commenting on this purchase by Jefferson (Anti-Federalist or Republican) when there was no express clause in the Constitution to warrant it, John Quincy Adams, whose father (Federalist) had been a spirited opponent of the great strict-constructionist, said: "It naturalizes foreign nations in a mass. It makes French and Spanish laws a part of the laws of the Union. . . . And all this done by an administration which came in blowing a trumpet against implied powers!"

One other great illustration, out of many cases, will suffice. In 1791 the Bank of the United States was created by Congress in support of Hamilton's financial policy for making stable the currency and establishing the National credit. No power to charter banks or corporations is expressed in the Constitution. In 1818 Maryland passed a law taxing the paper used in issuing money by all banks not chartered by its legislature. This affected the operations of a branch in Maryland of the Bank of the United States and brought a direct conflict of authority between the State and the Nation. The Supreme Court of the United States, in an opinion written by Chief Justice Marshall, held (1) that in pursuance of its fiscal or financial policy Congress had power to establish a national bank, and (2) that the State could not hamper or burden the proper activities of the Nation.

As to every one of the twenty grants of power Congress has from time to time enacted laws which it deemed necessary to make the power effectual. Indeed, as before indicated, this is what has fitted the Constitution to new or unforeseen conditions as they arose, and kept it the controlling force in the development of thirteen scattered agricultural communities into a Nation of forty-eight great States of immeasurable material wealth, of unexampled political freedom, and of the highest educational and social advantages.

Section 9. The Migration or Importation of such Persons as any of the States now existing shall think proper to admit, shall not be prohibited by the Congress prior to the Year one thousand eight hundred and eight, but a Tax or duty may be imposed on such Importation, not exceeding ten dollars for each Person.[61]

[61] As the preceding section deals with the affirmative powers of Congress, this section has to do with what has been called its negative powers. It enumerates ten things which Congress may not do.

In Section 9 a legislative body was for the first time restrained. Kings had been curbed by charters, but never a legislature. Parliament was often tyrannical. American statesmen feared the legislature. " An elective despotism was not the government we fought for," wrote Jefferson. Madison argued that " the people ought to indulge all their jealousy and exhaust all their precautions " in self-defense. So the first American invention in government was a curb upon legislative power, as was the second (Note 97).

The Privilege of the Writ of Habeas Corpus shall not be suspended, unless when in Cases of Rebellion or Invasion the public Safety may require it.[62]

[62] By the ancient writ of *habeas corpus* (have the body) an English court commanded the jailor or other officer having a prisoner in charge to bring him before the bar for inquiry as to the legality of his restraint from liberty. Men had been cast into prison without formal charge and left there without hearing or trial. In the Petition of Right to which Charles I was obliged to assent (1628) the sovereign was charged with violation of this privilege, which ante-

dated Magna Charta (1215). It was prayed in the Petition that "freemen be imprisoned or disseized only by the law of the land, or by due process of law, and not by the King's special command without any charge." In the reign of Charles II (1679) the first Habeas Corpus Act was passed to make more definite the rights of Englishmen which had been disregarded on one pretext or another. In the reign of George III the first act, relating to charges of crime, was supplemented by an act dealing with deprivation of liberty for any other reason.

Knowing in how many ways this right of the Englishman and the English colonist in America had been defeated, the framers of our Constitution forbade suspension of the privilege except in two similar contingencies; but even in time of (1) rebellion or (2) invasion the privilege is not to be suspended unless the public safety may require it.

As this clause is in Article I of the Constitution, relating to legislative powers, and as the subject is not mentioned in Article II, dealing with the powers of the Executive (President), it was held by Chief Justice Taney shortly after the outbreak of the Civil War that President Lincoln did not have power to suspend the privilege of the writ, Congress alone possessing that authority. The President had suspended the privilege in several instances where former officers of the army or the government had gone over to the Confederacy and were active in the North against the Union. Such persons were put in prison and held without trial.

To set the matter at rest Congress later authorized President Lincoln to suspend the privilege of the writ of *habeas corpus*.

In England a *habeas corpus* Suspension Act often is passed which partially annuls the operation of the celebrated Habeas Corpus Act of Charles II (1679). The Suspension Act makes it hopeless for any person imprisoned under a warrant signed by the Secretary of State on a charge of high treason or on *suspicion* of treason to insist upon being either discharged or put on trial. The Government of England may defer indefinitely the formal accusation and public trial of persons imprisoned on suspicion of treasonable practices. That cannot be done in the United States.

No Bill of Attainder [63]

[63] The bill of attainder in England was an act of Parliament by which a man was tried, convicted, and disposed of without a jury, without a hearing in court, generally without hearing the witnesses against him, and without regard to the rules of evidence. His blood was attainted or corrupted legally so that he could not inherit property from others nor could his children inherit property from him. This deprivation of property was contrary to the charter of Edward III (1327–1377), which said that no one should be "put out of his lands or possessions, . . . or disinherited, . . . without being brought to answer by due process of law." Bills of attainder were first passed by Parliament in 1459 and were often employed during the time of the Tudors (1485–1603). In the reign of Henry VIII (1509–1547) they were much employed to punish those who had incurred the King's displeasure and many fell victims who could not have been charged with any offence under existing law. During the Long Parliament (nearly twenty years) beginning in the reign of Charles I (1625–1649) Parliament itself made effective use of the bill of attainder to dispose of objectionable persons. In the reign of William III and Mary (1690) an act was passed "for the attainder of divers rebels"; and Macaulay says that "it was not even pretended that there had been any inquiry into the guilt of those who were thus proscribed." In 1870 forfeiture was abolished by the English Government except upon outlawry, and it was provided that "no judgment of or for any treason or felony shall cause any corruption of blood or any forfeiture or escheat." For his activities and

writings in behalf of colonial rights Jefferson's name was included in a bill of attainder presented in Parliament, but it was not pressed to a vote.

The convenience of the bill of attainder when ruthless power found in its way legal safeguards to the man was well illustrated in the case of Thomas Wentworth, Earl of Strafford and chief adviser of Charles I, who was impeached (1640) and tried before the House of Lords on the charge of attempting to subvert the liberties of England. As the evidence seemed insufficient, and as Strafford defended himself with great ability, his prosecutors, foreseeing an acquittal, withdrew the impeachment and subsequently attacked him by a bill of attainder which passed both Houses and received, under the pressure of public opinion, the unwilling signature of the King. Strafford was beheaded.

Bills of attainder were known in America in colonial times. In 1777 Thomas Jefferson wrote a bill of attainder for an outlaw in Virginia. This method of punishment was often used during the Revolution. In Lecky's "England in the Eighteenth Century" it is mentioned that in the State of New York an act confiscated all the goods of fiftynine royalists, including three women, and in a footnote the author makes reference to "a long list of these acts of attainder."

Having beheld the injustice of such punishment, the framers of our Constitution put in the instrument two prohibitions of bills of attainder, this one to curb the National Government, and one in the section following (Note 71) preventing such legislation by the government of a State.

or ex post facto Law shall be passed.[64]

[64] An act is *ex post facto* (after the deed or fact) when it (1) makes a criminal offence of what was innocent when done, or when it (2) aggravates a crime, making it greater than it was when committed, or when it (3) inflicts a greater punishment than was prescribed at the time the

crime was perpetrated, or when it (4) alters the rules of evidence in order to secure a conviction, or when it in effect if not in purpose (5) deprives the accused of some protection to which he had become entitled. Thus a law changing the number in a jury from twelve to eight after a crime had been committed was held *ex post facto* as to the accused, who could not be deprived of his liberty unless by a jury of twelve. And an act passed after a man nad been convicted and sentenced to death, requiring that persons under such sentence be kept in solitary confinement, was held *ex post facto* as to him because imposing additional punishment. But acts changing punishment from hanging to electrocution have been held by several courts not to be *ex post facto*, for, as one of the courts said, the act, so far as it could tell, might have mitigated rather than increased the punishment.

Nor was the law of a State *ex post facto* which gave the State an appeal in criminal cases which did not exist at the time the crime was committed, the appeal of the State resulting in a conviction of the defendant, the Supreme Court of the United States holding that the legislation of the State did not make criminal what was innocent, or aggravate an offence, or alter the rules of evidence, or otherwise deprive the accused of a substantial right.

Near the close of the Civil War an act was passed by Congress that no attorney should be permitted to practice in the Supreme Court of the United States or any other Federal court, or be heard by virtue of any previous admission, until he had first taken an oath that he had not voluntarily given aid, counsel, or encouragement to persons engaged in armed hostility to the United States and that he had not sought or accepted office in hostility to the National Government. A man who had served in both the House and the Senate of the Confederate States of America received a pardon from the President in 1865. He applied for readmission to practice in the Supreme Court without being required to take the oath mentioned, which of course he could not take. He contended that the act was unconstitutional because *ex post facto*, and he also claimed the right under his pardon. The Supreme Court held that as the oath could not be taken, the act operated "as a legislative decree of perpetual exclusion", a method of punishment which did not exist at the time the acts of the applicant were done.

No Capitation, or other direct, Tax shall be laid, unless in Proportion to the Census or Enumeration herein before directed to be taken.[65]

[65] A capitation (*caput*, meaning head) or poll (head) tax is one levied upon the individual without regard to his possessions in lands or personal property. The poll or capitation tax was common in early New England. While condemning the capitation tax in "The Federalist", and expressing the belief that taxes should be raised indirectly, Hamilton was nevertheless in favor of the constitutional provision permitting the laying of head taxes in case of emergency; for he mentioned that the sources of revenue then were few. This clause forbids Congress to lay a tax upon individuals except uniformly, and in proportion to the census provided for (Note 10) in Article I, Section 2, Clause 3, where this subject is first mentioned.

No Tax or Duty shall be laid on Articles exported from any State.[66]

[66] This is the only prohibition in the Constitution upon the taxing power of Congress. A like prohibition as to taxing either imports or exports is declared (Note 73) against the State legislature in Section 10, Clause 2, below.

This provision was demanded by the Carolinas and Georgia. They waived their objections to taxes on imports in consideration of this clause. Some of the agricultural States were in much fear of the taxing power.

A tax of one cent a pound on all filled cheese manufactured

was held by the Supreme Court not violative of this clause as to owners of cheese which was exported, for the tax cast no more burden on exported articles than was borne by those not exported. So during the Civil War a tax was imposed on all cotton and tobacco. It was contended by men producing and owning that as the larger part of those products was exported the tax was unconstitutional; but of course the tax was not laid because of the exportation — the commodities were called upon to pay the tax regardless of their entering foreign commerce. However, an act of Congress (1898) to meet the expenditures of the War with Spain was held (1901) unconstitutional under this clause as to a stamp tax imposed on a bill of lading covering shipments of grain for export, that being a tax imposed on the exporter only and for the reason that he exported, a tax plainly prohibited by this clause.

No Preference shall be given by any Regulation of Commerce or Revenue to the Ports of one State over those of another: nor shall Vessels bound to, or from, one State, be obliged to enter, clear, or pay Duties in another.[67]

[67] This proposal was placed before the Constitutional Convention by the delegates from Maryland, their fear being that congressional legislation might prefer Chesapeake Bay ports of Virginia to those of their State. Under the Articles of Confederation, as has been seen, each State was free to impose duties and make regulations to the disadvantage of others, and it was desired that equality in commerce be maintained in the future.

No Money shall be drawn from the Treasury, but in Consequence of Appropriations made by Law; and a regular Statement and Account of the Receipts and Expenditures of all public Money shall be published from time to time.[68]

[68] In this clause is repeated the lesson of English history that it should not be in the power of the Executive alone or of the legislature alone to raise or spend money at will. In Section 7 preceding (Note 37) is the requirement that all bills for raising money must originate in the House of Representatives; but they must then pass the Senate and be signed by the President. For over half a century the expression "appropriations made by law" was construed to mean by a bill passed by both Houses and signed by the President. In 1842 Congress began to make appropriations by joint resolution; but as that also must be signed by the President (Note 39), there is no real difference.

No Title of Nobility shall be granted by the United States: And no Person holding any Office of Profit or Trust under them, shall, without the Consent of the Congress, accept of any present, Emolument, Office, or Title, of any kind whatever, from any King, Prince, or foreign State.[69]

[69] "A wise jealousy of foreign influences in the affairs of government," says a writer on our Constitution, "will amply justify this provision."

A provision in almost the same words was in the first section of Article VI of the Articles of Confederation. It permitted persons holding office under a State to accept, with the assent of Congress, the objectionable gifts or distinctions; but the constitutions of at least two of the States at that time forbade them altogether. Of course, a republic born of the misrule of a monarchy should not grant titles of nobility. The institution called nobility had possessed itself of most of the posts of trust and honor to the hopeless exclusion of the rest of the people, and by prestige and by the favoritism of the government of which it was so large a part it had gained the greater share of the lands and other wealth of England and of the continental countries.

A gift from the King of France to our ambassador

during the Revolution is said to have suggested this provision. "Any present . . . of any kind whatever" was said by the Attorney-General's office in 1902 to prevent the acceptance of photographs from Prince Henry of Prussia, brother of the Emperor of Germany, by civil and military officers of the United States. But while Jefferson was President he accepted (1806) from Alexander I of Russia a bust of that Emperor, which he said would be "one of the most valued ornaments of the retreat I am preparing for myself at my native home." He said that he had laid it down as a law of his official conduct not to accept anything but books, pamphlets, or other things of minor value; but his "particular esteem" for the Emperor "places his image in my mind above the scope of law."

This prohibition of the granting of titles of nobility by the Nation is repeated (Note 72) as to the States in the first clause of the next section.

By the charter issued to Lord Baltimore in 1632 he was authorized to grant titles of nobility in Maryland. A claim to like authority was made under one or two other colonial charters.

In 1810 Congress proposed an amendment to add a heavy penalty to this clause by making any person "cease to be a citizen of the United States" and "incapable of holding any office of trust or profit" who should, without the consent of Congress, accept "any title of nobility or honor", or "any present, pension, office, or emolument of any kind whatever from any emperor, king, prince, or foreign power." At that time a brother of the Emperor Napoleon of France was in the United States. The proposed amendment lacked the necessary ratifying vote of only one State.

Section 10. No State shall enter into any Treaty, Alliance, or Confederation; grant Letters of Marque and Reprisal; coin Money; emit Bills of Credit; [70]

[70] All the powers in this section denied to the States are in Section 8 granted to the Nation. As the exercise of such powers by the States had helped to wreck the Government under the Articles of Confederation, the double precaution was taken by the people of granting them to the Nation in Section 8 of this Article of the Constitution and denying them to the States in Section 10. Those things are essentially National. In several places in the Constitution this double-statement of power is employed. By this section the States yielded to the Nation some powers which they had previously exercised.

Under the Articles of Confederation the worst of all the troubles, probably, sprang from the lack of National control of money and credits, and it was frequently stated in the Constitutional Convention that those evils — what Madison called "the pestilent effects of paper money" — must be abated forever. Nevertheless, many attempts have been made by States to issue paper money, that is to "emit bills of credit" to be passed as money. Those acts of the States have, of course, been held unconstitutional, in some instances by the courts of the issuing States — for the Constitution provides (Note 134) that "the judges in every State shall be bound thereby [by the National Constitution], anything in the Constitution or laws of any State to the contrary notwithstanding." But bills of credit or certificates of indebtedness which are not intended by the State to circulate as money do not fall within the prohibition of this clause.

make any Thing but gold and silver Coin a Tender in Payment of Debts; pass any Bill of Attainder, ex post facto Law, or Law impairing the Obligation of Contracts,[71]

[71] The command in the preceding section, that Congress shall not enact attainders or *ex post facto* laws, is here repeated as to the States, with the addition that the State

shall not impair the obligation of contracts. This was added when it was pointed out that the term *ex post facto* relates only to criminal law. The provision was accordingly framed to fit civil cases. Therefore the State may not change the legal standing of a citizen with respect either to his personal conduct or to his contracts. A contract which was permissible and valid at the time that it was entered into cannot be rendered void or be in any wise impaired by subsequent legislation by the State, or by the county or the city acting under powers received from the State. The obligation of a contract is its binding force on the party making it which the law at the time it was made would effectuate. It involves the promise of the party and the sanction of the law that the promise shall be carried out. The contracts of the State as well as those of the individual are covered by this clause. Many cases have arisen in which States have attempted to evade the obligations of contracts made by them with citizens. To illustrate, where a State chartered a bank and profited from its operations, and the law creating the bank provided that the bills or money issued by it should be receivable in payment of debts due to the State, such as taxes, a subsequent act of the legislature repealing this provision of the Bank Act was held (1850) by the Supreme Court of the United States to violate this clause of the Constitution. When the citizen accepted the inducement of the State to use its bank's money for its benefit a contract arose under which the State was obliged to render to him the advantage which it had promised and for which it had received a consideration.

One of the purposes of the provision was to prevent States from permitting the payment of debts in paper money. Another purpose was to prevent the passage of insolvency laws and stay laws which would release debtors from their present obligation to pay. In addition to those matters, contracts of States themselves had been repudiated. "The separate legislatures have so often abused the obligation of contracts," wrote Jefferson, "that the citizens themselves chose to trust it to the general [National] rather than to their own [State] authorities." On the same subject Chief Justice Marshall said "a course of legislation had prevailed in the States which weakened confidence of man in man."

No provision of the Constitution has received more frequent consideration by the Supreme Court of the United States and by the Supreme Courts of the States.

In 1758 the remnant of the Delaware Indians in New Jersey were given a tract of land by the State in consideration of their leaving lands which they were occupying; and it was agreed by the State that the lands to be given to the Indians aforesaid "shall not be subject to any tax, any law, usage, or custom to the contrary notwithstanding." In 1801 the legislature of New Jersey attempted to revoke the tax exemption after the lands had been sold by the Indians, but the Supreme Court of the United States held (1812) that the act of revocation was void for conflict with this provision. The Court said that the privilege to be free from taxation was, by the terms which created it, annexed "to the land itself." The exemption therefore went with the land to the purchaser, who could not be deprived of it.

The Dartmouth College case is perhaps the most celebrated of the early cases arising under this clause. In 1769, after an application to the King of England for a charter to incorporate a religious and literary institution, and upon the representation by the applicants that large contributions had been promised for the project, which would be conferred upon the corporation as soon as chartered, George III issued a charter. On the faith of that grant the property promised was conveyed to the corporation. Gifts of land and money were received and many rights acquired. In 1816 the legislature of New Hampshire passed "an Act to Amend the Charter and Enlarge and Improve the Corporation of Dartmouth College." The Act changed the name college to university, and the reorganization was such as to put the property and the franchise in the possession and control of another organization. The trustees of Dartmouth College refused to recognize the amended charter and brought a proceeding to see whether the acts of the legislature "are valid in law . . . or whether the same acts are repugnant to the Constitution of the United States, and so void." Daniel Webster, who had been educated at Dartmouth, was counsel for the college. The Supreme Court held (1819) that the legislation of New Hampshire impaired the obligation of the contract under which the college came into existence and was to continue in its course, and that it was therefore unconstitutional and void.

The withdrawal for a time of the remedy of a creditor by the enactment of a stay law is unconstitutional. So is any law which, under the pretence of changing the remedy, undertakes to compel a person to accept something different in the place of that for which he had contracted. Any law which gives a preference in payment of one creditor to another which did not exist when the contracts were made is invalid, even though the preferred creditor is the State itself. This is true of any law which takes away from the creditor a substantial right which the contract assured to him, as the right to the possession of mortgaged lands until the mortgage debt is paid. A law which increases the exemptions from executions issued on judgments so as seriously to impair the value of the remedy and reduce the possibilities of collection is void under this clause.

Contracts for the purchase price of slaves were enforced after Emancipation, notwithstanding the provision in the State constitution that such debts should not be paid; for the constitutional provision of the State was a "law" which impaired the obligation of a contract which was legally valid at the time that it was made.

The contractual right of the owner of a house or an apartment to the possession of the premises upon the expiration of the term agreed upon in the tenant's lease was held (1921) by the Supreme Court of the United States not unconstitutionally impaired by a rent law of New York (1920) de claring the existence of a housing emergency and providing that in a city of a million population or more no action should be maintainable to recover possession of premises occupied as a dwelling by a tenant desiring to remain and pay a reasonable rent, except that the owner might have the dwelling for his personal possession or to tear it down for the construction of a new building. Contracts are made said the court, "subject to this exercise of the power of the State when otherwise justified", referring to the police power, which is exerted for the health, safety, and wellbeing of the people.

Nor did the law operate to deprive the owner of property in violation of the Fourteenth Amendment (Note 173), for in many cases restrictions upon property rights for the general welfare have been upheld as warranted under the police power of the State. It has long been established, the court pointed out, that the owner of property may be restricted in his income or rental, as by laws imposing an excess profits tax, or an income tax, or by laws prohibiting usurious interest.

In the leading case on the power of the State to regulate the rates which may be charged the public for the use of private property, the Supreme Court stated (1876) the governing principle as follows :

"Property does become clothed with a public interest when used in a manner to make it of public consequence, and affect the community at large. When, therefore, one devotes his property to a use in which the public has an interest, he, in effect, grants to the public an interest in that use, and must submit to be controlled by the public for the common good, to the extent of the interest he has thus created. He may withdraw his grant by discontinuing the use ; but, so long as he maintains the use, he must submit to the control."

or grant any Title of Nobility.[72]

[72] In the preceding section (Note 69) the Nation is forbidden to grant titles of nobility. The repetition of the commandment as to the State shows the dislike which the Fathers had for that institution which, more than anything else, had made life for the Colonies under English rule impossible. All the repressive and burdensome plans of the Government of George III found prompt and generally unanimous support in the House of Lords, then the organized expression of intolerant and intractable nobility. The Constitutional Convention was determined that this noxious thing never should be found in the United States.

Titles of nobility have been conferred by the sovereign of England upon citizens of Canada.

No State shall, without the Consent of the Congress, lay any Imposts or Duties on Imports or Exports, except what may be absolutely necessary for executing it s inspection Laws: and the net Produce of all Duties and Imposts, laid by any State on Imports or Exports, shall be for the Use of the Treasury of the United States; and all such Laws shall be subject to the Revision and controul of the Congress.[73]

[73] Here is another recurrence to the National prerogative under the commerce clause (Note 45) to regulate trade. Every precaution was taken to keep the State from such interferences as those which had defeated the Union under the Articles of Confederation.

No State shall, without the Consent of Congress, lay any duty of Tonnage, keep Troops, or Ships of War in time of Peace, enter into any Agreement or Compact with another State, or with a foreign Power, or engage in War, unless actually invaded, or in such imminent Danger as will not·admit of delay.[74]

[74] In this sentence are four bars, none of which the State may cross without the permission of Congress: it may not (1) lay any duty of tonnage (tax upon the cubical capacity of a ship), for that might work a hindrance to commerce and bring conflict with the regulatory power of the Nation under the commerce clause; it may not (2) keep troops or ships of war (the State militia, organized for discipline, and belonging to civil life, not being troops within this clause), for standing troops within a State might bring conflicts with other States or other governments, or even with the Nation; it may not (3) enter into agreements (political) with other States or with foreign powers, for thereby the National Government might be embarrassed; and it may not (4) engage in war except in self-defence. Each one of those powers is inherent in any independent government. For the good of the Union and themselves the people of the States, in ratifying the Constitution, disclaimed those powers in favor of the Nation.

The Presidential Oath: "I do solemnly swear that I will faithfully execute the office of President of the United States, and will to the best of my ability, preserve, protect and defend the Constitution of the United States"

ARTICLE II

Section 1. The executive Power shall be vested in a President of the United States of America. He shall hold his Office during the Term of four Years, and, together with the Vice President, chosen for the same Term,[75]

[75] In Woodrow Wilson's "History of the American People" (Vol. 3, p. 71) it is pointed out that the laws of the new government were to be imperative instead of advisory: "It was provided with the Executive the Confederation had lacked; a person in whose authority should be concentrated the whole administrative force of its government."

In Green's "History of the English People" it is stated that Cromwell's experience with the Long Parliament (1640–1660) confirmed his belief in the need of an executive power, entirely apart from the legislature, "as a condition of civil liberty."

In the examination of Article I, relating to the Legislative Department of the government, it has been seen that the President has great power in that department as well as in his own, in approving or vetoing bills passed by the Senate and the House of Representatives. He has an influence in the Judicial Department, too, for he appoints (Note 89) the judges; but, of course, only with the approval of the Senate.

He is as much a creation of the Constitution as the Legislative Department (Congress) or the Judicial Department (the Supreme and inferior courts), and he is therefore as independent of both as they are of each other and of him.

But for misconduct he may be impeached by the House and tried by the Senate, the Chief Justice presiding (Note 17) at the trial.

It was the intention of the Founders of the Republic that the Executive (President) should be a strong branch of the government. While the Colonies had had more than enough of a kingly executive wielding great and arbitrary power in a stubborn way, they had later learned from experience with governors of the States under the Articles of Confederation (1781–1789) that an executive with defined and limited powers is an essential to good government. In those days the legislature was most feared as a possible usurper of power. The lawless record of the Long Parliament of England was only a century and a half away, while many acts of later Parliaments were believed to be transgressions of both constitutional and natural rights. James Otis and other colonial leaders declared that Parliament enacted laws against the Colonies "which neither God nor man ever empowered them to make." Hence the check of the President's veto, and the numerous definite limitations upon the power of Congress.

When the work of framing Article II had been done some thought that a monarch had been set up in the President; but, of course, that was unreasonable, as the Constitution provides for his election by popular vote, as he cannot raise a dollar for an army or for any other purpose, as he cannot declare war, as he is subject to removal by impeachment, and as he can do but very little beyond executing the laws of the Legislative Department (Congress). But within his sphere he is powerful and independent. "Abraham Lincoln," wrote James Bryce, "wielded more authority than any single Englishman has done since Oliver Cromwell." But much of Lincoln's war power, and particularly that for the use of which he was most criticised, the suspension of the privilege of the writ of *habeas corpus*, was given to him by Congress for the term of the war only. So in 1917 Congress gave to President Wilson extraordinary powers for prosecuting the war against Germany.

In the Constitutional Convention many favored a plural Executive, consisting of two or more men. Jefferson, who was not in the Convention, favored a one-man Executive, pointing out that "A Committee of the States" provided for in the Articles of Confederation to act during recess of Congress "quarreled very soon, split into two parties, abandoned their post, and left the Government without any visible head until the next meeting of Congress." In the "Federalist" a single executive was advocated by Hamilton because of "decision, activity, secrecy, and dispatch" and because plurality "tends to conceal faults and destroy responsibility."

The length of the term and whether there should be more than one term were much debated. A resolution was passed by the Convention that the President be not eligible for reëlection, Washington voting against it. Jefferson wrote strongly for one term, but he lived to change his mind and serve two terms. Later, he wrote that the example of four Presidents retiring at the end of eight years would have "the force of precedent and usage" against any man who might seek a third term. President Grant sought a third term in 1880, but he was defeated in the Republican nominating convention. Theodore Roosevelt, who served three years of the second term of McKinley and a four-year term thereafter, sought a third in 1912. Failing to secure the nomination in the Republican convention, he ran on a third-party ticket and lost. Franklin D. Roosevelt was the first president to be elected for a third term, when he ran for a third time in 1940.

Although the Constitutional Convention passed a resolution for one term, the committee to which it was finally referred never reported it back. Terms were proposed ranging in length from during good behavior down to three years. The Convention fixed the term at seven years, but the report came back from the committee showing four years, not disclosing, however, the reason for the change.

The President of France is elected for seven years and he may be reëlected.

In Chile the term of the President is five years and he is not eligible for reëlection. He cannot, without the permission of Congress, leave the Republic during his term or for one year thereafter.

The term of the President of the United States of Brazil is six years, and he is forbidden to leave the country during his incumbency under penalty of forfeiture of office.

In the first Congress under the new order (1789) consideration was given to choosing titles for the President and Vice President. "His Excellency" and "His Highness" and other titles were suggested, but as the House of Representatives had already addressed him simply as The President, it was finally resolved to adhere to his constitutional title, "President of the United States of America."

be elected, as follows [76]

[76] Over and over the Constitutional Convention debated the question of how the President should be elected. It was proposed that he be chosen by Congress; by "electors chosen by the people in election districts"; by the governors of the States; by the Senate; and by the votes of all the people. The suggestion that the people could choose a President was described as "vicious", while Mr. Wilson of Pennsylvania stood stanchly for the popular vote. James Madison said that "if it is a fundamental principle of free government that the legislative, executive and judiciary powers shall be *separately* exercised, it is equally so that they be independently exercised"; and he declared that there is even greater reason why the Executive should be independent of the Legislative branch than why the Judiciary should be. Although at first the Convention voted that Congress elect the President, it was, after full

discussion of a question "the most difficult of all which we have had to decide", concluded to choose by the electors mentioned in the next paragraph, probably following the provision of the Constitution of Maryland for the election of State senators.

Each State shall appoint, in such Manner as the Legislature thereof may direct, a Number of Electors, equal to the whole Number of Senators and Representatives to which the State may be entitled in the Congress: [77]

[77] This is the "electoral vote" of a State. Those of all the States together make the vote of the so-called "electoral college." The vote of a State consists of one vote for each of the two senators and one vote for each representative. When the number of members in the National House of Representatives is changed by the growth of population, this necessarily increases the number of votes in the "electoral college." When Washington was first elected (1788) there was a total of sixty-nine electoral votes, that being the number of senators and representatives of the States participating, New York having failed to choose electors and Rhode Island and North Carolina not yet having ratified the Constitution. In 1936 there were five hundred thirty-one electoral votes in all the United States, based on the census of 1930.

It was the intention of the Constitutional Convention that the electors, chosen as each State might think the best way, should meet and vote their individual preferences, thus excluding the influence of Congress, and also the influence of the voters at large, who were thought incompetent to choose a President; and that is the way Washington was elected twice and Adams once. But during the administration of Adams friends of Jefferson in Congress held a conference or caucus and announced him as their candidate. This became the settled method of announcement.   Later the caucus was superseded by the party convention, which adopted a platform and nominated candidates, a method which still prevails.

In the beginning some of the States chose their electors by their legislatures, some according to districts, and some otherwise.   Now they are chosen by ballot of the whole people.   On the same ballot are the names of the presidential and vice-presidential candidates of the party, for whom the electors are expected (though not obliged by the Constitution) to vote.

but no Senator or Representative, or Person holding an Office of Trust or Profit under the United States, shall be appointed an Elector.

[The Electors shall meet in their respective States, and vote by Ballot for two persons, of whom one at least shall not be an Inhabitant of the same State with themselves.   And they shall make a List of all the Persons voted for, and of the Number of Votes for each; which List they shall sign and certify, and transmit sealed to the Seat of the Government of the United States, directed to the President of the Senate.   The President of the Senate shall, in the Presence of the Senate and House of Representatives, open all the Certificates, and the Votes shall then be counted.   The Person having the greatest Number of Votes shall be the President, if such Number be a Majority of the whole Number of Electors appointed; and if there be more than one who have such Majority, and have an equal Number of Votes, then the House of Representatives shall immediately chuse by Ballot one of them for President; and if no Person have a Majority, then from the five highest on the List the said House shall in like Manner chuse the President.

But in chusing the President, the Votes shall be taken
by States, the Representation from each State having one Vote; A quorum for this Purpose shall consist of a Member or Members from two-thirds of the
States, and a Majority of all the States shall be necessary to a Choice. In every Case, after the Choice
of the President, the Person having the greatest
Number of Votes of the Electors shall be the Vice
President. But if there should remain two or more
who have equal Votes, the Senate shall chuse from
them by Ballot the Vice President.] [78]

[78] This paragraph in brackets was superseded on September
25, 1804, when the Twelfth Amendment was promulgated.
The paragraph is retained here for its historic value. The
electors then voted for persons, not for a President and a
Vice President. Of the persons voted for they could not
designate the one they preferred for the chief office and the
one for second place. The candidate receiving the highest
number of votes became President. The next highest number made the Vice President regardless of political belief.
Thus *all* the electors voted for George Washington. The
next number in size voted for John Adams. That made
Washington President and Adams Vice President. By
that method John Adams of the Federalist (or National)
party later (1797) became President, receiving seventy-one
electoral votes, and Thomas Jefferson, an intense anti-
Federalist, Vice President, sixty-eight votes being the next
highest number. The anti-Federalists were, in addition to
being opposed to a strong National (as distinguished from
State) government, in favor of intimate relations with the
new Republic of France, while the Federalists declared
that all foreign alliances must be avoided. In his Farewell
Address (September 17, 1796) Washington spoke repeatedly
and powerfully against implicating ourselves in European

affairs.   Such conflict of opinion and the consequent want
of harmony within the administration made an amendment
to the Constitution necessary.   In the presidential election
of 1800 Thomas Jefferson and Aaron Burr received seventy-
three electoral votes each. The election therefore went
to the House of Representatives, in which, after thirty-five
ballotings, Jefferson was chosen.   That made Burr Vice
President, for "in every Case, after the Choice of the
President, the Person having the greatest Number of
Votes of the Electors shall be Vice President."   The
changes made will be considered in the study of the Twelfth
Amendment (Note 165).

**The Congress may determine the Time of chusing
the Electors, and the Day on which they shall give
their Votes; which Day shall be the same throughout
the United States.**[79]

[79] As elections in different States were held at different
times, Congress acted (1872) under this clause and directed
that the electors be appointed in each State "on the Tuesday
next after the first Monday in November in every fourth
year"; and the electors are required to "meet and give
their votes on the second Monday in January next following
their appointment at such place in each State as the legislature of such State shall direct", usually the capital being
by the State legislature designated as the place.

**No person except a natural born Citizen, or a Citi-
zen of the United States, at the time of the Adoption
of this Constitution,**[80] **shall be eligible to the Office of
President; neither shall any Person be eligible to
that Office who shall not have attained to the Age of
thirty-five Years, and been fourteen Years a Resident within the United States.**

[80] Many of foreign birth who had helped to create the
United States would have been rendered ineligible had

not the provision been inserted making eligible those of foreign birth who at the time of the adoption of the Constitution were citizens of the United States. The lapse of time long since removed that class and left the excepting clause the mere record of an interesting historic fact.

Seven of the signers of the Constitution were foreign born: James Wilson, Robert Morris and Thomas Fitzsimons of Pennsylvania, Alexander Hamilton of New York, William Paterson of New Jersey, James McHenry of Maryland, and Pierce Butler of South Carolina.

Some members of the Constitutional Convention argued for a financial qualification also. It was suggested that the President should be worth in property at least $100,000. The proposal was rejected. The first President was a man of large means. Most of the Presidents have been poor in property.

It is an interesting fact that the one-House Congress sitting under the Articles of Confederation passed, while the Constitutional Convention was in session (July 13, 1787), "an ordinance for the government of the territory northwest of the river Ohio" (now Ohio, Indiana, Illinois, Michigan, and Wisconsin) in which it was provided that the governor to be appointed by Congress should, besides being a resident of the district, "have a freehold estate therein in 500 acres of land while in the exercise of his office." The judges of the court created were each required to own a like area. The belief then was common that ownership of property added to stability of character and citizenship.

In Case of the Removal of the President from Office, or of his Death, Resignation, or Inability to discharge the Powers and Duties of the said Office, the same shall devolve on the Vice President, and the Congress may by Law provide for the Case of Removal, Death, Resignation or Inability, both of the President and

Vice President, declaring what Officer shall then act
as President, and such Officer shall act accordingly,
until the Disability be removed, or a President shall
be elected.[81]

[81] Congress has made no provision, evidently believing
it unnecessary under the foregoing language, for the performance of the duties of the President in time of his inability alone.

For nearly three months after being shot (July 2, 1881)
President Garfield was unable to perform the duties of his
place, but Vice President Arthur did not because of that
"inability" assume "the powers or duties of the said office."
After the President's death (September 19, 1881) Mr. Arthur
succeeded to the post. In 1919–1920 President Wilson's
sickness caused such "inability" for several months that
not even Cabinet officers or representatives of foreign nations were permitted to see him. The language of the Constitution clearly expresses the intent that in case of such
inability, even when temporary, the Vice President shall
discharge the duties of the office. The Supreme Court of
New Hampshire held under a similar provision in the constitution of that State that the governor's office was
"vacant" when his temporary inability from sickness and
the needs of public service required the duties to be performed by a substitute, and that in such circumstances the
President of the State Senate could be compelled by writ
of mandamus from court to assume and discharge the
duties. In 1948 Congress enacted that if for reason of
death, resignation, removal, inability, or failure to qualify,
there is neither President nor Vice President to discharge
the office, the Speaker of the House shall resign and act
as President; if there be no Speaker, the President pro
tempore of the Senate shall resign and act: in either case
to the end of the term. On failure of both President-elect
and Vice President-elect to qualify, any officer named shall

serve only until a President or a Vice President qualifies. Should there be no President pro tempore to act, a member of the Cabinet shall serve, beginning with the Secretary of State.

The Constitution of the United States of Brazil (1890) is more clear than ours and provides that the Vice President shall take the place of the President "in case of *temporary* disability and succeed him in case of vacancy."

The President shall, at stated Times, receive for his Services, a Compensation, which shall neither be encreased nor diminished during the Period for which he shall have been elected, [82]

[82] The first Congress, by an Act of September 24, 1789, fixed the salary of the President at $25,000 a year.

The Act of March 3, 1873, doubled President Grant's salary the day before his second term began and increased those of the Vice President, the members of the Cabinet, the Justices of the Supreme Court, and the members of Congress themselves. It was made retroactive as to Congressmen. This was contrary to popular opinion and also to the practice of legislators in the States not to increase their compensation during the term for which they were elected. Owing to public disapproval, one of the first steps of the next Congress was to reduce (January 20, 1874) all of the advances of salaries except those of the President and the Justices of the Supreme Court, the Constitution forbidding (Note 98) Congress to diminish those. In 1909 the salary of the President was advanced to $75,000, with an allowance from time to time for traveling expenses such as Congress may deem necessary and not exceeding $25,000 a year. President Washington declined a salary.

The Australian Governor General, who is appointed by the sovereign of England instead of being elected, receives a salary of $50,000 a year.

See Note 33 for advances of Congressional salaries.

and he shall not receive within that Period any other Emolument from the United States, or any of them.[83]

[83] Of the provisions of this paragraph Alexander Hamilton wrote in the "Federalist" (No. LXXIII): ".They [Congress] can neither weaken his fortitude by operating upon his necessities, nor corrupt his integrity by appealing to his avarice. . . . , Nor will he be at liberty to receive any other emolument than that which may have been determined by the first act. He can, of course, have no pecuniary inducement to renounce or desert the independence intended for him by the Constitution."

Before he enter on the Execution of his Office, he shall take the following Oath [84] or Affirmation: — " I do solemnly swear (or affirm) that I will faithfully execute the Office of President of the United States, and will to the best of my Ability, preserve, protect and defend the Constitution of the United States."

[84] The oath is usually administered at the Capitol by the Chief Justice of the United States "before" the President-elect takes office on Jan. 20. But it may be taken elsewhere and before any officer empowered by law to administer oaths. President Grant's second term expired on Sunday, March 4, 1877, and Rutherford B. Hayes took the oath at the White House on Saturday and again at the Capitol on Monday. Upon the death of President Garfield (September 19, 1881) the oath was taken by Vice President Arthur in New York City and later he took it again in Washington.

Section 2. The President shall be Commander in Chief of the Army and Navy of the United States, and of the Militia of the several States, when called into the actual Service of the United States; [85]

[85] This is a constitutional right which Congress has no power to diminish. In the Convention it was proposed

that he be not permitted to head an army in the field, but the proposal was rejected. In practice, however, no President has led an army or commanded a navy. The Secretary of War and the Secretary of the Navy carry out the wishes of the commander in chief. The experience of General Washington during the Revolution with the dilatory methods of Congress probably brought the Convention to the idea that there should be no divided authority when troops are "called into the actual service of the United States." Some of the early Constitutions of the States made the governors commanders; and the ordinance creating Northwest Territory (1787) made the governor "commander in chief of the militia", with authority to "appoint and commission officers in the same below the rank of general officers."

Formerly some of the States thought that they should determine whether the militia should be sent to the service of the Nation, but the Supreme Court of the United States held that "the authority to decide whether the exigency has arisen belongs exclusively to the President and his decision is conclusive upon all other persons." If many States were to come to many conclusions upon such a subject the Nation might in the meanwhile be destroyed.

In time of war much of the power exercised by the President is delegated to him by Congress for the time being. During the Civil War Congress so aided the President that it was described as "a giant committee of ways and means." In 1862 it authorized President Lincoln to take possession of railroads when necessary for public safety. In World War I Congress authorized the President to take over and operate the railroads as an instrumentality of war, which he did. It passed many acts giving him extraordinary powers, such as the Conservation of Food Act, the War Finance Corporation Act, the Trading with the Enemy Act, and many others. Such authority expires either by a time limit in the act itself or by subsequent repeal by Congress.

he may require the Opinion, in writing, of the principal Officer in each of the executive Departments, upon any subject relating to the Duties of their respective Offices,[86]

[86] The "principal officer" is a member of the President's Cabinet. At least twice the Constitutional Convention refused to hamper the President by an advisory council which might influence his conclusions. In Colonial times the royal governor had a council with a considerable power. But in the course of events there has grown up a cabinet somewhat resembling the council which the Convention rejected. However, it is not a Constitutional body, and the President is in no way bound by the opinion of his cabinet, nor is he obliged to consult it at all. Some Presidents, knowing that the majority of the members of the cabinet were not in sympathy with a particular policy, have gone forward without consulting them. Others have listened to suggestions and then acted at pleasure. Jefferson called for a vote in cabinet meetings, his vote counting one with the others. But he believed that he had the right to independent action. Lincoln wrote the Emancipation Proclamation without consulting his cabinet; but he read it during a meeting for suggestions and amendments.

The first "principal officer" created under this clause was the Secretary of State, brought into being by an act of the first Congress, July 27, 1789. His department was then called the Department of Foreign Affairs. Next came the Secretary of War (August 7, 1789), the Secretary of the Treasury (September 2, 1789), the Attorney-General (September 24, 1789), the Postmaster General (May 8, 1794), the Secretary of the Navy (April 30, 1798), the Secretary of the Interior (March 3, 1849), the Secretary of Agriculture (May 15, 1862), the Secretary of Commerce (February 14, 1903), and the Secretary of Labor (March 4, 1913).

In Chile there is a Council of State resembling our President's cabinet, made up of three persons chosen by the Senate, three by the House of Deputies, and five by the President. Its duties are advisory, except in some cases in which the Constitution requires submission to the Council. Thus to a degree the President is restricted.

In Canada, in Australia, and in South Africa there is a council chosen by the Governor General and holding piace at his pleasure.

and he shall have Power to grant Reprieves and Pardons for Offences against the United States, except in Cases of Impeachment. [87]

[87] With one exception the power to pardon is absolute. The judgment of the United States Senate in an impeachment trial (Note 25) is beyond the reach of executive clemency. Otherwise an appointee of the President who might be convicted in an impeachment trial could be pardoned and reappointed to the office for which he had been adjudged unfit. Such was the method of the sovereign of England in protecting his favorites from punishment. In the Act of Settlement (1701) providing for a successor to Queen Anne, the Parliament declared that no pardon by the King could be used to exculpate one who had been impeached "by the Commons in Parliament."

On Christmas day, 1868, President Johnson issued a general proclamation granting full pardon "unconditionally and without reservation" to those who had acted against the Union in the Civil War. The judiciary committee of the Senate questioned his power, but the Senate took no action. The Supreme Court has said that the President's pardoning power is beyond control or limitation by Congress.

He shall have Power, by and with the Advice and Consent of the Senate, to make Treaties, provided two-thirds of the Senators present concur; [88]

[88] A treaty is a written contract between two governments respecting matters of mutual welfare, such as peace, the acquisition of territory, the defining of boundaries, the needs of trade, the rights of citizenship, the ownership or inheritance of property, the benefits of copyrights and patents, or any other subject.

During the time of the Continental Congress (1774–1781) many treaties were made by it on behalf of the States by name. The Congress was then the only governmental authority. While the Articles of Confederation were in effect (1781–1789) the one-House Congress, even after creating a Department of Foreign Affairs (1781), retained supervisory power over treaties and some other international matters; and it was by this method that the Treaty of Paris (1783), by which England recognized the independence of the United States, was negotiated. Twelve other treaties were entered into by Congress. But when the present Constitution was framed, creating a President and a Congress of two Houses, it was determined to let the President, the executive head of the Nation, negotiate treaties with other governments and to empower the Senate to ratify or reject them.

In the Constitutional Convention a committee's report gave to the Senate the full power to make treaties. One delegate favored giving the power to the two Houses of Congress. Probably as a compromise the method stated in the Constitution was adopted. The subject received no more than ordinary consideration. It was pointed out in the "Federalist" by Alexander Hamilton that treaty-making is neither legislative nor executive, but that it appeared that the executive is "the more fit agent in those transactions, while the vast importance of the trust and the operation of the treaties as laws plead strongly for the participation of the whole or a portion of the legislative body in the office of making them." The Senate must finally approve a treaty by a two-thirds majority before it

"He shall have Power, by and with the Advice and Consent of the Senate, to make Treaties . . ." U. S. delegates sign United Nations Charter at San Francisco

"The President shall be Commander in Chief of the Army and Navy of the United States

can become effective. The reason for this given by Alexander Hamilton was that a man raised from humble station to the height and power of the Presidency might be unable to withstand the temptation of avarice or ambition by aiding a foreign power to the detriment of the United States.

Once a treaty is made, it requires both branches of Congress to abrogate it; that is, the President and the Senate cannot undo their work.

A precedent for thus abrogating a treaty made by the President and approved by the Senate may be found as far back as July 7, 1789, when Congress passed "An Act to Declare the Treaties heretofore Concluded with France no longer Obligatory on the United States" because they "have been repeatedly violated on the part of the French government." As a law of Congress may thus supersede a treaty, so a treaty may supplant an act of Congress, the latest expression of the National will being controlling.

While in this clause the Constitution names the President and the Senate as the makers of a treaty, other provisions sometimes require the concurrence of the House of Representatives; for as all money bills must originate in that House (Note 37), it may refuse to provide the means for effectuating the treaty. Of course, many treaties need no such aid from the House; but the House may constitutionally render null a treaty in which it disbelieves and which cannot be effectual without the expenditure of money.

The Reverdy Johnson–Lord Clarendon Treaty of 1869, which attempted to settle all differences with England from 1853 down, was rejected by the Senate by a vote of 54 to 1, largely because it was felt that Johnson should have exacted an apology for acts done by England during the Civil War in claimed violation of neutrality.

On February 16, 1893, just before the expiration of his term, President Harrison sent a treaty to the Senate for the annexation of Hawaii. When President Cleveland took office he withdrew the treaty, as he questioned the validity of the revolutionary provisional government which had been set up under the protection of marines from a man-of-war of the United States lying in the harbor of Honolulu.

In Cleveland's administration (1897) the Senate declined to approve a treaty made with England because it proposed to submit American "interests in all cases to the decisions of an outside tribunal." The treaty was drawn after a very serious dispute with England regarding the boundary between British Guiana and Venezuela, our government interposing under the Monroe Doctrine for the protection of the last-named State.

President Washington consulted with the Senate respecting treaties which he intended to negotiate. The practice has not been generally followed by his successors, though from time to time it has been adopted. In 1846, in the midst of a threatening controversy with Great Britain respecting the northwest boundary of the United States from the Rocky Mountains to the Pacific Coast, which negotiations in 1818, in 1824, in 1826, and in 1844 had failed to settle, President Polk transmitted to the Senate a proposal "of Her Britannic Majesty for the adjustment of the Oregon question" and asked for its advice. Referring to Washington's practice as "rarely resorted to in later times", he said that it "was, in my judgment, eminently wise and may on occasion of great importance be properly revived."

These were his reasons :

"The Senate are a branch of the treaty-making power, and by consulting them in advance of his own action upon important measures of foreign policy which may ultimately come before them for their consideration, the President secures harmony of action between that body and himself. The Senate are, moreover, a branch of the war-making power, and it may be eminently proper for the Executive to take the opinion and advice of that body in advance upon any great question which may involve in its decision the issue of peace or war."

President Polk concluded the message by saying that if the majority of the Senate necessary to ratify (two thirds) should "advise the acceptance of this proposition . . . I shall conform my action to their advice." But he said that should the Senate by a two-thirds vote decline to give advice or express an opinion, then he would "consider it my duty to reject the offer." On June 12, 1846, two days later, the Senate passed a resolution that "the President of the United States be, and he is hereby, advised to accept the proposal of the British Government . . . for a convention to settle boundaries."

After the Spanish War President McKinley sent three senators to the peace conference at Paris. A resolution of disapproval was introduced in the Senate, but it was not passed. One objection was that such a course would tend to give the President an undue influence over the Senate, probably because senators serving with the President in the negotiation of a treaty might be less inclined to independent judgment when the treaty should come up in the Senate for ratification.

At the close of the War of 1812 with England two members of Congress were appointed by President Madison to attend the peace conference at Ghent, the Speaker of the House, Henry Clay, and Senator James A. Bayard of Delaware. Believing that they could not serve in two capacities, they resigned from Congress.

President Harding appointed two senators as delegates to the Washington Conference (November 12, 1921–February 6, 1922), in which nine nations drafted treaties, some for the reduction of armaments and others respecting the general peace of the world.

The Senate may (1) approve, (2) reject, (3) approve with amendments, (4) approve upon condition that specified changes will be made, and (5) approve with reservations or interpretations. In some instances it has failed to act at all. In 1795 the Senate approved the Jay Treaty with

Great Britain "on condition" that certain changes be made to our commercial advantage; and the British Government accepted the conditions.

The rejection of a treaty by the Senate "can be the subject of no complaint", said our State Department to Great Britain when the treaty of 1869 regarding the Alabama Claims was not approved, "and can give no occasion for dissatisfaction or criticism." In 1804 Secretary of State Madison had occasion to give Spain a like hint. "When peculiarities of this sort in the structure of a government are sufficiently known to other governments", said he, "they have no right to take exception at the inevitable effect of them."

Many treaties have been approved by the Senate and many disapproved. Treaties suggesting any modification of or departure from our Constitutional system have been rejected. Thus in President Roosevelt's administration a number of arbitration treaties negotiated by Secretary of State Hay with various countries provided for referring to The Hague Tribunal [1] questions of a Constitutional nature and also disputes respecting the interpretation of treaties themselves. As the reference to the Tribunal would be by the President, the Senate would be shorn, it believed,

[1] The Hague Tribunal arose out of conferences in 1899 and 1907 held at the capital of Holland upon the suggestion of Nicholas II of Russia, who recommended an "understanding not to increase for a fixed period the present effectives of the armed military and naval forces and at the same time not to increase the budgets pertaining thereto, and a preliminary examination of the means by which even a reduction may be effected in the future in the forces and budgets above mentioned." The first conference was attended by representatives of twenty-six nations. Forty-four nations were represented in the conference of 1907. Owing to the opposition of Germany, the subject of excessive armaments was abandoned. But many plans for the improvement of international practices were put in motion. The first question to be decided by The Hague Tribunal was submitted by the United States, relating to a fund owing to Californians by Mexico. Many questions of the kind formerly settled by war have been disposed of at The Hague.

of part of its Constitutional duties in treaty-making matters. When the Senate amended the treaties so as to retain what it conceived to be its Constitutional jurisdiction of the subject, the President refused to go further.

The most notable disagreement of this kind arose in 1919, when the treaty negotiated by President Wilson at Paris (June 28, 1919) closing the World War and constructing a League of Nations was laid before the Senate. It was believed by the Senate that the proposals to submit to an international tribunal certain questions would change our Constitutional form of government — would require the United States to go to war without a declaration by Congress (Note 55); would commit the Nation to the expenditure of money which Congress might not wish to appropriate (Note 37); and would turn over to the balloting of nations the disposition of many of our most important Constitutional affairs. The Senate therefore proposed to ratify the treaty "with reservations and understandings."

The Senate reserved to Congress the right to withdraw from the League and to be the sole judge as to whether its obligations had been fulfilled; declined to assume any obligation to preserve the territorial integrity or political independence of any other country, or to use the military or naval forces except as Congress might desire to do; declined to accept any mandate or guardianship over another nation except as Congress might determine; reserved to the Government of the United States exclusively the determination of domestic and political questions; declined to submit to arbitration or to the Council of the League of Nations the "long established policy commonly known as the Monroe Doctrine"; withheld its assent to the article of the treaty giving the Chinese province of Shantung to Japan; and declined to be limited in armament except as Congress might direct. Some other reservations were made. When the treaty with the reservations came to final vote in the Senate on March 19, 1920, it received forty-nine yeas and thirty-five nays, or seven votes fewer than the necessary two thirds to make a ratification. President Wilson declined to offer any concessions to the views of the Senate.

and he shall nominate, and by and with the Advice and Consent of the Senate, shall appoint Ambassadors, other public Ministers and Consuls, Judges of the supreme Court, and all other Officers of the United States, whose Appointments are not herein otherwise provided for, and which shall be established by Law: [89] **but the Congress may by Law vest the Appointment of such inferior Officers, as they think proper, in the President alone, in the Courts of Law, or in the Heads of Departments.**

[89] In the Constitutional Convention serious objection was taken to this provision, as the President might refuse his assent to necessary measures of Congress until appointments objectionable to the Senate had been confirmed. It was argued that this authority to appoint would invest him with power leading toward monarchy. Benjamin Franklin was of this belief. However, in practice the plan has worked very well. It is probably true that some Presidents have to some extent used their appointing power to influence Congress, refusing to fill offices within the control of members until a bill favored by him had been passed. On the other hand, it is believed that the Senate has sometimes used its power to approve appointments to influence the President to conform to its wishes. In a message dated March 1, 1886, President Cleveland declined to inform the Senate why he had removed a United States attorney from office without its consent, declaring that it had no Constitutional authority in the matter; and he referred to "the threat proposed in the resolutions now before the Senate that no confirmation will be made unless the demands of that body be complied with" as insufficient to deter him

from his duty to maintain the Chief Magistracy "unimpaired in all its dignity and vigor."

For removing, in disregard of the Tenure of Office Act, Edwin M. Stanton, a hostile Secretary of War, President Johnson was impeached by the House, but the Senate failed to convict. The Tenure of Office Act was repealed on March 3, 1887, a year after the spirited message of President Cleveland just before mentioned, in which he spoke of the Act as by a Congress "overwhelmingly and bitterly opposed politically to the President" and "determined upon the subjugation of the Executive to legislative will." He considered the passage of the Act as an admission by Congress that it had no Constitutional basis for its claim.

The first appointment to the cabinet to be denied confirmation by the Senate was that of Roger B. Taney (later Chief Justice of the United States) to the Secretaryship of the Treasury in 1834. He had helped Jackson undo the United States Bank.

The President shall have Power to fill up all Vacancies that may happen during the Recess of the Senate, by granting Commissions which shall expire at the End of their next Session.[90]

[90] Like many another clause of the Constitution, this one was copied from a State. The Constitution of North Carolina had such a provision. When the Senate is not in session to confirm appointments, the President may nevertheless meet the needs of the public service. But should the Senate during its next session not confirm a recess appointment (as it is called) the appointment will expire with that session. This is to prevent the President from building up the executive power by putting in office men not deemed suitable by the Senate.

Section 3. He shall from time to time give to the Congress Information of the State of the Union,[91]

[91] This mandate has been carried out by the annual and the special messages of the Presidents, the annual message at the opening of Congress in December and the special message when a matter of unusual importance comes up, such as a disagreement with a foreign government, or a disaster calling for the granting of relief, or the conservation of the forests and minerals, and the like. Washington and Adams delivered their messages orally. Jefferson, who was not a ready speaker, asked leave to submit his in writing, saying that Congress might then consider a message at its convenience. The written message remained the practice until 1913, when President Wilson revived the oral address to Congress.

Because the President is required by the Constitution to give information to Congress from time to time, Congress from the beginning has claimed, conversely, the right to ask the President for information. Washington was called upon by the House of Representatives for papers regarding the defeat of General St. Clair's forces in 1791 by the Miami Indians. After a three-day consideration of the question by Washington and his cabinet, which was regarded as of the greatest importance as a precedent, it was decided that the House had a right to copies of the papers. In 1909 President Roosevelt refused to permit the Attorney-General to make answer to a resolution of the Senate asking why no legal proceedings had been begun against a corporation named for violation of the Sherman Anti-Trust law.

A clause similar to this was in the Constitution of New York of 1777.

and recommend to their Consideration such Measures as he shall judge necessary and expedient; [92]

[92] In England the Parliament is supreme, and the King must sign any bill submitted to him, even his own death warrant, as one writer on English law expressed it. Therefore, English authorities have been astonished by the ac-

tivity of our President in legislation, which often amounts (in the opinion of some) to domination. But it was the intention of the Fathers of the Republic that the President should be an active power. In addition to conferring upon him unqualified authority to sign or veto bills passed by Congress (Note 38), they command him in this clause to recommend to the consideration of Congress such legislation as he should judge necessary and expedient. Through the reports of the members of his cabinet his information on the state of the country is complete, and he is therefore probably better equipped to make recommendations than any other man. At any rate, he is made by the Constitution an important part of the legislative mechanism of our government.

he may, on extraordinary Occasions, convene both Houses, or either of them,[93]

[93] The Senate convenes in extra session immediately after the new President has taken the oath, to confirm his appointments, especially those of his cabinet officials. The House of Representatives never has been called in session alone. Both Houses have been called in special session, but not often. The first special session was called by President John Adams (1797) because of violations by France of the law of neutrality with respect to American commerce during a war with England. President Madison (1809) called a special session because of violations of neutrality by England, and later (1813) he called a special session regarding peace with England after the War of 1812. President Van Buren (1837) called a special session on account of financial troubles following the suspension, in Jackson's term, of the National Bank. Eighteen days after calling (1841) for financial reasons a special session President Harrison died. A special session was called by President Pierce because of the failure of the previous session "to make provision for the support of the Army" and on account of many troubles

with the Indians.   The great special session was that called by President Lincoln for July 4, 1861, preparatory to conducting the Civil War.   President Hayes (1877) called a special session because the previous one had failed to support the Army, and later (1879) he called another because the preceding Congress had failed to make an appropriation for the Legislative, the Judicial, and the Executive departments of the Government.   President Cleveland called a special session (1893) on account of "the existence of an alarming and extraordinary business situation", which was caused by the act requiring the Government to purchase a fixed quantity of silver each year.   President McKinley called a special session (1897) for the reason that "for more than three years" current expenditures had been greater than receipts, and he advocated a tariff law to raise the necessary revenue.

This clause may have been borrowed from an early constitution of New York or from that of Massachusetts.

and in Case of Disagreement between them, with Respect to the Time of Adjournment, he may adjourn them to such Time as he shall think proper; [94]

[94] It never has been necessary for the President to exercise this authority.   The working of a written constitution furnishes many like illustrations of the potency of the mere existence of a clearly defined power.   Having in mind the very serious dissensions between the King of England and Parliament, and between the two Houses of Parliament themselves, respecting convening and adjourning, and the length of sessions, and the legal rights of one another, the framers of our Constitution provided that Congress shall assemble at least once a year (Note 27); that neither House shall adjourn for more than three days without the consent of the other, nor to any other place than that in which the two Houses shall be sitting (Note 31); and that, finally.

if they cannot agree upon adjournment (but only when there is disagreement), the President may adjourn them.

Charles I was determined that his ministers should not be responsible to Parliament. "Remember," he said, "that Parliaments are altogether in my power for their calling, sitting, and dissolution; and, therefore, as I find the fruits of them to be good or evil they are to continue or not to be." When in March, 1629, Charles sent orders for the dissolution of Parliament, the Speaker of the House of Commons was forcibly prevented from leaving the chair until the House had voted resolutions in condemnation of the King's illegal practices. "None have gone about to break Parliaments," declared John Eliot, in words which proved to be prophetic of the beheading of Charles, "but in the end Parliaments have broken them."

he shall receive Ambassadors and other public Ministers; [95]

[95] This merely makes definite a matter of formality in international relations. Each government has some one to deal with the representatives of other nations, and the Constitution makes the President that one in this country The Secretary of State acts for him in most affairs. He may refuse to receive a representative deemed objectionable. He may also dismiss an ambassador by giving him passports to leave the country, as has happened where the conduct of a representative has been openly offensive. President Cleveland (1888) gave the ambassador from England his passports because he wrote a letter during the presidential political campaign which was widely published and which made comments adverse to the Cleveland administration. The ambassador from Austria was so dismissed by President Wilson for interference in our affairs before we entered the World War. An objectionable minister who has not flagrantly offended may be quietly recalled by his government upon the request of the President.

Almonte, the Mexican minister at Washington, demanded his passports and went home when (1845) Congress passed a resolution to accept the proposal of the Republic of Texas to come into the Union as a State.

When the Department of State (first called Foreign Affairs) was established by Congress the law provided that the principal officer of the Department, now the Secretary of State, should carry on correspondence with other governments "in such manner that the President of the United States shall from time to time order or instruct." President Grant felt that his prerogative in this respect had been invaded by a joint resolution of Congress directing the Secretary of State "to acknowledge a dispatch of congratulation from the Argentine Republic and the high appreciation of Congress of the compliment thus conveyed." The President vetoed the resolution and said that the "adoption has inadvertently involved the exercise of a power which infringes upon the Constitutional rights of the executive."

he shall take Care that the Laws be faithfully executed,[96] and shall Commission all the Officers of the United States.

[96] This Constitution and the laws of Congress made in pursuance of it, and the treaties, are declared to be (Note 133) "the supreme law of the land, . . . anything in the constitution or laws of any State to the contrary notwithstanding." These National laws are over all. The courts in every State are "bound thereby." It is made the duty of the President to "take care" that these laws are observed and fully executed.

Contrasting the Constitution with the Articles of Confederation in this respect, Woodrow Wilson's "History of the American People" (Vol. 3, p. 71) says: "It conferred upon the Federal Government powers which would make it at once strong and independent. . . . Its laws were to be, not advisory, but imperative, and were to operate, not upon the States, but directly upon individuals, like the laws of any sovereign."

Ruling that a United States marshal who had killed a man in the act of assaulting a Federal judge traveling in the performance of his duty could not be tried on a charge of murder under the laws of California, where the deed was done, the Supreme Court of the United States said (1890):

"We hold it to be an incontrovertible principle that the Government of the United States may, by means of physical force, exercised through its official agents, execute on every foot of American soil the powers and functions that belong to it."

When physical force is not necessary the United States executes the Constitution and its laws and treaties through its judicial tribunals and its marshals. Thus where the Supreme Court of a State undertook to release by *habeas corpus* a man in the custody of a United States officer on a charge of having violated an Act of Congress, its action was reversed (1858) by the Supreme Court of the United States, Chief Justice Taney saying: "For no one will suppose that a government which has now lasted nearly seventy years, enforcing its laws by its own tribunals and preserving the union of the States, could have lasted a single year or fulfilled the high trusts committed to it if offenses against its laws could not have been punished without the consent of the State in which the culprit was found. . . . And the powers of the General Government, and of the States, although both exist and are exercised within the same territorial limits, are yet separate and distinct sovereignties, acting separately and independently of each other within their respective spheres. And the sphere of action appropriated to the United States is as far beyond the reach of the judicial process issued by a State judge or a State court as if the line of division was traced by landmarks and monuments visible to the eye."

The duty of the President "to take care that the laws be faithfully executed" cannot be interfered with by the Judicial Department. In 1867 the Supreme Court of the United States held that it had no jurisdiction to entertain a bill for injunction presented by the State of Mississippi to prevent President Johnson and General Ord from executing two laws of Congress passed on March 2 and March 23 of that year over the President's veto and known as the Reconstruction Acts. The first of those acts recited that no legal government or adequate protection for life and property existed in Mississippi and some other southern States and that it was necessary that peace and good order be enforced until a loyal republican State government could be established, and it accordingly divided the States into five military districts and made it the duty of the President to assign an officer of the army to each district with a sufficient military force to maintain order and punish offenders. The second act provided machinery for registering voters and forming new constitutions in the States. "But we are fully satisfied that this court has no jurisdiction of a bill to enjoin the President in the performance of his official duties," said Chief Justice Taney in denying the application.

In 1864 a citizen of Indiana was arrested by the military authorities, tried by a military court on the charge of disloyal acts, when the civil courts were "open and in the proper and unobstructed exercise of their judicial functions", and sentenced to be hanged. He was not a resident of a seceded State, nor a prisoner of war, nor a person in the military or naval service. The sentence had been under consideration by President Lincoln before his death, and it was finally approved by President Johnson as commander in chief (Note 85) of the military forces. Holding that the prisoner should be discharged by writ of *habeas corpus* because the military tribunal had no legal existence, that "it **is the birthright of every American citizen when charged** with crime to be tried and punished according to law", and that "if in Indiana he conspired with bad men to assist the enemy he is punishable for it in the courts of Indiana", the Supreme Court of the United States made (1866) this comment upon the contention that the approval of the sentence by the President gave it legal value: "He is controlled by law and has his appropriate sphere of duty, which is to execute, not to make, the laws."

Section 4. The President, Vice President and all civil Officers of the United States, shall be removed from Office on Impeachment for, and Conviction of, Treason, Bribery, or other high Crimes and Misdemeanors.[96a]

[96a] Treason and bribery were the worst offences in the public life of England at that time. By a later provision of the Constitution (Note 113) the many and vague treasons in English law were reduced in this country to two definite faults: (1) waging war against the United States, or (2) adhering to its enemies. In 1787, while the Constitutional Convention was in session, Warren Hastings, the first Governor General of Bengal, was by the House of Commons impeached "of high crimes and misdemeanors." Hence, probably, the same words in our Constitution. As the charges against Hastings were of confiscation of property and oppressiveness in government, the English definition of the words may be inferred from the accusation. The managers of the impeachment of President Johnson contended that "an impeachable crime or misdemeanor . . . may consist of a violation of the Constitution, of law, of an official oath, or of duty, by an act committed or omitted, or, without violating a positive law, by abuse of discretionary powers from improper motives, or from any improper purpose."

"The Judicial Power . . . shall be vested in one supreme Court . . ."

ARTICLE III

Section 1. The judicial Power of the United States, shall be vested in one supreme Court, and in such inferior Courts as the Congress may from time to time ordain and establish.[97]

[97] "But for this system of United States courts extended throughout the States and supreme within its own sphere," says Fiske ("Critical Period American History", p. 300), "the Federal Constitution could never have been put into practical working order. . . . This intrusting to the judiciary the whole interpretation of the fundamental instrument of the government is the most peculiarly American feature of the work done by the convention, and to the stability of such a federation as ours, covering as it does the greater part of a huge continent, it was absolutely indispensable."

The first session of the first Congress (Sept. 24, 1789) provided for a Supreme Court with "a chief justice and five associate justices", four of whom should constitute a quorum. In February, 1801, the number of associates was reduced to four. On April 29, 1802, the Court was enlarged to six associate justices. The number of associates was increased to eight on March 3, 1837. On March 3, 1861, Congress increased the Court by making it consist of a chief justice and nine associates, and Stephen J. Field of California was appointed by President Lincoln to the new associate justiceship. To prevent President Johnson from appointing Attorney-General Stanbery to fill a vacancy on the bench, Congress reduced the number of associates to six on July 23, 1866. The number of associates was increased to eight, six of whom are a quorum, by an act of April 10, 1869, about a month after Johnson's term expired. One of the appointees of President Grant to the two new places was rejected by the Senate, and the other, Edwin M. Stanton, died before he could take his seat. Thus a court of seven decided the first Legal Tender Case on February 7, 1870, holding that paper money ("Greenbacks", so called) could not under the Constitution (see Note 44), be made a legal tender in place of coin in payment of debts. On the same day President Grant appointed William Strong of Pennsylvania, and Joseph P. Bradley of New Jersey, and in May, 1871, another Legal Tender Case coming up, the first decision was overruled. At present (1940) the Supreme Court consists of a chief justice and eight associates.

In 1937 President Roosevelt submitted to Congress a bill for reform of the Supreme Court, providing for the increase of the number of judges to 15, by appointing one additional judge for each incumbent eligible to retire. This bill was rejected by Congress, and a milder one substituted, and subsequently passed. This provides for a change in procedure, allowing the Attorney General to take part in any suit in the federal courts involving the constitutionality of a federal Act, and allowing him to appeal directly to the Supreme Court from any inferior federal court decision against the constitutionality of an Act.

"Inferior courts" were established under this clause by the first Congress and called Circuit Courts. They sit throughout the States for the trial of causes arising under the Constitution, the laws of Congress, and treaties.

In 1890 Congress created under this clause, for the relief of the overburdened Supreme Court, a Circuit Court of Appeals consisting of three judges in each of the nine circuits into which it divided the United States and its territories. To illustrate, the First Circuit contains Rhode Island, Massachusetts, New Hampshire, Maine, and Porto Rico; and the Ninth embraces Arizona, California, Oregon, Nevada, Washington, Idaho, Montana, and Hawaii. In many cases the decision of a Circuit Court of Appeals is final and the litigation therefore never reaches the Supreme Court.

Below the Circuit Courts of Appeals (the Circuit trial courts having been abolished) are the United States District Courts (over eighty), there being one or more districts in a State, according to the needs of the population. These courts try civil and criminal cases, and appeals lie from them to the Circuit Courts of Appeals in most cases, but in a few (involving Federal questions) directly to the Supreme Court.

In 1855 a Court of Claims was created by Congress to hear cases against the United States, as the sovereign can be sued only upon its consent.

In 1909 Congress established a Court of Customs Appeals to review decisions of the Board of General Appraisers on questions arising out of import duties.

In China and some other countries consular courts have been created by Congress, in which the American consul sits to effectuate treaties and try certain causes.

In organized territories of the United States, like Alaska and Hawaii, the courts are created by Congress; but when the territory is admitted as a State, then the Federal courts are superseded by courts of the State's creation.

The Interstate Commerce Commission was created in 1887 to regulate commerce among the States by railway, telegraph, telephone or any other means; and so in 1914 the Federal Trade Commission was created to prevent unfair methods and unfair competition in interstate trade. While these tribunals are not courts, they are mentioned here because of their great importance.

The Judges, both of the supreme and inferior Courts, shall hold their Offices during good Behaviour, and shall, at stated Times, receive for their Services a Compensation which shall not be diminished during their Continuance in Office.[98]

[98] The Colonial Declaration of Rights of October 14, 1774, complained that judges were "dependent on the Crown alone for their salaries."

A complaint in the Declaration of Independence was that King George III "has made judges dependent on his will alone for the tenure of their office and the amount and payment of their salaries."

Lecky mentions in "England in the Eighteenth Century" that there was "a long and bitter quarrel about the position of the judges" in the Colonies. He says that the colonists wished the judges to hold their office during good behavior and thus be beyond the control of the home government

The King of England, becoming dissatisfied with the conduct of the colonists, demanded the surrender of their charters. This being resisted, a proceeding in *quo warranto* (inquiring by what warrant they claimed rights) was instituted in the courts of England "and", as Story well said, "it terminated, as in that age it might well be supposed it would, in a judgment pronounced in 1624 by judges holding their office during his pleasure."

Most of the constitutions of other nations which have been drafted since ours have adopted the provision making the term of judges during good behavior, and many of them prohibit the intimidation of the judge by the reduction of his salary. By the constitutions of Belgium (1831–1873) and Brazil (1890) judges are appointed for life. In Argentine (1853, 1860) and Chile (1833–1893) the judges hold during good behavior. It is significant that the constitutions of the three great British dependencies, those of the Dominion of Canada (1867), the Commonwealth of Australia (1900), and the Union of South Africa (1909), follow explicitly that of the United States in requiring that judges be appointed, that they hold office during good behavior, and that their salaries be not reduced. Canada had seen the practical operation of this clause of our Constitution for over three quarters of a century. It was more than a century and a decade old when Australia followed it. In 1909, when the Union of South Africa was established, this constitutional provision had served for 120 years the great purpose for which it was designed.

In December, 1919, the United States District Court of Kentucky, in a suit brought by another district judge, held that the Income Tax Act of September 24, 1919, imposing a tax upon salaries, including those of the judges of the Federal courts, was not intended to and therefore did not diminish the compensation of judges within the meaning of this clause.

On June 1, 1920, the Supreme Court reversed that decision, holding that the tax on the salaries of judges "was imposed contrary to the Constitutional prohibition and so must be adjudged invalid." The Court expressed "regret that its solution falls to us, and this although each member [of the Supreme Court] has been paying the tax in respect of his salary voluntarily and in regular course." But, it added, "jurisdiction of the present case cannot be declined or renounced; the plaintiff was entitled by law to invoke our decision." However, construing an act (1932) taxing the salaries of judges "taking office after" the enactment, the Supreme Court, really overruling the decision just examined, held (1939) that the tax would not work a "diminution of salary" within the prohibition of this clause.

Under like constitutional provisions in Pennsylvania, Louisiana, and North Carolina, the rulings had been that the judicial salary cannot be touched even by a tax. Up to 1862 no attempt had been made to tax the salaries of judges. When Chief Justice Taney raised the question, the Government discontinued the Civil War income tax as to Federal judges and refunded to the judges what had been withheld by the Treasurer of the United States. In the Income Tax Act of 1894 the salaries of the judges were not mentioned. In the acts of 1913, 1916, and 1917 they were expressly excepted from the income tax. But in the

Act of 1919 income was made to include for taxation "the compensation received as such" by "the President of the United States, the judges of the Supreme and inferior courts of the United States", and some others.

In 1937 the Supreme Court Retirement Act was passed, giving the Justices the privilege of retiring upon reaching the age of 70, a privilege previously accorded to judges of inferior Federal courts.

Section 2. The judicial Power shall extend to all Cases, in Law and Equity, arising under this Constitution, the Laws of the United States, and Treaties made, or which shall be made, under their Authority; [99]

[99] By the "judicial power", as distinguished from the legislative power and the executive power, is meant the authority to hear and determine controversies as to law or fact between the government and individuals, or between individual parties. "That power is capable of acting," said the Supreme Court, "only when the subject is submitted to it by a party who asserts his rights in the form prescribed by law; it then becomes a *case*." The Constitution of the Commonwealth of Australia (1900), which copies this paragraph almost verbatim, defines judicial power as "a power to declare and apply the laws of the Commonwealth." A court does not express an opinion upon the Constitution, a law of Congress, or a treaty except in a "case" — when its judicial power has been invoked by some one asserting a right. Nor does a court ever decide a constitutional question if it can be avoided; that is, if the case may be disposed of by the decision of other questions the constitutional question will be passed. The purpose in this clause is that essentially National questions shall be tried in National courts.

"One great object in the establishment of the courts of

the United States and regulating their jurisdiction," said the Supreme Court, "was to have a tribunal in each State presumed to be free from local influence and to which all who were non-residents or aliens might resort for legal redress."

Under the Articles of Confederation there were no such tribunals as the present National (Federal, so called) courts, and experience had taught the positive need of them.

The judicial power does not extend to a determination of political questions, such as whether a State has a republican form of government.

When a case arises in a State court and involves a question of the Constitution, or of an act of Congress, or of a treaty, it is the duty of the court to follow and enforce the National law; for the Constitution explicitly and emphatically requires (Note 134) that "the judges in every State shall be bound thereby, anything in the Constitution or laws of any State to the contrary notwithstanding." Should a State law, for example, deny "the equal protection of the laws" by favoring one class of citizens as against another; or should a State pass an *ex post facto* law, or tax exports, or interfere with commerce among the States, or take private property for public use without compensation, or do any other of many things forbidden by the Constitution which have been done: and should the Supreme Court of the State uphold such a law in a case brought by a citizen claiming to be wronged, then "the judicial power of the United States" would "extend" to such a case and it would be the duty of the Supreme Court of the Nation to reverse the ruling of the tribunal of the State and to declare the law of the State to be void and inoperative because of conflict with "the supreme law of the land." In the course of our history the Supreme Court of the United States has been under the necessity of deciding many such cases.

Alexander Hamilton discussed in the "Federalist" the relative powers of the Legislative Department, the Executive Department, and the Judicial Department. "The Executive not only dispenses the honors," he said, "but holds the sword of the community. The Legislative not only commands the purse, but prescribes the rules by which the duties and rights of every citizen are to be regulated. The Judiciary, on the contrary, has no influence over either the sword or the purse . . . and can take no active resolution whatever. It may truly be said to have neither force nor will, but merely judgment. This simple view of the matter suggests several important consequences — it proves incontestably that the judiciary is beyond comparison the weakest of the three departments of power, that it can never attack with success either of the others, and that all possible care is requisite to enable it to defend itself against their attacks."

In Canada the Supreme Court of the Dominion passes upon legislation of the Provinces and of the Dominion just as ours determines whether an act of a State legislature or an act of Congress goes beyond the bounds fixed by the Constitution. Many acts of legislation in Canada have been held void for conflict with the Constitution, the British North America Act of Parliament of 1867, which follows closely in general plan the Constitution of the United States. This statement may be repeated about Australia and its constitution of 1900. A decision of the Supreme Court of Canada may be (and many decisions have been) reviewed and sustained or reversed by the Privy Council in London, the court of last resort of the British colonies, except Australia, which refused in 1900 to permit Parliament to insert in its constitution a provision for such appeal. It contended that experience in the United States with a court of final resort justified its opposition to the plan.

— to all cases Affecting Ambassadors, other public Ministers, and Consuls; [100]

[100] It is fitting that the representatives of nations should

have a hearing in our National courts when their rights have been drawn into question.

— to all Cases of admiralty and maritime Jurisdiction; [101]

[101] These cases arise out of the law of the sea and often involve rights of citizens of other countries. Therefore National jurisdiction of the subject is preferable to what might be differing decisions by State courts.

— to Controversies to which the United States shall be a Party; [102]

[102] The United States is the moving party in its own courts against violators of the revenue laws and the many other acts of Congress contained in what is called the penal code. It also brings civil suits in its courts to enforce its rights, as to set aside a patent to public land obtained by fraud, or to cancel a certificate of naturalization secured by an alien who did not intend to be loyal to the United States, or to enforce any rights of contract, or to collect money owing to it. The cases which the United States litigates in its courts are of great number and variety. Were there no Federal courts the Nation might not always secure speedy and adequate relief in the courts of the States.

But because the Government enters its courts at pleasure to seek redress from individuals or corporations, or to punish them under its penal laws, it by no means follows that individuals or corporations may in like manner bring actions against it. The sovereign cannot be sued except upon its consent, and the United States has established a special tribunal (the Court of Claims) for the trial of special cases, particularly claims for money.

Nor because the Nation may sue a State, as it has done to settle a boundary dispute between a State and a Territory, does it follow that a State may sue the Nation. Thus the Supreme Court held (1907) that the State of Kansas could not maintain in that court under this clause a suit against the United States respecting grants of railroad right of way through Indian lands of which the State claimed to be the trustee. It was said that public policy forbids that the sovereign be sued without its consent. That consent was given as to some cases (but not all) by the creation of the Court of Claims.

Where revenue agents of the United States, acting in pursuance of the National prohibitory law, were indicted in the State of Oregon for involuntary manslaughter, they having unintentionally killed a man while they were engaged in the performance of a lawful act, it was held (1920) by the United States District Court that the State had no right to prevent the removal of the case to a Federal court under acts of Congress dating back to 1833, when South Carolina undertook to prevent the collection of National revenue, and Congress provided for the trial in Federal courts of criminal charges against Federal officers. During the Civil War (1863) it was considered necessary, owing to the difficulties which beset officers of the Government in the southern and in some of the northern States, to make the act include civil cases as well as criminal. The National Government takes care in its own courts of litigation in which it or its representatives are concerned.

— to Controversies between two or more States; [103]

[103] In an early case the Supreme Court said that the Constitution had made justiciable — that is, properly triable or disposable in a court rather than by the sword, by treaty, or otherwise — some matters "which were not known as such at the common law; such, for example, as controversies between States as to boundary lines, and other questions admitting of judicial solutions." That is another example of entirely new methods devised and presented to mankind by the Fathers of the Republic. Beginning in 1799, with a controversy between New York and Connecticut, many

Chief Justice John Marshall raised the Supreme Court to power and majesty as guardian and interpreter of the Constitution

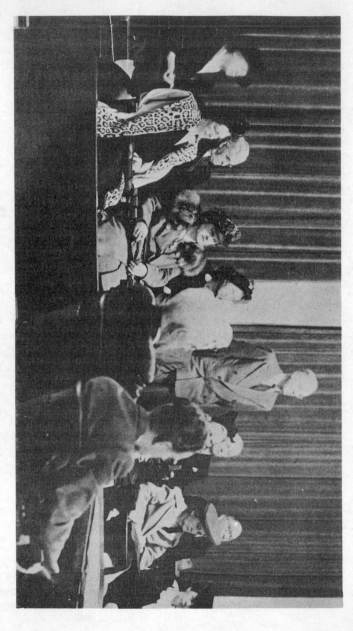

"The Trial of all Crimes, except in Cases of Impeachment, shall be by Jury"

disputes between States respecting boundaries have been disposed of by the Supreme Court.

"Instead of reserving the right to seek redress for injustice from another State by their sovereign powers," wrote Chief Justice Taney, "they [the States] have bound themselves to submit to the decision of this court, and to abide by its judgment. And it is not out of place to say, here, that experience has demonstrated that this power was not unwisely surrendered by the States; for in the time that has already elapsed since this government came into existence, several irritating and angry controversies have taken place between adjoining States, in relation to their respective boundaries, and which have sometimes threatened to end in force and violence, but for the power vested in this court to hear them and decide between them."

Other cases, as that of Kansas against Colorado for draining by irrigation the Arkansas River (1907) to the damage of farmers in the complaining State, in which it was found that "little if any detriment" had been worked to "the great body of the valley" because the large flow is underground, have been heard by the Supreme Court. So Missouri was held (1906) not to have sustained its allegations against Illinois regarding the pollution of the waters of the Mississippi by the Chicago drainage canal, although in 1930 a decision was handed down that Chicago must reduce her water diversion to 1,500 cu. ft.

— between a State and Citizens of another State;[104]

[104] It is manifest that in a controversy between a State and a citizen of another State the citizen should have the right to remove the case against him from the court of the suing State to a court of the Nation. The citizen of a State is also a citizen of the United States, and that should entitle him to litigate in a court of the United States when a State is plaintiff. The language of this clause imports that a citizen of one State may sue another (not his own) State.

This objection was raised when the Constitution was before the States for adoption. James Madison (afterward President) and John Marshall (afterward Chief Justice) said that an individual could not "call any State into Court." Nevertheless, in 1793 the Supreme Court held in a historic case (Chisholm, a citizen of South Carolina, against Georgia) that he could. As many of the States were in poor financial condition and liable to suits for money, that decision, though logical under the language of the clause, was threatening as a precedent. It caused a great commotion, which resulted in the adoption of the Eleventh Amendment (Note 164) on January 8, 1798, declaring that "the judicial power of the United States" should not be construed to extend to a suit against a State by a citizen of another State, or by a citizen or subject of any foreign State.

The Constitution of Australia grants jurisdiction to the High (Supreme) Court where a citizen desires to sue a State.

In our country a person having a claim against a State must apply to the legislature for relief, unless the State has established a Court of Claims, which some States have done.

— between Citizens of different States,[105]

[105] Several States have passed laws to prevent the removal under this clause to Federal courts of suits begun in the courts of the States against non-residents, but these acts have been held void for conflict with the Constitution. In one such case (1908) the Supreme Court said: "A State cannot tie up a citizen of another State having property within its territory, invaded by unauthorized acts of its own officers, to suits for redress in its own courts." The dispute between citizens of different States is one in which the Nation is properly concerned; the contesting parties are citizens of the Nation as distinguished from citizens of a State. The practical need for this clause was early learned by the Government itself. When South Carolina called (1832)

a convention and adopted an ordinance to resist the collection of duties imposed by a tariff law of Congress, and the legislature of the State passed " An Act to Carry into Effect in Part an Ordinance to Nullify Certain Acts of the Congress of the United States", the revenue officers of the Nation were so badly dealt with that Congress (1833) passed "An Act Further to provide for the Collection of Duties on Imports" which gave a right of action in a Federal court to a revenue officer injured in person or property and also gave him the right to remove from a State court to a Federal court any suit or prosecution brought against him. And in the midst of the Civil War (March 3, 1863), three months after the Emancipation of the Negro, an act was passed by Congress providing for the removal to Federal courts of any civil or criminal case brought in a State court against "any person who is denied or cannot enforce in the judicial tribunals of the State . . . any right secured to him by any law providing for the equal civil rights of citizens of the United States." In the Civil War, again, the draft officers of the Nation were protected by the Federal courts where public feeling was against the Union.

"The Constitution was not formed merely to guard the States against danger from foreign nations, but mainly to secure union and harmony at home, for if this object could be attained there would be but little danger from abroad," said the Supreme Court of the United States in reversing the decision of the highest court of a State which had undertaken to release by its writ of *habeas corpus* a man in the custody of a United States marshal on a charge of violating an act of Congress; "and to accomplish this purpose, it was felt by the statesmen who framed the Constitution, and by the people who adopted it, that it was necessary that many of the rights of sovereignty which the States then possessed should be ceded to the general government; and that, in the sphere of action assigned to it, it should be supreme, and strong enough to execute its own laws by its own tribunals, without interruption from a State or from State authorities. And it was evident that anything short of this would be inadequate to the main objects for which the government was established; and that local interests, local passions or prejudices, incited and fostered by individuals for sinister purposes, would lead to acts of aggression and injustice by one State upon the rights of another, which would ultimately terminate in violence and force, unless there was a common arbiter between them, armed with power enough to protect and guard the rights of all, by appropriate laws, to be carried into execution peacefully by its judicial tribunals."

— between Citizens of the same State claiming Lands under Grants of different States,[106]

[106] This is only a landmark now. In 1787 there were many and serious disputes among persons claiming lands which had been granted by different States, the boundaries of States being very vaguely defined.

and between a State, or the Citizens thereof, and foreign States, Citizens or Subjects.[107]

[107] Any foreign Nation, or any citizen thereof, is entitled to sue any American citizen in one of our Federal courts. In like manner a citizen of the United States may sue a foreign State or a citizen of a foreign State in a court of the United States — but of course he must first find the party on American soil. A writer on the jurisdiction of Federal courts states that he advised the Governor General of Canada that Queen Victoria might bring a suit in the Supreme Court of the United States to determine the liability of the State of New York on a claim of tribes of Indians which had gone from that State to Canada.

In all Cases affecting Ambassadors, other public Ministers and Consuls, and those in which a State shall be Party, the supreme Court shall have original Jurisdiction.[108]

[108] That is, the action, suit, or proceeding must be begun in the Supreme Court.

In all the other Cases before mentioned, the supreme Court shall have appellate Jurisdiction,[109] **both as to Law and Fact, with such Exceptions, and under such Regulations as the Congress shall make.**

[109] This means that the proceeding must originate in an inferior court and be there brought to decision or judgment. After that the case may be taken to the Supreme Court for review.

The Supreme Court of the Dominion of Canada is not the court of last resort. Cases involving questions of constitutional law (such as a controversy between two provinces, or between a province and the Dominion, regarding power) are finally heard by the Privy Council in London. This practice obtains generally in other British colonies, except Australia, which omitted from its draft of a constitution (1900) a provision for such appeal. The Supreme Court of Canada, precisely after the manner of ours, passes upon the constitutionality of laws enacted by the provincial parliaments and by the Dominion Parliament. So in Australia.

The Trial of all Crimes, except in Cases of Impeachment, shall be by Jury; [110]

[110] In the Colonial Declaration of Rights of October 19, 1765, it was said "that trial by jury is the inherent and invaluable right of every British subject in these Colonies", and there was condemned an act of Parliament "extending the jurisdiction of the courts of the admiralty beyond its ancient limits" so as to try colonists for various offences without a jury. In the Declaration of October 14, 1774, it was said that the colonists were entitled "to the great and inestimable privilege of being tried by their peers of the vicinage."

The jury trial is given here and in the Sixth Amendment (Note 153) only in criminal cases, but the Seventh Amendment guarantees a jury in civil cases (Note 157) in which the amount in controversy exceeds twenty dollars. While this provision relates to trials in Federal courts only, the constitutions of the States have similar provisions. Indeed, such a clause was in the constitutions of many of the States before 'ie National Constitution was drafted. The jury of the Constitution is the jury of the England of that day. It consists of twelve men and their verdict must be unanimous.

The Declaration of Independence arraigned the English Government for "depriving us in many cases of the benefit of a trial by jury."

Referring to the provisions of the Constitution guaranteeing to the citizen a public trial by jury, with witnesses and counsel in his defense, the Supreme Court of the United States, holding (1866) that a citizen of Indiana who had not been in the military service, but who had been sentenced (1864) by a military tribunal to be hanged for disloyal conduct during the Civil War, should have been tried before a jury in a court of law, the courts of Indiana never having been closed by the War, employed this language:

"Time has proven the discernment of our ancestors; for even these provisions, expressed in such plain English words that it would seem the ingenuity of man could not evade them, are *now* after the lapse of more than seventy years, sought to be avoided. Those great and good men foresaw that troublous times would arise, when rulers and people would become restive under restraint, and seek by sharp and decisive measures to accomplish ends deemed just and proper, and that the principles of constitutional liberty would be in peril unless established by irrepealable law. The history of the world had taught them that what was done in the past might be attempted in the future. The Constitution of the United States is a law for rulers and people, equally in war and peace, and covers with the shield of its protection all classes of men, at all times, and under all circumstances. No doctrine involving more pernicious consequences was ever invented by the wit of man than that any of its provisions can be suspended during any of the great exigencies of government. Such a doctrine leads directly to anarchy or despotism."

and such Trial shall be held in the State where the said Crimes shall have been committed; [111]

[111] In the Colonial Declaration of Rights of October 14, 1774, an act of Parliament of the twelfth year of George III, for the protection of the King's docks and munitions in the Colonies, was condemned because it "declares a new offense in America and deprives the American subject of a constitutional trial by jury of the vicinage by authorizing the trial of any person charged with the committing of any offense described in the said act, out of the realm, to be indicted and tried for the same in any shire or county within the realm", that is, in any county of England or Scotland; and it was recited in the preamble that Parliament had lately resolved that, by the force of a statute passed in the thirty-fifth year of the reign of Henry VIII, "colonists may be transported to England and tried there upon accusations for treasons and misprisions, or concealments of treasons committed in the Colonies, and by a late statute such trials have been directed in cases therein mentioned."

The Declaration of Independence complained of King George III that "he has combined with others to subject us to a jurisdiction foreign to our Constitution and unacknowledged by our laws"; and it said that he had given "his assent to their acts of pretended legislation . . . for transporting us beyond seas to be tried for pretended offenses." This provision of our Constitution has been strictly enforced by the courts whenever attempts have been made (and they have been numerous) to take an accused person from his home to a distant jurisdiction for trial.

In President Grant's administration (1873) an attempt was made to take to Washington for trial on a charge of libel the editor of a paper published in New York and circulated in the National capital. The court, finding that the defendant "if removed to the District of Columbia would be tried in a manner forbidden by the Constitution", refused to grant a warrant for removing him. In the administration of President Roosevelt (1909) a like dispute originated. An attempt was made by officers of the United States to take to Washington for trial on a charge of criminal libel editors living in Indianapolis who had questioned the motive of the Government in changing its plan for an Isthmian canal from the Nicaraguan route to the Panama route after a committee had reported in favor of the former, which could be purchased for $40,000,000, while the latter was to cost $100,000,000. The United States District Court at Indianapolis denied the application for the removal of the defendants, and said: "To my mind that man has read the history of our institutions to little purpose who does not look with grave apprehension upon the possibility of the success of a proceeding such as this. . . . If the prosecuting officers have the right to select the tribunal . . . if the government has that power, and can drag citizens from distant States to the capital of the Nation there to be tried, then, as Judge Cooley says, this is a strange result of a revolution where one of the grievances complained of was the assertion of the right to send parties abroad for trial." (See Note 153.)

but when not committed within any State,[112] the Trial shall be at such Place or Places as the Congress may by Law have directed.

[112] As on the high seas.

Section 3. Treason against the United States, shall consist only in levying War against them, or in adhering to their Enemies, giving them Aid and Comfort.[113]

[113] William Blackstone, whose lectures (1758) at the University of Oxford became the great text-book on English law, with which lectures the members of the Constitutional Convention were very familiar, gives a statement of the law of treason which embraced at least seventeen acts punishable by death — death in a "very solemn and terrible" way, the commentator says, by hanging, followed by disembowelling and quartering. Hallam ("Constitutional History of England"), dealing with civil government in the reign of Elizabeth (1558–1603), refers to "those glaring transgressions of natural as well as positive law that reduced our courts of justice in cases of treason to little better than the caverns of murderers." That is enough to make clear why the Founders of the Republic defined treason — the only crime defined in the Constitution — and limited it to two offenses. A proposal to let Congress define treason, as the English Parliament had always done, was rejected by the Constitutional Convention. The Constitution defined it and Congress cannot change it. Treason "shall consist *only*" of the Constitutional specifications.

In the celebrated trial of Aaron Burr (1807) on a charge of treason in the United States Circuit Court at Richmond, Virginia, the meaning of "levying war" was discussed by Chief Justice Marshall, who presided in that circuit, in the light of a full review of English history; for this clause was borrowed from an elaborate act of Parliament of the reign of Edward III (1352) saying that "if a man do levy war against our lord the King and his realm", or "if a man be adherent to the King's enemies in his realm, giving to them aid and comfort in the realm or elsewhere", he should be guilty of treason. Marshall said that it is not enough to be leagued in a conspiracy; it is necessary to perform a part. That part may be minute, and it may not be actual appearance in arms, but it must be a part of the plan and must be performed by the person charged. Notwithstanding the great efforts of the Jefferson administration to secure the conviction of Burr, the jury was directed by Marshall to return a verdict of not guilty because the testimony offered by the Government was "irrelevant until there be proof of the overt act by two witnesses." Burr had been charged with raising troops against the Government, but no proof of overt acts was produced. The feeling ran so high that Marshall was hanged in effigy, but the search of historians has failed to find evidence sufficient under this section to convict Burr of treason.

Upon our entering the World War a proclamation was issued (April 16, 1917) by President Wilson stating the acts which had been held to be within the Constitutional definition of treason, and warning both citizens and aliens not to do them. In part it was as follows:

"The courts of the United States have stated the following acts to be treasonable:

"The use or attempted use of any force or violence against the Government of the United States, or its military or naval forces;

"The acquisition, use or disposal of any property with knowledge that it is to be, or with intent that it shall be, of assistance to the enemy in their hostilities against the United States;

"The performance of any act or the publication of statements or information which will give or supply in any way. aid and comfort to the enemies of the United States;

"The direction, aiding, counseling, or countenancing of any of the foregoing acts;

"Such acts are held to be treasonable whether committed within the United States or elsewhere; whether committed by a citizen of the United States, or by an alien domiciled, or residing, in the United States, inasmuch as resident aliens, as well as citizens, owe allegiance to the United States and its laws."

There may be treason against a State under its constitution or laws, which the State may punish. Thus John Brown was executed by the State of Virginia for treason committed by his attack upon the State arsenal at Harper's Ferry.

No Person shall be convicted of Treason unless on the Testimony of two Witnesses to the same overt Act,[114] or on Confession in open Court.

[114] Referring to the execution of Sir Walter Raleigh (1618) for high treason, under a sentence passed fifteen years before, which "stained the reign of James I", Hallam says: "His conviction was obtained on the single deposition [written testimony] of the Lord Cobham, an accomplice, a prisoner, not examined in court, and known to have already retracted his accusation." Hallam states that while some contended "that less than two witnesses ought not to be received in a case of treason", it is doubtful whether any one had been allowed the benefit of that contention. Two witnesses to the same act are required by our Constitution, and of course the accused must be (Sixth Amendment, Note 155) "confronted with the witnesses against him." The written statement of one absentee, such as lost Raleigh his life, will not do in the United States. The "overt act" is one which discloses a purpose to levy war or to aid the enemy.

In the eleventh year of Queen Victoria (1848) the Treason-Felony Act of Parliament reduced the number of treasons and fixed penal servitude instead of death as punishment in many cases.

The Congress shall have Power to declare the Punishment of Treason,[115]

[115] In 1790 Congress prescribed death by hanging as the punishment of treason. In 1862 Congress enacted that treason be punishable by death and the liberation of the traitor's slaves, or by imprisonment of not less than five years and a fine of not less than $10,000 and the liberation of slaves. The punishment now is death, or imprisonment and fine, with the loss of right to hold office under the United States.

but no Attainder of Treason shall work Corruption of Blood, or Forfeiture except during the Life of the Person attainted.[116]

[116] Congress ran counter to this limitation during the Civil War. It passed (July 17, 1862) an act "to suppress insurrection, to punish treason and rebellion, to seize and confiscate the property of rebels", and for some other purposes, which was called the Confiscation Act. To insure the speedy termination of the war it was made the duty of the President to seize the property and money of officers of the Confederate army and of the president and other officials of the Confederate States.

President Lincoln had prepared a draft of a message objecting to this Act as violative of this clause. But before it was presented to Congress a joint resolution was passed to the effect that the Act "shall be so construed as not . . . to work a forfeiture of the real estate of the offender beyond his natural life." In view of the resolution President Lincoln signed the bill and it became a law. Notwithstanding the resolution, purchasers of real estate under the Confiscation Act claimed full title. In one of the first cases to reach the Supreme Court, reference was made to the qualifying resolution by Congress, and it was said that had Congress undertaken to convey title beyond the life of the offender, "it would have transcended its jurisdiction." Where the property of a Confederate general had been seized and sold and he left a son as heir, the Supreme Court held that under this clause the purchaser could take no interest beyond the lifetime of the original owner, upon whose death the son had legal title to the land. Several cases of this kind arose and the decisions were uniformly as stated — that the purchaser of property under the Confiscation Act could acquire an interest only during the life of the offender, punishment for whose offence could not be visited upon his children.

Sessions of the Constitutional Convention of 1787 were held in Philadelphia's historic old Independence Hall

Capitol in Dover, Delaware, first State to ratify the Constitution. Other small State, Rhode Island, was last

ARTICLE IV

Section 1. Full Faith and Credit shall be given in each State to the public Acts, Records, and judicial Proceedings of every other State.[117]

[117] This is a command to the States which they must obey. It is another of the nationalizing clauses of the Constitution. "The public acts [that is, the laws], records and judicial proceedings" (judgments and decrees of courts) of one State must be given in every other State "the force and effect to which" they are "entitled in the State where rendered." Thus a copy (properly authenticated or proved) of a judgment against a man for money, obtained in a court of the State of New York, may be presented to a court in California (the defendant having moved to the latter State, perhaps to escape the obligation) and a judgment will be there entered against him and enforced as it would have been in New York had he remained there. It is not necessary again to bear the trouble and expense of bringing witnesses and proving a case.

Substantially the same language was in a resolution passed in 1777 by the Continental Congress, and it reappeared in the Articles of Confederation

The first Congress under the Constitution passed an act (May 26, 1790) to effectuate this clause by prescribing how records should be authenticated and declaring that they should have such faith and credit in every State as they had in the State from which they were taken.

Full faith and credit was held by the Supreme Court of the United States (1903) not to have been denied by the courts of Massachusetts in permitting the first wife of a man, rather than the second, to administer his estate upon his death, as the law of Massachusetts made invalid in that State a divorce which he went to South Dakota to procure. Full faith and credit did not require that a decree of divorce granted in South Dakota should be respected and made operative against the public policy of Massachusetts.

And the Congress may by general Laws prescribe the Manner in which such Acts, Records and Proceedings shall be proved, and the Effect thereof.[118]

[118] Thus an Act of Congress provides that an act of a legislative body is authenticated for use in another State "by having the seal of such Territory, State, or country affixed thereto." A copy of a judgment or decree of court rendered in any State "shall be proved or admitted in any other court within the United States by the attestation of the clerk and the seal of the court annexed, if there be a seal, together with a certificate of the judge . . . that the said attestation is in due form."

Section 2. The Citizens of each State shall be entitled to all Privileges and Immunities of Citizens in the several States.[119]

[119] Provisions of this kind were in the colonial charters. The colonists of Virginia, for example, who received (1606) the first charter from the English sovereign, were by that writing guaranteed "all liberties, franchises and immunities within any of our dominions to all intents and purposes as if they had been abiding and born within this our realm of England."

"The better to secure and perpetuate mutual friendship and intercourse among the people of the different States in this Union," ran the Articles of Confederation, "the free inhabitants of each of these States (paupers, vagabonds and fugitives from justice excepted) shall be entitled to all the privileges and immunities of free citizens in the several States."

A citizen of one State going to or transacting business in another is entitled in the latter State to the privileges and immunities enjoyed by its citizens. The State cannot legislate against him or otherwise disfavor him. The intent was that the citizen of one State should not be an alien in another. In any State he has the protection of the government of that State, the enjoyment of life and liberty with the right to acquire and possess property, the right to pursue and obtain happiness, to institute actions in court, and generally to possess what the citizen of the State possesses. Numerous cases have arisen under this clause where States have attempted to favor their own citizens to the prejudice of the citizens of other States. Such laws are void for conflict with this clause.

After the Negro was emancipated there was adopted the Fourteenth Amendment (1868), one of the provisions of which (Note 172) is that "no State shall . . . abridge the privileges or immunities of citizens of the United States." Thus, putting the two clauses together, the State is forbidden to abridge the privileges and immunities of (1) the citizen of another State, and of (2) the citizen of the United States. For there are two citizenships and two loyalties.

A State cannot take away the right of citizens of other States to sue in the Federal courts of that State. This clause was held not to warrant an act of Congress prescribing punishment of *persons* for conspiring to deprive others (liberated Negroes) of equal privileges or immunities, as the guaranty of the Constitution is against wrongs done by *States* and not by persons. Wrongs done in a State by persons must be dealt with by the State in the exercise of its police power, and not by the Nation.

A Person charged in any State with Treason, Felony, or other Crime, who shall flee from Justice, and be found in another State, shall on demand of the executive Authority of the State from which he fled, be delivered up, to be removed to the State having Jurisdiction of the Crime.[120]

[120] This returning of a fugitive charged with crime to the place of his misdeed for trial is called interstate extradition. International extradition was probably aided in development by the practical operation of this clause. It was more than half a century after it was written in 1787 that England entered into a treaty of extradition (1842) with the United States. This was followed from time to time by treaties among leading countries. Previously to those treaties a fugitive too often found safety in a foreign country, although sometimes a government would surrender a fugitive as a matter of courtesy. Thus Spain delivered to the United States for trial a fugitive who had been indicted (1871) for taking the funds of the City of New York.

The "shall . . . be delivered up" in this clause is not mandatory. Congress has provided no remedy should a State refuse to deliver, and there have been many instances of refusal where, in the opinion of the Governor, substantial justice did not require surrender. The Governor of Ohio refused (1860) to deliver to Kentucky a man charged with aiding the escape of a slave, and the Supreme Court of the United States held that the Act of Congress of 1793, passed under this clause, declaring it to be the duty of a State to deliver upon a sufficient showing, was not mandatory. Therefore, a Federal court would not issue a mandate to compel the governor to obey.

The State will not deliver the fugitive until it has examined the record against the accused and found it regular and legal. If it appears that the proceeding was brought to force a settlement of a private demand, or to bring back the accused to be tried on some other charge, or otherwise to misuse legal writ or process, the application will be denied. And even after the State has determined to surrender the fugitive, he may secure, by the writ of *habeas corpus*, a hearing in court as to whether, on the record exhibited against him, he is legally restrained of his liberty.

One who while a fugitive commits an offence against the laws of the asylum State must stand trial there before being surrendered, and if convicted must serve sentence. To be a fugitive within the meaning of this clause it is enough to have left the demanding State after having committed a crime. One who goes into another State and commits a crime and then returns home is a fugitive. To be "charged" with crime within the language of the clause so as to warrant extradition one must be accused by a person having knowledge of the offence and stating it under oath; or if he has been convicted in the demanding State, then a record of the trial must be submitted to the Governor of the asylum State.

It is the duty of the Federal courts to see that this power be not extended to fields and exercised in classes of cases not clearly within the Constitution.

The "felony or other crime" of this clause includes any indictable offence under the present laws of the demanding State — that is, it is not limited to the offences known to the common law at the time the Constitution was adopted.

The governor of the asylum State should not attempt to pass upon the guilt of the accused — it is enough to determine that an extraditable offence has been regularly charged.

The international rule of treaty, that a fugitive surrendered by a foreign country cannot, on being taken home, be tried for an offence not embraced in the demand, does not generally apply to interstate extraditions under this clause, although some of the States follow that rule.

Where a criminal who had fled to another State was taken back forcibly without extradition papers, the Supreme Court of the United States held that the governor of the asylum State had no authority under the Constitution to demand his return, a fugitive having no right to asylum in any State.

A person may be arrested and detained for a reasonable time by the asylum State in order that the other State may prepare papers and make a demand.

No Person held to Service or Labor in one State, under the Laws thereof, escaping into another, shall, in Consequence of any Law or Regulation therein, be discharged from such Service or Labor, but shall be delivered up on Claim of the Party to whom such Service or labor may be due.[121]

[121] This is the last of the three (Notes 11 and 61) compromises respecting slavery. Time has made it obsolete. It related to the fugitive slave. It was designed to overcome the decision (1772) of Lord Mansfield, Chief Justice of the King's Bench, fifteen years before in the celebrated case of the Negro, Somerset, that a slave brought by his master from Virginia to England became free. This was held notwithstanding that slavery was common then in the English colonies and that traffic in slaves was one of the foremost of English activities in trade. To apply that principle in America would liberate the slave who might flee to a northern State. Therefore this protecting clause was necessary to secure from the slave-holding States their ratification of the Constitution.

In 1793 Congress effectuated this clause by "An Act Respecting Fugitives from Justice and Persons Escaping from the Service of Their Masters." In 1850, when the rumblings of the coming Civil War were rising, Congress passed another Fugitive Slave Law requiring, among many things, "all good citizens" to "aid in the prompt and efficient execution of this law", and authorizing officers "to summon and call to their aid the bystanders." In a case arising in Wisconsin, in which a man was charged with aiding in the escape of a fugitive slave in violation of this Act, it was held (1858) by the Supreme Court that under this clause Congress had authority to enact the Fugitive Slave Law.

"I say that the South has been injured in this respect," said Daniel Webster of Massachusetts in the Senate in 1850, "and has a right to complain; and the North has been too careless of what I think the Constitution peremptorily and emphatically enjoins upon her as a duty."

Many northern States enacted laws to aid the fugitive slave. Although the Ordinance of the Congress under the Articles of Confederation creating the Northwest Territory — reënacted by the first Congress (August 7, 1789) under the Constitution — forbade slavery, it nevertheless provided for the return of fugitive slaves to their owners.

Section 3. New States may be admitted by the Congress into this Union; [122]

[122] Even before the Constitution, provision was made for the admission of new States. The Ordinance (1787) of the Congress under the Articles of Confederation which created the Northwest Territory provided for a temporary government until the population should reach five thousand, when a representative would be admitted to Congress; and when the population should reach sixty thousand a State would be admitted to remain in the Union forever, upholding a republican form of government, and prohibiting slavery. The Articles of Confederation provided (Art. XI) that "Canada, acceding to this Confederation, and joining in the measures of the United States, shall be admitted into and entitled to all the advantages of this Union; but no other colony shall be admitted into the same unless such admission be agreed to by nine States."

For nearly four years (November 17, 1777, to March 1, 1781) the adoption of the Articles of Confederation was delayed by a dispute over the lands lying west of the original colonies. The grants from the crown had extended to the west indefinitely. They were intercepted at the Mississippi by claims to that valley based on French explorations. Thus Virginia claimed what afterward became West Virginia, Kentucky, and also the greater part of Ohio, Indiana, and Illinois, and part of northern Michigan, Wisconsin, and Minnesota. Jumping across eastern New York to Oswego and a line thence south, Massachusetts claimed western New York and what later became the lower half of Michigan and the lower half of Wisconsin. Connecticut claimed what is now the northern. part of Ohio, Indiana, and Illinois. North Carolina, South Carolina, and Georgia extended to the Mississippi. Some of the landless States, notably Maryland, contended that as those lands had been wrested from English dominion by common endeavor and sacrifice, they should become the property of the Union and not go to the enrichment of a few States. They finally carried their point. New York, which claimed but little, and Virginia, with a vast area, led the way (1781) by ceding their lands, and the others followed. Immediately Maryland. which had blocked the way, ratified the Articles of Confederation and they went into operation as successor to the provisional government maintained by the Continental Congress. That Congress had promised by resolution the year before (October 10, 1780) that lands which might be ceded to the Union by the State would be "disposed of for the common benefit of the United States", and also that they would be "settled and formed into distinct republican States which shall become members of the Federal Union."

Later (1803), by the Louisiana Purchase from Napoleon of France, the vast territory between the Mississippi and the Rocky Mountains was added by President Jefferson

to the domain.   In 1819 Florida was secured by President
Monroe from Spain.   Texas was admitted (1845) in the
term of President Polk.   The war with Mexico (1846–1847)
was followed by the purchase from that country by President Polk of the region west of the Rocky Mountains for
$15,000,000 in cash and the assumption by the United States
of all debts owing from the Mexican Government to American citizens, not to exceed $3,500,000.   In 1867 Alaska
was purchased of Russia for $7,200,000 by President John-
son, and following the war with Spain (1898) Puerto Rico
and the Philippines came under the dominion of the United
States during the term of President McKinley.

Usually the people of a Territory have adopted a constitution and submitted it to Congress for approval.   When
all conditions have been satisfactory Congress has passed
an act admitting the Territory as a State.   The admission
of Utah was once denied because of local religious customs.
Many conditions were imposed by Congress after the Civil
War upon the right of returning States to representation
in Congress, such as the repudiation of the debt of the
Confederacy, and the permission of the Negro to vote.

**but no new State shall be formed or erected within
the Jurisdiction of any other State ;** [123]

[123] But in the case of what is now West Virginia, the
people of which remained loyal during the Civil War, Congress decided that the part remaining loyal "might maintain a loyal State for the government of the whole State",
and that that government could give its consent to the
erection of a new State within the limits of the old, which
was done.

The territory of Vermont, the first State to be admitted
into the Union (March 4, 1791), was claimed by both New
York and New Hampshire; but as the claim was never
maintained by either State, the admission of Vermont
was not the erection of a new State "within the jurisdic-

tion of any other State ", prohibited by the foregoing clause.

The joint resolution of Congress (March 1, 1845) "for annexing Texas to the United States" authorized the creation of "new States, of convenient size, not exceeding four in number, in addition to said State of Texas."

nor any State be formed by the Junction of two or more States, or parts of States, without the Consent of the Legislatures of the States concerned as well as of the Congress.[124]

[124] "The particular precaution against the erection of new States by the partition of a State without its consent," wrote Alexander Hamilton, "quiets the jealousy of the larger States, as that of the smaller is quieted by a like precaution against a junction of States without their consent."

The Congress shall have Power to dispose of and make all needful Rules and Regulations respecting the Territory or other Property belonging to the United States; [125]

[125] Under this power Congress has erected Territories out of the public domain, provided for the government of them (usually by an elective legislature and an appointive executive and judiciary) until they were ready for statehood, and admitted them to the Union upon their presenting satisfactory constitutions for a republican form of government. Many Territories so governed grew populous and prosperous. Indeed, the opinion has been expressed by many residents of Territories that the territorial form of government is less expensive than that of a State and otherwise preferable to it. Part of the expenses of a Territorial government are paid by the National treasury. But as the governor and the other executive officers are appointed by the President and the people have no vote

in National elections, the desire for home rule and participation in National affairs has outweighed all such benefits of Territorial government.

and nothing in this Constitution shall be so construed as to Prejudice any Claims of the United States, or of any particular State.[126]

[126] "The proviso annexed is proper in itself," wrote Madison, "and was probably rendered absolutely necessary by jealousies and questions concerning the western territory sufficiently known to the public." At the time the Constitution was drafted, North Carolina and Georgia had not ceded to the Nation their western lands.

Section 4. The United States shall guarantee to every State in this Union a Republican Form of Government,[127] **and shall protect each of them against Invasion;**

[127] "In the light of the undoubted fact that by the Revolution it was expected and intended to throw off monarchical and aristocratic forms," says Cooley ("Principles of Constitutional Law"), "there could be no question but that by a republican form of government was intended a government in which not only would the people's representatives make the laws and their agents administer them, but the people would also directly or indirectly choose the executive."

This clause requires the Nation to protect the State from invasion by a foreign power, and also from domestic insurrection (Note 57), like the Dorr Rebellion, in Rhode Island, when the President announced that should it be necessary he would support the older government.

What is a republican form of government or whether one exists in a State is determinable by the political power (legislative) of the United States and not by the judicial This question arose out of the Dorr Rebellion (1842), when persons in the military service of the State broke into and searched the rooms of persons who were in insurrection. In an action for damages brought by persons whose rooms had been entered, the defendants justified on the ground that as officers of the State they were helping it defend itself from insurrection under the declaration by it of martial law. The plaintiff rejoined that the former State government "had been displaced and annulled by the people of Rhode Island" and that the persons who were said to be in insurrection and whose houses were broken into were in fact "engaged in supporting the lawful authority of the State." In a decision written by Chief Justice Taney in 1848 it was said that in forming the constitutions of the different States after the Declaration of Independence. and in the various changes and alterations which had since been made, "the political department has always determined whether the proposed constitution or amendment was ratified or not by the people of the State, and the judicial power has followed its decision."

In 1867 the State of Georgia filed a bill for injunction in the Supreme Court of the United States against Edwin M. Stanton, Secretary of War, General Grant, and Major General Pope, to restrain them from carrying out the provisions of the Reconstruction Acts of Congress (Note 96) for maintaining order in the southern States and holding elections for the adoption of new constitutions. The bill for injunction recited that Major General Pope had been placed in command of the military district in which Georgia was situated for the purpose of carrying out these Acts of Congress, although at the close of the war military forces had been withdrawn and the civil government of the State had been revived and reorganized with the consent of the President as Commander in Chief of the army, all that was lacking for complete rehabilitation being representation in the Senate and the House of Representatives. The Supreme Court dismissed the bill for want of jurisdiction, saying that its authority related to "the rights of persons or property, not merely political rights, which do not belong to the jurisdiction of a court, either in law or equity."

In 1912 a tax-payer in Oregon brought this question again to the attention of the Supreme Court, claiming that the amendment of 1902 to the constitution of Oregon, by which the people reserved to themselves the right to propose amendments to the Constitution and to enact or reject at the polls laws or amendments independent of the legislative assembly, had destroyed the republican form of government which had been guaranteed by this section of the National Constitution. It was contended that such government by the people directly is democracy and not the representative or republican form which the framers of the Constitution had in mind. The Supreme Court said that the questions presented "have long since by this court been definitely determined to be political and governmental and embraced within the scope of the powers conferred upon Congress, and not therefore within the reach of the judicial power."

and on Application of the Legislature, or of the Executive (when the Legislature cannot be convened) against domestic Violence.[128]

[128] The President is to determine when "domestic violenc " warrants his sending troops to a State. The Nation will not act as a policeman. Where a State had no militia with which to preserve order the President sent troops upon the call of the governor (the legislature not being in session), but then the President insisted that the legislature must sit and make preparations without delay so that he might withdraw the troops. During the disorders of a country-wide railway strike in 1894, which, in Chicago, interfered with the transportation of United States mail, President Cleveland sent troops to maintain order not only without the request of the Governor of Illinois, but also against his protest. Under the clause

(Note 51) putting post offices and post roads in the care of the Nation the Federal Government could take any steps necessary anywhere to keep the post roads open.

During Dorr's Rebellion in Rhode Island in 1842, when two rival organizations were claiming to be the legal government, Governor King of the older government called upon President Tyler for assistance. The President said that he hoped that intervention might not be necessary for the restoration of order, but that he would "not be found to shrink from the performance of a duty which, while it would be the most painful, is at the same time the most imperative." As between the contending parties, he said that it would be his duty "to respect the requisition of that government which had been recognized as the existing government of the State through all time past until I shall be advised, in regular manner, that it has been altered and abolished and another substituted in its place by legal and peaceable proceedings." That declaration virtually ended the rebellion.

In the Constitutional Convention there was much discussion and revision before this clause was finally so nicely balanced between National and State authority.

ARTICLE V

The Congress, whenever two-thirds of both Houses shall deem it necessary, shall propose Amendments to this Constitution, or, on the Application of the Legislatures of two-thirds of the several States, shall call a Convention for proposing Amendments, which, in either Case, shall be valid to all Intents and Purposes, as part of this Constitution, when ratified by the Legislatures of three-fourths of the several States, or by Conventions in three-fourths thereof, as the one or the other Mode of Ratification may be proposed by the Congress; [129]

[129] In this Article there is prevented for the future one of the failures in practice of the Articles of Confederation. They provided (Article XIII) that no alteration at any time should be made unless agreed to in the Congress of the United States "and be afterward confirmed by the legislature of *every* State." Three important attempts to amend the Articles failed on account of that provision for unanimity. Rhode Island alone prevented an amendment by which the Government could raise money on import duties. New York alone defeated another amendment for a general revenue plan. A third important amendment thus defeated related to commerce. The framers of our Constitution removed that obstacle.

Here, for the first time in history, a government provided for its own change without turbulence or bloodshed.

All the Amendments to the Constitution thus far adopted were proposed by Congress and not by the legislatures of the States; and only one ratification (that of Amendment XXI) has been effected by conventions rather than by State legislatures. The Constitution itself was ratified (Note

James Madison did much drafting of the Constitution; his notes on debates are best record of the Convention

Alexander Hamilton; though a delegate to the Convention, his chief service was in securing Constitution's adoption

137), not by the legislatures, but by conventions of the people in the States. New Jersey ratified the Fourteenth Amendment on September 11, 1866, and attempted on March 27, 1868, to rescind its action; and in January, 1868, Ohio attempted to rescind its ratification of that Amendment, which was given on January 11, 1867. Secretary of State Seward announced the ratification of the Fourteenth Amendment by three fourths of the States, and mentioned those attempts at rescission. Congress thereupon passed a concurrent resolution that the ratifications made the Amendment a part of the Constitution. Oregon tried to withdraw its ratification of the Fourteenth Amendment after its adoption had been proclaimed by the Secretary of State New York undertook to withdraw its ratification of the Fifteenth Amendment. The governing principle seems to be that when the legislature took the step of ratifying under the Constitution it exercised its constitutional authority, exhausted its power in the premises, and could do nothing further.

In 1919 the Supreme Judicial Court of Maine, in answer to a question propounded by the Governor, declared that the legislature could not rescind its ratification of the Eighteenth Amendment, establishing prohibition.

In 1920, in six cases, arising in New Jersey, Rhode Island, Massachusetts, Kentucky, Wisconsin, and Missouri under the Eighteenth Amendment, the Supreme Court of the United States held that the referendum provisions in the constitutions of some States cannot be applied under this article to the ratification or rejection of amendments — the requirement being that the legislature, or a convention, and not the voters, must ratify or reject an Amendment.

On December 20, 1860, South Carolina, in the State convention, repealed or withdrew the ratification of the Constitution which it gave in 1788 and undertook to return to its former status.

Praising our Constitution as superior to that of England

because time and consideration are required to make an amendment, Lecky ("Democracy and Liberty") says that "an appetite for organic change is one of the worst diseases that can affect a nation."

Fenet, the French statesman, in making a report for the revision of the law of France and the adoption of a civil code, and having in mind the failure of the French Revolution in its effort to take leave of past thought and achievement and to set up a new social and governmental system based upon supposedly new ideas, gave expression to this maxim, which should not be forgotten : "It is better to preserve what it is not necessary to destroy."

In his Farewell Address (1796), caution is given by Washington to resist "the spirit of innovation" upon the principles of the Constitution, "however specious the pretexts." He said that "facility in changes upon the credit of mere hypothesis and opinion exposes to perpetual change from the endless variety of hypothesis and opinion"; and that in any event, should a "modification of the Constitutional powers" be necessary, it should be made "by an amendment in the way which the Constitution designates."

"But let there be no change by usurpation." he warned.

Every one of the twelve constitutions of France adopted since 1789 has been made difficult to amend. To illustrate, one provided that no amendment could be made until three successive legislative assemblies should have expressed the wish for a change in some article.

The Parliament of Australia can alter certain articles but not others. The Parliament of the Dominion of Canada cannot change the constitution, which is alterable by the Parliament of England. But in New Zealand almost all the articles are amendable by the local Parliament.

In the Argentine Republic, which followed our Constitution closely, amendments are first declared by a two-thirds vote of Congress to be necessary, and then the subject is dealt with in a convention for the purpose.

In Brazil, as with us, amendments may be initiated by either Congress or the legislatures of the States.

From time to time Presidents have suggested to Congress the propriety of proposing amendments to the Constitution. Jefferson, who had questioned the constitutional power to make the purchase of Louisiana in 1803, suggested to Congress (1806) that an amendment be proposed authorizing the spending of surplus National funds for education throughout the States, for the construction of roads, the opening of rivers and the digging of canals. President Monroe suggested (1817) the propriety of an amendment authorizing the establishment of seminaries throughout the land. In 1829 President Jackson recommended an amendment permitting the distribution of surplus National revenue among the States so as to avoid what he considered the illegal appropriation of public money for non-National purposes. On December 3, 1860, the month after Lincoln was elected, President Buchanan asked Congress to propose an "explanatory amendment" (1) recognizing property in slaves where they then were held or might afterward be owned; (2) protecting the right of slave owners to hold slaves in Territories, the right thereafter to be determined by a vote of the people; and (3) recognizing the right of an owner to his fugitive slave and declaring all State laws void which were designed to impair or defeat his rights. In 1868 President Johnson asked Congress to propose an amendment for the election of the President by the direct vote of the people, limiting his term to six years, and forbidding reëlection. President Grant desired (1873) an amendment authorizing the President to veto any item of a bill to which he might object without negativing the whole bill; and in 1882 President Arthur made a like request, calling the attention of Congress to the fact that fourteen States had at that time made such provision for the veto of legislative bills by their governors. President Grant also (1873) requested the proposal of an amendment that a special session of Congress be forbidden to deal with any subject except that for which it had been specially convoked.

To illustrate how closely the applicability of the Constitution has always been studied it may be mentioned that from April to November, 1921, there were offered in the first session of the Sixty-seventh Congress twenty-five resolutions to amend it, some of them being substantially repetitions of others. One was for making the term of the President six years and prohibiting his reëlection; another would authorize him to veto any provision of a bill and approve the remaining ones; another would empower Congress to regulate the employment of children under sixteen years of age (see Note 45); another would extend the word "elections" in the Constitution to include primaries (see Note 26); another would submit to a vote of the people the question of declaring war (Note 55); another would extend the constitutional definition of treason (Note 113) to include acts of injury in time of war to the military, physical, or financial resources of the United States; another would require the ratification of an Amendment by the voters of the country to the exclusion of the legislatures of the States; and more of various kinds. It has been said that over 2000 amendments have been proposed in the course of our National life.

Provided that no Amendment which may be made prior to the Year One thousand eight hundred and eight shall in any Manner affect the first and fourth Clauses [Notes 61 and 65] in the Ninth Section of the first Article; [130] and that no State, without its

[130] This relates to slavery.

Consent, shall be deprived of its equal Suffrage in the Senate.[131]

[131] Once more the small State is guaranteed against being prejudiced by the large ones. In the Brazilian Constitution it is provided that bills to abolish the republican federative form of government, or to destroy equality of representation in the Senate, are not subjects of deliberation. (See Note 18.)

ARTICLE VI

All Debts contracted and Engagements entered into, before the Adoption of this Constitution, shall be as valid against the United States under this Constitution as under the Confederation.[132]

[132] This was "a solemn assurance to public creditors and to the world that the public faith would be inviolably kept by the United States under its changed government."

Hamilton put the debt of the Union at $11,710,378 owing in foreign countries and $42,414,085 of domestic debt. The States themselves owed $25,000,000, making debts in the aggregate of $79,000,000.

The credit of the Colonies had sunk so low during the Revolution that had it not been for bankers in Holland and France the war for freedom must have failed. Thereafter the young States issued so much paper money and passed so many laws making it difficult for creditors to collect debts that it was considered necessary to give assurance to the world that the Nation would pay.

In like manner the Dominion of Canada assumed in its Constitution (1867) responsibility for existing debts.

This Constitution, and the Laws of the United States which shall be made in Pursuance thereof; and all Treaties made, or which shall be made, under the Authority of the United States, shall be the supreme Law of the Land; [133]

[133] This means that the Constitution itself is a law which it is the duty of the courts (State as well as National) to

uphold and enforce as they do all other laws. A law of Congress to be one of the supreme laws must be "made in pursuance thereof" and not in conflict with the Constitution. When not made in pursuance thereof it is of course unconstitutional and of no effect.

"If the State governments had not been restrained from encroaching on the powers vested in the National Government," wrote President Monroe, "the Constitution, like the Confederation, would soon have been set at naught; and it was not within the limit of the human mind to devise any plan for the accomplishment of the object other than by making a National Constitution which should be to the extent of its powers the supreme law of the land."

"Legislators have their authority measured by the Constitution," says Cooley; "they are chosen to do what it permits, and nothing more, and they take solemn oath to obey and support it. . . . To pass an act when they are in doubt whether it does not violate the Constitution is to treat as of no force the most imperative obligations any person can assume."

Before this supreme law the acts of Congress, the acts of State legislatures, and the constitutions of States, when conflicting with it, go down. When the people express their will in the National Constitution all conflicting expressions of will of an inferior sort go for nothing. An excellent illustration of the absolute supremacy of the Constitution was presented in the Eighteenth Amendment, prohibiting the manufacture and sale of intoxicating liquors, because at the time of its adoption there were not only many States with laws permitting the manufacture and sale of liquors, but there were also acts of Congress, and, moreover, the National treasury derived large revenue from licenses and taxes respecting liquors. But all those fell and were nothing the instant that the Eighteenth Amendment, the supreme law, took effect. "The first section of the Amendment," said the Supreme

Court of the United States, disposing (June 7, 1920) in one decision of cases which arose in New Jersey, Rhode Island, Massachusetts, Kentucky, Wisconsin, and Missouri, "the one embodying the prohibition, is operative throughout the entire territorial limits of the United States, binds all legislative bodies, courts, public officers, and individuals within those limits, and of its own force invalidates every legislative act — whether by Congress, by a State legislature, or by a Territorial assembly — which authorizes or sanctions what the section prohibits."

A good illustration of the statement in the Constitution that a treaty (along with the Constitution itself, and the acts of Congress made in the pursuance of it) is the supreme law of the land, before which National laws, State laws, and judicial decisions must fall, is found in the Migratory Bird Case, in which the Supreme Court held (1920) that, upon our making a treaty in 1916 with Great Britain for the protection of birds passing between the United States and Canada, the States ceased to have regulatory power. When the supervisory power was given to Congress by a treaty, the treaty and the act to carry it out became the supreme law of the land. Of the three elements entering into what the Constitution declares to be the "supreme law of the land", namely, "this Constitution, and the laws of the United States which shall be made in pursuance thereof, and all treaties made or which shall be made under the authority of the United States", the treaty is second to no other. The laws of Congress are not the supreme law of the land unless they "shall be made in pursuance thereof" — of the Constitution. But the treaty is the supreme law of the land when made "under the authority of the United States" — that is, when negotiated by the President and approved by the Senate. The people having expressed their National will in a treaty, the will of a State respecting the subject must conform to the superior will.

Of the coöperation which should prevail between the State and the Nation and of the proper relation of the two governments to each other the Supreme Court said (1858):

"Nor is there anything in this supremacy of the general government, or the jurisdiction of its judicial tribunals, to awaken the jealousy or offend the natural and just pride of State sovereignty. Neither this government, nor the powers of which we are speaking, were forced upon the States. The Constitution of the United States, with all the powers conferred by it on the general government, and surrendered by the States, was the voluntary act of the people of the several States, deliberately done, for their own protection and safety against injustice from one another."

and the Judges in every State shall be bound thereby, any Thing in the Constitution or Laws of any State to the Contrary notwithstanding.[134]

[134] Every judge in every court of the States is under oath or affirmation to support the Constitution of the United States. When any litigation arises out of the constitution of his State or out of any of its laws it is by this clause made his duty to "be bound" by the National Constitution and laws and in a proper case to hold the State constitution or law to be void for conflict with "the supreme law of the land." This the courts of the States have done from the beginning down in almost countless cases, as where a State constitution or law has interfered with or assumed to control interstate commerce, or to deal discriminatively with the citizens of other States or of the United States, or to emit bills of credit or paper money, or to prescribe *ex post facto* punishment, or to impair the obligations of contracts, and so on. But when a State court fails in this respect its action is reviewable and reversible by the Supreme Court of the United States.

Discussing this clause, Dicey, the distinguished English legist, mentions that while French constitutionalists endeavored by many and strict provisions to "confine the power of the legislature", they failed to recognize and provide for "the fact that enactments of the legislature might, without being in so many words opposed to the Constitution, yet be of dubious constitutionality, and that some means would be needed for determining whether a given law was or was not in opposition to the *principles* of the Constitution." He states that "a constitution may be undermined by the passing of laws which, without nominally changing its provisions, violate its principles." George Washington adverted to this in his Farewell Address and said that "one method of assault may be to effect in the form of the Constitution alterations which will impair the energy of the system and thus to undermine what cannot be directly overthrown."

Dicey declares that the Americans solved the problem. They "directed their attention, not so much to preventing Congress and other legislatures from making laws in excess of their powers, as to the invention of means by which the effect of unconstitutional laws may be nullified; and this result they have achieved by making it the duty of every judge throughout the Union to treat as void any enactment which violates the Constitution, and thus have given to the restrictions contained in the Constitution on the legislative authority either of Congress or the State legislature the character of real laws, that is, of rules enforced by the courts. This system, which makes the judges the guardians of the Constitution, provides the only adequate safeguard which has hitherto been invented against unconstitutional legislation."

In another chapter Dicey returns to the subject and points out that "in no country has greater skill been expended" in the construction of a judicial system, and he mentions again that "the guardianship of the Constitution is in America confided not only to the Supreme Court, but to every judge throughout the land."

"The power, moreover, of the courts which maintains the articles of the Constitution as the law of the land," quoting Dicey further, "and thereby keeps each authority within its proper sphere, is exerted with an ease and regularity which has astounded and perplexed Continental critics. The explanation is that while the judges of the United States control the action of the Constitution, they nevertheless perform purely judicial functions, since they never decide anything but the cases before them."

That is, they do not have the initiative to interfere. A "case" must be brought before they can act. All the decisions of the courts have disposed, not of theoretic or academic questions, but of actual and weighty controversies between men with respect to life, liberty, or property. One party has claimed a right under the Constitution, or under an act of Congress, or under a treaty. The other party has contested the claim. The court has decided the contention. Except where a case is thus brought for judgment before a court by contesting parties, the judiciary has no power to render any decision or to make any pronouncement whatsoever. Both the Legislative Department and the Executive Department have vast initiative — the Judicial Department has none at all.

The Constitution of Australia is declared, like ours, to be the supreme law of the land, and that "it shall be binding on the courts, judges, and the peoples of every State and of every part of the Commonwealth, notwithstanding anything in the law of any State." The High Court of Australia, like our Supreme Court, and like the Supreme Court of Canada, declares invalid a legislative act in conflict with the Constitution.

The Senators and Representatives before mentioned, and the Members of the several State Legis-

latures, and all executive and judicial Officers, both
of the United States and of the several States, shall
be bound by Oath or Affirmation, to support this Constitution; [135]

[135] In the oath taken by a State officer he first swears to
uphold and defend the Constitution and the laws of the
United States, and next he swears to support those of his
State.

The first oath prescribed by Congress (June 1, 1789)
was simply to support the Constitution, and it contained
no invocation to God. During the Civil War (July 2,
1862) the oath was changed by Congress to what was
called the "iron-clad oath", and the affiant was required
to say that he had not borne arms against the United
States or given aid or encouragement to hostile forces,
or held office under hostile authority; and he was made
to declare that he would support and defend the Constitution against all enemies, that he took the oath without
mental reservation or evasion, and that he would faithfully discharge the duties of the office, "so help me God."
So far as this Act prevented a man from resuming his
practice as an attorney before the Supreme Court after
he had been pardoned by the President for holding office
under the Confederate States it was held to be unconstitutional because *ex post facto*, imposing a punishment which
was not prescribed at the time of the misconduct. It
operated as a bill of attainder because a person was, without trial, adjudged guilty of a crime and sentenced to
exclusion from civil rights. In 1868 Congress made a
modification of the foregoing oath for those who had
"participated in the late rebellion and from whom all
legal disabilities" had been "removed by Act of Congress."

"This is the last and closing clause of the Constitution,"
said the Supreme Court (1858), disposing of a case in
which the Supreme Court of a State had undertaken to

release a man in the custody of a United States marshal
who was holding him under a warrant issued by a
United States District Court in pursuance of an act of
Congress, "and inserted when the whole frame of government, with the powers hereinbefore specified, had been
adopted by the Convention; and it was in that form,
and with these powers, that the Constitution was submitted to the people of the several States, for their consideration and decision. . . . In the emphatic language
of the pledge required, it is *to support this Constitution.*
And no power is more clearly conferred by the Constitution and laws of the United States than the power of
this court to decide, ultimately and finally, all cases
arising under such Constitution and laws."

Writing of the approaching civil war between Charles I
and Parliament, in which the House of Lords would probably favor the King, the historian Green ("English People,"
Sec. 1036) portrayed in a sentence the dire consequences of
a lack of clearly defined powers of government and of the
binding of all officers of government to follow absolutely
the written charter:

"The legal antiquarians of the older constitutional school
stood helpless before such a conflict of coördinate powers,
a conflict for which no provision had been made by the
law, and on which precedents threw only a doubtful and
conflicting light."

**but no religious Test shall ever be required as a
Qualification to any Office or public Trust under the
United States.**[136]

[136] By the oaths prescribed by some of the States the
person entering office was required to express belief in
"one God, the creator of the universe, the rewarder of the
good and the punisher of the wicked"; or to declare belief in the "divine inspiration" of the Scriptures, or "faith
in God the Father and in Jesus Christ, His only Son", and

so on. Such oaths excluded from office those whose belief prevented them from so swearing, and they were con-
sequently the "religious test" forbidden by this clause
of the Constitution. This clause was added by motion
in the Constitutional Convention to the language requiring an oath by all officials, both National and State, and
its adoption was unanimous. The clause, however, is not
a prohibition upon the States. But most if not all of the
constitutions of the States have a like provision.

This subject comes up again in another form in the
First Amendment, which forbids (Note 141) Congress
(not the States) to make any "law respecting an establishment of religion or prohibiting the free exercise thereof."
The First Amendment also, or the substance of it, is in
the constitutions of the States, though some were slow in
adopting it.

ARTICLE VII

The Ratification of the Conventions of nine States shall be sufficient for the Establishment of this Constitution between the States so ratifying the Same.[137]

[137] As the Articles of Confederation (Art. XIII) provided that no alteration should ever be made in them unless "agreed to in a Congress of the United States and be afterwards confirmed by the legislature of *every* State ", this complete superseding of the Articles by the action, not of "a congress", but of a Constitutional Convention, and the ratifying of that action by nine States instead of every one of the thirteen, has been described as revolutionary. However, the people ratified the Constitution as prepared, and it was within their power to make any change that seemed desirable. It has been seen (Note 129) that the provision requiring unanimity of State action was in practice destructive of government. It was the belief in the Constitutional Convention that the new instrument could not at first secure the approval of every State. That was correct. The Constitution went into operation with George Washington as President and a Congress of two Houses sitting before North Carolina and Rhode Island ratified it. "To have required the unanimous ratification of the thirteen States," wrote Madison in "The Federalist", . . . "would have marked a want of foresight in the Convention which our own experience would have rendered inexcusable." There was much debate over a proposal that the Constitution be submitted for ratification to the legislatures of the States instead of to "conventions", but the proposal was rejected. Some feared that

the legislatures might not ratify. It has been seen, however (Note 129), that amendments to the Constitution may be ratified in either way.

On September 20, 1787, three days after the Constitutional Convention had finished at Philadelphia the drafting of a Constitution, a copy of the new instrument was laid before the Congress, sitting in New York, accompanied by a letter from George Washington, who had presided over the Convention. "And thus the Constitution," he wrote, referring to the many conflicting opinions and interests which had been adjusted, "which we now present is the result of a spirit of amity, and of that mutual deference and concession which the peculiarity of our political situation rendered indispensable." Congress at once sent a copy of the Constitution, with a copy of Washington's letter, to the legislature of each State and urged the calling of ratifying conventions. Then began the great battle in each of the thirteen States over ratification. The little State of Delaware, the only fear of which had been removed by the grant of a vote in the Senate equal to that of the largest State (Notes 18 and 131), was the first to ratify, on December 16, less than three months after the Constitutional Convention adjourned But in Pennsylvania, New York, Massachusetts, Virginia, and Maryland the opposition was strong and it had able leadership — although most of the objections raised look unimportant now when viewed in the light of experience. It was objected that the vote in each House of Congress was to be by individuals instead of by States ; that Congress was to have an unlimited power of taxation ; that too much power was given to the National judiciary ; that paying the salaries of senators and representatives out of the National treasury would make them independent of their own States ; that an oath of allegiance to the National Government was to be required ; that laws impairing the obligation of contracts were to be prohibited ; that the document was the production of "visionary young men", like Hamilton and Madison; that the election of members of the House of Representatives for so long a term as two years would be dangerous; that the new Congress might make itself a perpetual oligarchy and tax the people at will; that a National capital in so vast an area as ten miles square (the District of Columbia), independent of the State, would foster tyranny; that the power to maintain an army would bring oppression; that Congress would use the power granted with respect to elections to destroy freedom of the ballot; that assent should not be given to the continuance of the slave trade until 1808; that the Constitution contained no bill of rights; and that it gave no recognition to the existence of God.

Ratification was vigorously opposed by such men as Patrick Henry, Benjamin Harrison, John Tyler, and Richard Henry Lee of Virginia, Elbridge Gerry of Massachusetts, Luther Martin and Samuel Chase of Maryland, Thomas Sumter of South Carolina, and George Clinton and Melanchton Smith of New York.

While much pamphleteering and debating was done in Pennsylvania and elsewhere, the great battle was waged in New York. Not only was that State necessary to the Union because it lay between northern and southern States which had already ratified and which could not be close commercially or politically if divided by a foreign State, but more than two thirds of the members of the convention called in New York to ratify or reject were opposed to the Constitution. Alexander Hamilton conceived the idea of explaining each part of the Constitution in a series of short articles which appeared in different publications. James Madison and John Jay aided in the work. Of the eighty-five letters published and signed Publius, five were written by Jay, twenty-nine by Madison, and fifty-one by Hamilton. They helped to carry the day, and New York entered the Union on July 26, 1788, of which it became the Empire State. In book form those letters are known as the "Federalist", the most brilliant work on our Constitution. During the French Revolution, which followed ours, the "Federalist" was translated into French. Later it appeared in German during dreams of a republic. It appeared in Spanish and Portuguese in South America, for fifteen republics south of us framed constitutions after ours. While the correspondence of the time throws much light upon the workings of the Constitutional Convention, the sessions of which were secret, like those of the British Parliament, the main source of information is the Madison Papers or the Madison Journal, made up from the shorthand notes of the great delegate from Virginia. Congress caused the publication of the notes in 1843.

"No man could say whether argument or interest had won the fight for the Constitution," says Woodrow Wilson ("A History of the American People", Vol. 3, p. 98), referring to the "Federalist" and the other discussions of the time, "but it was at least certain that nothing had been done hastily or in a corner to change the forms of Union. These close encounters of debate had at least made the country fully conscious of what it did. The new Constitution had been cordially put through its public ordeal. All knew what it was and for what purpose it was to be set up. Opinion had made it, not force or intrigue; and it was to be tried as a thing the whole country had shown itself willing to see put to the test."

DONE in Convention by the Unanimous Consent of the States present [138]

[138] Rhode Island was not present. While there was "unanimous consent of the States present", some delegates of States refused to sign. For New York the only signature was that of Alexander Hamilton.

Only fifty-five of the sixty-five delegates chosen by the States sat in the Constitutional Convention. Of those, forty-two were present at the signing. Three of those present (Randolph and Mason of Virginia and Gerry of Massachusetts) refused to sign because they believed that too much power was taken away from the States.

the Seventeenth Day of September in the Year of our Lord, one thousand seven hundred and Eighty seven and of the Independence of the United States of America the Twelfth. IN WITNESS whereof We have hereunto subscribed our Names,

(Signed by)   G⁰ Washington
Presidt and deputy from Virginia

New Hampshire.

John Langdon	Nicholas Gilman

Massachusetts.

Nathaniel Gorham	Rufus King

Connecticut.

Wm Saml Johnson	Roger Sherman

New York.

Alexander Hamilton

New Jersey.

Wil: Livingston	Wm Patterson
David Brearley.	Jona: Dayton

Pennsylvania.

B. Franklin	Thomas Mifflin
Robt. Morris	Geo. Clymer
Thos. Fitzsimons	Jared Ingersoll
James Wilson	Gouv Morris

Delaware.

Geo: Read	Gunning Bedford jun.
John Dickinson	Richard Bassett
Jaco: Broom	

Maryland.

James McHenry   Dan : of St Thos Jenifer
Danl Carroll

Virginia.

John Blair —   James Madison Jr.

North Carolina.

Wm Blount   Richd Dobbs Spaight,
Hu Williamson

South Carolina.

J. Rutledge   Charles Cotesworth Pinckney
Charles Pinckney   Pierce Butler.

Georgia.

William Few   ⸌   Abr Baldwin
Attest : William Jackson, *Secretary.* [139]

[139] "Thus after four months of anxious toil," says Fiske ("Critical Period of American History", p. 304), "through the whole of a scorching Philadelphia summer, after earnest but sometimes bitter discussion, in which more than once the meeting had seemed on the point of breaking up, a colossal work had at last been accomplished, the results of which were most powerfully to affect the whole future career of the human race so long as it shall dwell upon the earth."

The calculation has been made that the Constitutional Convention spent upon its task eighty-six working days.

"The establishment of our institutions," wrote President Monroe, "forms the most important epoch that history hath recorded. They extend unexampled felicity to the whole body of our fellow-citizens, and are the admiration of other nations. To preserve and hand them down in their utmost purity to the remotest ages will require the existence and practice of virtues and talents equal to those which were displayed in acquiring them. It is ardently hoped and confidently believed that these will not be wanting."

How The Constitution Was Ratified ·

The course of the thirteen States in ratifying the new Constitution presents an interesting study :

1787			*Unanimous*	*For*	*Against*
Dec.	7	Delaware [1]	u		
	12	Pennsylvania		43	23
	18	New Jersey	u		
1788					
Jan.	2	Georgia	u		
	9	Connecticut		128	40
Feb.	6	Massachusetts [2]		187	168
Apr.	28	Maryland		63	11
May	23	South Carolina [3]		149	73
June	21	New Hampshire [4]		57	46
	26	Virginia [5]		89	79
July	26	New York [6]		30	27
1789					
Nov.	21	North Carolina [7]		194	77
1790					
May	29	Rhode Island [8]		34	32

[1] The small State having had its great fear dispelled by the guarantee of a vote in the Senate equal to that of the largest. Delaware quickly led in ratifying.

[2] In the ratifying convention of Massachusetts there was strong opposition to those clauses of the Constitution (Notes 11, 61, and 121) which made concessions to slavery. And there was dislike of the clause (Note 136) forbidding a religious test for the person holding office. While a bill of rights also was desired, Massachusetts set the good example of ratifying "in full confidence that the amendments proposed will soon become a part of the system", as they did.

[3] Ratification by South Carolina destroyed the hope of some Virginians for a separate confederacy of southern States. They were opposed to the National powers granted by the Constitution.

[4] On July 2 Congress received word that the ninth State had ratified. In September it fixed the first Wednesday in January,

1789, for the choice of electors, the first Wednesday in February for balloting for a President and a Vice President, and the first Wednesday in March (March 4, as it happened and as the date remained until 1933) for the commencement of the new government.

⁵ In addition to opposing a strong National government as against the dominance of the State, Virginians, led by Patrick Henry, objected to the clause (Note 71) preventing a State from impairing the obligation of a contract. At that time Virginian planters owed to English merchants over ten million dollars and the legislature of Virginia had suspended their right to sue for their money in the courts of that State.

⁶ New York, in the port of which more than one half of the goods consumed in Connecticut, New Jersey, Vermont, and western Massachusetts paid duties or other taxes, stubbornly opposed the Constitution because of the commerce clause (Note 45). Opposition in the ratifying convention was led by Governor Clinton. In support of the Constitution the imperishable "Federalist" papers were written by Hamilton, Madison, and Jay. Chief Justice Morris and Chancellor Livingston aided in the struggle for the Constitution.

⁷ North Carolina did not enter the Union until after the new government was well on its way. The first convention (July. 1788) refused, by a vote of 184 to 84, to ratify the Constitution because of the lack of a Bill of Rights and in the fear that the strong National government would in time overbear State authority.

⁸ Rhode Island, which did not send delegates to the Constitutional Convention, and which long refused to ratify, knocked at the door for admission after the new government began to deal with it as a foreign country and subjected it to taxes on its exports.

An early procession in honor of the Federal Constitution after ratification, passing by New York's Bowling Green

ARTICLES
IN ADDITION TO, AND AMENDMENT OF,
THE CONSTITUTION OF THE UNITED STATES
OF AMERICA, [140]

Proposed by Congress, and Ratified by the Legislatures
of the Several States, Pursuant to the Fifth Article
of the Original Constitution.

First ten Amendments (of twelve) proposed by Congress September 25, 1789; adopted June 15, 1790.

[140] During the first session of the first Congress under the new Constitution this self-explanatory resolution was passed:

"*The Conventions of a number of the States having at the time of their adopting the Constitution expressed a desire, in order to prevent misconstruction or abuse of its powers, that further declaratory and restrictive clauses should be added: And as extending the ground of public confidence in the government will best insure the beneficent ends of its institution —*

"Resolved *by the Senate and House of Representatives of the United States of America in Congress assembled, two-thirds of both Houses concurring,* That the following articles be proposed to the legislatures of the several States, as amendments to the Constitution of the United States, all or any of which articles, when ratified by three-fourths of the said legislatures, to be valid to all intents and purposes, as part of the said Constitution, viz.:

"Articles in addition to, and amendment of, the Constitution of the United States of America, proposed by Congress and ratified by the legislatures of the several States, pursuant to the fifth article of the original Constitution."

Then followed twelve proposed amendments, the first two of which failed of adoption. The first related to membership in the House of Representatives by population, and the second was against the taking effect of a law varying the compensation of senators and representatives until an election should have intervened.

The ten Amendments adopted make the so-called American Bill of Rights. It has been seen that the Petition of Right and the Declaration of Rights and the Bill of Rights were favorites of the English. Following the practice in the mother country, the colonists issued a Declaration of Rights through their first Continental (Stamp Act) Congress in 1765. More than fifteen years before the adoption of these Amendments a Declaration of Rights had been issued (1774) by the Colonies through deputies sitting "in general congress" at Philadelphia. Reciting that they were "justly alarmed by these arbitrary proceedings of Parliament", which they denounced as "unconstitutional" and "formed to enslave America", they took "into their most serious consideration the best means of attaining" their rights and concluded to "do, in the first place, as Englishmen their ancestors in like cases have usually done for asserting and vindicating their rights and liberties." Then they made specific declarations, among them being that the foundation of liberty is the right to participate in legislative councils; that they were entitled to the "immunities and privileges" given by the colonial charters; that a standing army in the Colonies was "against law"; that restraint of "the right peaceably to assemble . . . and petition" is "illegal"; that "it is indispensably necessary to good government" that the "branches of the legislature be independent of each other" and that therefore a legislative council appointed at the pleasure of the King "is unconstitutional, dangerous and destructive to the freedom of American legislation"; and that Acts of Parliament directing that "colonists be transported to England and tried there upon accusations for treason" and other acts were "unjust and cruel, as well as unconstitutional."

The word "unconstitutional" appears in this Colonial Declaration of Rights again and again.

So Massachusetts, New York, Virginia, and some other States wanted a Bill of Rights in the Constitution, and with the tacit understanding that they would have one they ratified it. Some argued that all the guaranties in the Amendments already existed in the law transplanted from England; but that was a time of written charters and written constitutions, and, to remove every possibility of doubt, a Bill of Rights was wanted in plain writing. The very fact that a writing exists between men often prevents disputes. When both know definitely what the boundaries are neither is likely to make encroachments. That our forefathers were wise in not leaving such vital matters to inference, implication, or construction will be shown by an examination of the first ten Amendments.

"The executive in our governments is not the sole — it is scarcely the principal — object of my jealousy," wrote Jefferson from Paris, urging upon Madison the need of amendments making a Bill of Rights; "the tyranny of the legislatures is the most formidable dread at present, and will be for many years. That of the executive will come in its turn, but it will be at a remote period."

The Constitution already contained provisions belonging to a Bill of Rights, such as those forbidding *ex post facto* laws (Note 64) and bills of attainder (Note 63), prohibiting the suspension of the privilege of *habeas corpus* (Note 62), requiring trial by jury (Note 110) and at the place where the crime was committed, defining treason and limiting punishment (Notes 113–116), granting the immunities and privileges of all States to the citizens of each State (Note 119), and forbidding a religious test (Note 136) before admission to office.

The State constitutions which were adopted in 1776 after the Declaration of Independence contained elaborate bills of rights for the protection of the individual; and, as elsewhere observed, those constitutions were the source of much matter selected by the Constitutional Convention.

The additional safeguards which were given to the man by the so-called Bill of Rights will now be examined. They contain nothing novel. They embody "guaranties and immunities which are inherited from our English ancestors", the Supreme Court (1897) has said.

ARTICLE I.

Congress shall make no law respecting an establishment of religion, or prohibiting the free exercise thereof; [141]

[141] In the reign of Charles II, Parliament, for the purpose of compelling all persons to attend the established Church, passed (1665) the Conventicle Act making every one over sixteen years of age who attended a conventicle (any meeting for religious worship at which five persons were present besides the household) subject to imprisonment, with transportation beyond seas for the third offence. During the same reign it passed the Test Act requiring oaths in support of the established religion. Under those acts, which were not repealed until recent times, all nonconformists of whatever religious belief were very severely dealt with. Those acts hastened emigration to America, as did intolerance in continental countries.

"It is strange indeed," says Ridpath ("Popular History of the United States", p. 128), "that the very men who had so recently, through perils by sea and land, escaped with only their lives to find religious freedom in another continent, should have begun their career with intolerance and persecution."

The established Church of England had been set up in several of the Colonies and taxes were levied for its support.

Madison and Jefferson had waged (1784) a battle in Virginia against the establishment, finally securing the passage of a law declaring that any interference by the civil authority with religious opinion is against natural right.

A clause like this failed of adoption in the Constitutional Convention. As a member of the first House of Representatives under the new Constitution, Madison brought up this Amendment. After the House had adopted it the Senate rejected it, but it was later reinstated by that body.

When Madison became President he vetoed (1811) a bill passed by Congress for incorporating a church organization because he held it contrary to this Amendment, and shortly thereafter he vetoed another which would make a gift of public lands to a church.

Before the Constitutional Convention sat several of the States had put in their constitutions clauses for religious freedom. All of them have such clauses now. The prohibition under consideration is against the Nation and not the State.

In 1890 the Supreme Court of the United States, concluding a great contest begun in the District Court of the Territory of Utah in 1887, held that the National Government had "a perfect right to prohibit polygamy and all other open offenses against the enlightened sentiment of mankind, notwithstanding the pretense of religious convictions by which they may be advocated and practiced."

Let it be borne in mind that all of the first ten Amendments are of National effect and not binding upon the States.

or abridging the freedom of speech, or of the press; [142]

[142] "The liberty of the press consists. in a strict sense,"

says Hallam ("Constitutional History of England"), "merely in an exemption from the superintendence of a licenser."

He states that when, in the reign of Henry VIII (1509–1547), the political importance of the art of printing began to be apprehended, that monarch thought it necessary to take absolute control of it. Not only did he limit the privilege of keeping a press, but he also required previous inspection of the matter by a licenser. The same authority states that "the Long Parliament (1640–1660) did not hesitate to copy this precedent of a tyranny they had overthrown."

What our forefathers meant by the liberty of the press was defined by Blackstone (1758) two centuries after the time of Henry VIII as "in laying no *previous* restraints upon publications, and not in freedom from censure for criminal matter when published. Every freeman has an undoubted right to lay what sentiments he pleases before the public; . . . but if he publishes what is improper, mischievous, or illegal, he must take the consequence of his own temerity."

That is, he will be held accountable, by criminal proceeding or in civil action for damages, should he slander or libel another. And his oral and written speech is subject to restriction by the police power for the protection of the moral health of the community. Nor is he free to advocate the overthrow of civil order.

In 1771, following the publication of imperfect reports of the debates in Parliament, the sessions of which were then secret, the House of Commons issued a proclamation forbidding the publication of debates. A printer who disobeyed and who ignored a summons to appear at the bar of the House was arrested by its messenger. The magistrates of London released him on the ground that the proclamation was without legal force. Then the House sent the lord mayor of the city to the Tower, but the crowds that followed him showed to Parliament that public opinion was against it. Further attempt to prevent reports was not made. "The first great English journals," says Green ("The English People", Vol. 5, sec. 1504), "date from this time."

By the Sedition Law of 1798, which expired by limitation on March 3, 1801, the end of Adams's administration, Congress, in the opinion of many, went to the limit of its power under this clause; but in the cases which arose at the time the courts sustained the legislation. The law was designed to suppress seditious newspapers which were attacking the Government chiefly because it had, upon the declaration of war against England by the new Republic of France, issued a proclamation of neutrality, declaring a policy which has ever since been followed. There was such widespread sympathy in the United States with the French Revolution that people exulted in the guillotining (1793) of Louis XVI and of Queen Marie Antoinette, whose assistance had made American independence possible. The belief was that the United States should become involved in the European conflict and many foreigners were publishing papers assailing the Government for not doing so. The first minister from the French Republic and other emissaries had taken advantage of this sentiment and openly worked against our policy of neutrality. The Sedition Law forbade the publication of matter which was intended to defame the Government or to bring its officers into disrepute. The fact that Washington favored it explains the fear which was entertained by sober men that the end of all government and law which had come in France would eventually destroy the United States.

Freedom to speak and freedom to print, guaranteed by this clause, must be considered in the light of other clauses, for the Constitution is to be read as a whole and effectuated in all its parts, as nearly as may be done. Thus another clause (Note 56) empowers Congress to raise armies. May speaking or writing under the former clause impede or cripple the Nation in its measures of defense under the latter clause? The Supreme Court has answered No. And so a Federal court remarked (1921) that while it is very desirable to enforce the Eighteenth Amendment, that end must not be accomplished by searches and seizures in violation of the Fourth Amendment, or by making a citizen bear witness against himself in violation of the Fifth. And while under the clause respecting the post office the Government has almost absolute power and may exclude objectionable matter from the mails, it may not, in disregard of the Fourth Amendment, search or seize letters to find whether the sender has committed a crime. Those examples show how the various clauses of the Constitution must be coordinated and applied together.

Freedom of speech is not abridged by the prohibition of addresses in public parks or of the publication of libelous, indecent or blasphemous articles or matter injurious to public morals or private reputation.

In many States it has been held under similar constitutional provisions (for, as before mentioned, the First Amendment here restricts Congress only) that freedom of speech and printing is not abridged by State laws for the censoring of moving pictures.

Among the laws of Congress springing from the World War was the Espionage Act of June 15, 1917, which forbade any one wilfully to cause or attempt to cause insubordination, disloyalty, mutiny, or refusal of duty in the military or naval forces of the United States. Every one of those who spoke and wrote against our being in the war, or who tried to dissuade men from enlisting, promptly invoked in self-defense this constitutional provision for free speech. But the Espionage Act was upheld by the Supreme Court in the first case to reach it, and that declaration was repeated in many following cases of varying facts and circumstances. On March 1, 1920, affirming a sentence to the penitentiary of the editor of a foreign-language newspaper who had, during recruiting, published articles against our action in the War, abusing and belittling the American and his government, and showing up what he called "the failure of recruiting", the Supreme Court said:

"But simple as the [Espionage] law is, perilous to the country as disobedience to it was, offenders developed, and when it was exerted against them challenged it to decision as a violation of the right of free speech assured by the Constitution of the United States. A curious spectacle was presented: that great ordinance of government and orderly liberty was invoked to justify the activities of anarchy or of the enemies of the United States, and by a strange perversion of its precepts it was adduced against itself."

In March, 1921, the Supreme Court upheld the action of the Post Office Department in excluding from the mails during the World War a newspaper which had denounced our government as a "plutocratic republic", a financial and political autocracy, which denounced the Selective Service Law of Congress as unconstitutional, arbitrary, and oppressive, which denounced the President as an autocrat, and the war legislation as having been passed by "a rubber stamp Congress", and which contended that soldiers could not legally be sent outside of the country and that the United States was waging a war of conquest. The National Defense Act of 1917 said that any newspapers published in violation of its provisions should be "nonmailable" and "should not be conveyed in the mails or delivered from any post office or by any letter carrier." Pointing out that the published matter "was not designed to secure the amendment or repeal of the laws denounced . . . but to create hostility to and to encourage violation of them", the Supreme Court said:

"Congress shall make no law respecting an establishment of religion, or prohibiting the free exercise thereof."

"Congress shall make no law . . . abridging the freedom of speech . . . or the right of people peaceably to assemble".

"Freedom of the press may protect criticism and agitation for modification or repeal of laws, but it does not extend to protection of him who counsels and encourages the violation of the law as it exists. The Constitution was adopted to preserve our government, not to serve as a protecting screen for those who, while claiming its privileges, seek to destroy it."

In an earlier case (1892) it was held to have been no abridgment of the freedom of the press for Congress to exclude from the mails newspapers containing advertisements of lotteries, as the government could not be "compelled arbitrarily to assist in the dissemination of matters condemned by its judgment."

The State supreme courts, under State constitutional provisions guaranteeing freedom of speech and of the press, have stated the doctrine as it has been expressed in the foregoing decisions by the Supreme Court of the United States. Thus, the Constitution of New York provided for freedom in speaking and writing and prohibited restraint of the "liberty of speech or of the press"; but it made the citizen "responsible for the abuse of that right." The court of last resort in that State held (1902) that a seditious publication instigating revolution and murder and suggesting the persons in authority to be murdered was not protected by the State constitution, which, the court said, places "no restraint upon the power of the legislature to punish the publication of matter which is injurious to society according to the standard of the common law — it does not deprive the State of the primary right of self-preservation."

And in 1918 the Supreme Court of Minnesota upheld a law of that State (1917) which had been passed in aid of the Nation and which made it unlawful "for any person to print, publish, or circulate in any manner whatsoever" anything "that advocates or attempts to advocate that men should not enlist in the military or naval forces of the

United States or of the State of Minnesota." Persons had been convicted of violating the Act and circulating a pamphlet asserting that "this war was arbitrarily declared without the will of the people"; that "the President and Congress have forced this war upon the United States"; that now "they are attempting by military conscription to fight a war to which we are opposed"; that "the integrity of the country is being menaced"; that "this war was declared to protect the investments"; and so on. The Supreme Court of the State said that the Act was not in conflict with the Espionage Law of Congress because the citizens of the State (who are also citizens of the United States) owe a duty to the Nation, and that the State "owes a duty to the Nation to support, in full measure, the efforts of the national government." It was specifically held that the State statute did not abridge the freedom of National citizenship in violation of the Fourteenth Amendment to the Constitution of the United States.

In President Jackson's seventh annual message (December, 1835) he took cognizance of the abolitionist newspapers and magazines, the publication of which had begun in 1831, and called upon Congress to prevent the transmission of them by the Post Office Department, "under severe penalties," as they were "intended to instigate the slaves to insurrection." Although many in Congress shared his view, no bill was passed.

or the right of the people peaceably to assemble, and to petition the Government for a redress of grievances.[143]

[143] This right already existed in customary law. In the Colonial Declaration of Rights of October 19, 1765, it was said "that it is the right of British subjects in these Colonies to petition the King or either House of Parliament"; and in the Declaration of Rights of October

14, 1774, it was complained that "assemblies have been frequently dissolved, contrary to the rights of the people, when they attempted to deliberate on grievances." It was further said " that all prosecutions, prohibitory proclamations and commitments for the same are illegal." It was declared also that "their dutiful, humble, loyal, and reasonable petitions to the Crown for redress have been repeatedly treated with contempt by His Majesty's ministers of state."

In the Declaration of Rights submitted by Parliament to William III and Mary (1689) and accepted by them, it was said that the right to petition the King existed and that the prosecution of petitioners which had taken place was illegal. It was considered so valuable by our forefathers that it was protected by this express provision. Assemblies for the discussion of their rights and petitions for the correction of their wrongs had been repeatedly employed by the colonists.

"In every stage of these oppressions," says the Declaration of Independence, "we have petitioned for redress in the most humble terms; our repeated petitions have been answered by repeated injury." When this Constitution was written the right of assembly and petition was preserved in the constitutions of several States.

Van Buren's administration was marked by a struggle to prevent the receipt and consideration by Congress of petitions for the abolition of slavery. Senator Calhoun declared such petitions a violation of the Constitution.

The people must assemble "peaceably." Regulations for the preservation of order are not a denial of the right. Nor can the right to petition be employed for the purpose of visiting malice upon others. The petition must be for something within the authority of the body addressed, or the petitioners must in good faith believe it to be.

The petition in England was based on the fact that Parliament was a court as well as a legislative body. Indeed, at first it was more of a court than a legislature.

In 1839 the English Chartists (seeking an extension of suffrage, vote by ballot, pay for members of Parliament, and an abolition of property qualifications for suffrage) presented to the House of Commons a petition having 1,250,000 signatures.

While this First Amendment, and the nine following it, are prohibitions against encroachments upon liberties by the Nation (Note 141), it was held by the Supreme Court in 1937 that the Due Process Clause of the Fourteenth Amendment, written against the States after the Civil War, protects from infringement by a State "the right of the people peaceably to assemble". Holding the Syndicalism Act of Oregon of 1933 violative of the Due Process Clause of the Fourteenth Amendment as applied to a man who attended a meeting "under the auspices of the Communist Party" but said nothing toward "effecting industrial or political change or revolution", forbidden by the Act, the Court declared that "peaceable assembly for lawful dis- cussion cannot be made a crime".

ARTICLE II.

A well regulated Militia, being necessary to the security of a free State, the right of the people to keep and bear Arms shall not be infringed.[144]

[144] This means the arms necessary to a militia, and not the dirks, pistols, and other deadly weapons used by the lawless. In the Declaration of Rights it was complained that kings had disarmed the people. Of course the colo- nists were by force of early circumstances bearers of arms. This prohibition upon the Nation means that it can never interfere with the people who make the militia of the States; and that therefore the States will always have the means to check by physical force any usurpation of authority not given to the Nation by the Constitution. Maryland and Virginia had such provisions in their constitutions when the Constitutional Convention sat.

ARTICLE III.

No Soldier shall, in time of peace be quartered in any house, without the consent of the Owner, nor in time of war, but in a manner to be prescribed by law.[145]

[145] The Petition of Right of 1628, which Charles I was compelled to accept, complained that "companies of soldiers and mariners had been dispersed into divers counties, and the inhabitants, against their wills, had been compelled to take them into their houses and allow them there to sojourn against the laws and customs of this realm." The English Parliament required that the colonists provide quarters for troops, and when General Gage went from Halifax to Boston he demanded quarters, which were refused.

The Colonial Declaration of Rights of October 19, 1765, makes no mention of a standing army in the Colonies; but that of October 14, 1774, proclaimed "that the keeping of a standing army in these Colonies, in times of peace, without the consent of the legislature of that Colony in which the army is kept, is against law"; and an act of Parliament was condemned which required the colonists to provide "suitable quarters for officers and soldiers in His Majesty's service in North America." A complaint in the Declaration of Independence against George III was "for quartering large bodies of armed troops among us" and for "keeping among us in times of peace standing armies without the consent of our legislature."

"James II's army," says Burnet, "was kept for some time in the western counties, where they lived at free quarters, and treated all that they thought disaffected with rudeness and violence insufferable."

"Before the Revolution" (1688), says Macaulay ("History of England", Vol. 5, p. 234), "our ancestors had known a standing army only as an instrument of lawless power."

ARTICLE IV.

The right of the people to be secure in their persons, houses, papers, and effects, against unreasonable searches and seizures, shall not be violated, and no Warrants shall issue, but upon probable cause, supported by Oath or affirmation, and particularly describing the place to be searched, and the persons or things to be seized.[146]

[146] Hallam mentions that in the reign of Charles I the unconstitutional practice of committing to prison some of the most prominent people and searching their houses for papers was renewed. Cooley says that this constitutional provision probably resulted from the seizure (1683) of the papers of Algernon Sidney, which were used as a means of convicting him of treason; and of those of John Wilkes at about the time (1763) that the controversy between Great Britain and the Colonies was assuming threatening proportions. The general search warrant never was considered legal in England after the battle fought by Wilkes. The protection of this clause is not limited to one's dwelling house, but extends to his person and papers. Many cases have arisen, but the courts have invariably held that no vague or general warrant is sufficient and that the letter of the Constitution must be closely followed.

Even under the strict customs laws enacted by Congress, the burden of proof is on the claimant seeking to make seizure, and probable cause must be shown for the act; while the stringent acts of Congress regarding internal revenue require that upon the issuing of search warrants by the district court and the commissioners of courts, the internal revenue officer must make oath in writing that he has reason to believe and does believe that "a fraud upon the revenue has been or is being committed upon or by the use of said premises." An order of court requiring a person to produce an invoice of goods for the inspection of government officers and to be offered in evidence against him was held an unconstitutional exercise of authority.

James Otis of Massachusetts became celebrated in 1761 by contesting in court this form of tyranny through the use of Writs of Assistance. The English practice of personal search had become odious in the Colonies. "A person with this writ in the daytime," said Otis in his argument, "may enter all houses, shops, etc. at will, and command all to assist him." Further, he said, "Every man prompted by revenge, ill humor, or wantonness to inspect the inside of his neighbor's house may get a Writ of Assistance."

Every day magistrates refuse to issue search warrants because probable cause is not shown or because the oath required by this Amendment is not sufficiently definite and direct.

An actual entry of the premises is not necessary to a search; a compulsory production of books and papers for use in evidence against the owner of them was said by the Supreme Court to be a violation of the Fourth Amendment. And an act of Congress requiring a party to produce books and papers, and permitting the Government, in case of his refusal, to assume as true its allegations of what the books and papers contained, was held by the Supreme Court to be void for conflict with this Amendment.

"The protection of the Constitution is not, however, confined to the dwelling-house," says Cooley, "but it extends to one's person and papers, wherever they may be. It is justly assumed that every man may have secrets pertaining to his business, or his family or social relations, to which his books, papers, letters, or journals may bear testimony, but with which the public, or any individuals of the public who may have controversies with him, can have no legitimate concern; and if they happen to be disgraceful to him, they are nevertheless his secrets, and are not without justifiable occasion to be exposed. Moreover, it is as easy to abuse a search for the purpose of destroying evidence that might aid an accused party, as it is for obtaining evidence that would injure him, and the citizen needs protection on the one ground as much as on the other."

In 1920 the Supreme Court held that this Amendment protected a corporation and its officers from an unwarranted "sweep of all the books, papers, and documents" made by representatives of the Department of Justice of the United States under an invalid subpoena in the hands of the United States District Attorney. Admitting that the seizure was wrongful, the Government contended that it might use the information so obtained to make later a specific demand for papers which it was unable to make before. The Court said No.

ARTICLE V.

No person shall be held to answer for a capital, or otherwise infamous crime,[147]

[147] A capital crime is one punishable by death and an infamous crime is one punishable by death or imprisonment.

unless on a presentment or indictment of a Grand Jury,[148]

[148] The grand jury consists of not more than twenty-three men called in by the sheriff of the county (or by the United States marshal of the district) to hear witnesses respecting any subject that may properly be brought before them. If they believe that a person accused should be brought to trial, they return into court a "true bill" or indictment, which is a formal charge in writing that acts were done amounting to a crime; otherwise they write "no bill." The person indicted is later brought to trial in court before a petit jury of twelve, which, after hearing the evidence on both sides, returns a verdict of guilty or not guilty. The

grand jury originated when men were executed or imprisoned upon the order of the king or on the charge of his subordinates. It was designed to prevent unjust punishments. for the grand jurors (who sat secretly and, therefore, could not be called to account for opposing the Government) presumably would protect the accused from wrong. But it is out of time now and many States have abolished it. In those States an "information" is filed by the prosecuting attorney against the person whom he wishes to bring to trial. The information sets out the charges as the indictment of the grand jury does. The grand jury cannot be dispensed with as a National institution until this Amendment has been changed.

except in cases arising in the land or naval forces, or in the Militia, when in actual service in time of War or public danger; nor shall any person be subject for the same offence to be twice put in jeopardy of life or limb; [149]

[149] Where an Englishman had been indicted and put on trial and the evidence did not appear sufficient the court discharged the jury but ordered the prisoner to be held until more proof might come in. Hallam says that he was accordingly indicted again. When he pleaded that he had already been tried, the judges had the effrontery to deny that he had ever been put in jeopardy. A person is considered to have been once put in jeopardy when brought before a court of competent jurisdiction upon an indictment or information in sufficient form and a jury has been impanelled and sworn to try him. Of course he has not been put in jeopardy where a jury fails to agree and the jury has been discharged for that reason, or where a conviction has been reversed by an appellate court.

Nor can his trial be stopped after the jury has been sworn to try him should it then appear that the evidence against him is insufficient. The trial must proceed to verdict.

nor shall be compelled in any criminal case to be a witness against himself,[150]

[150] He cannot be required to testify either directly or indirectly. His papers and books cannot be made to speak against him. In this particular the Fourth and Fifth Amendments unite for one purpose. "This provision," says the Supreme Court, "had its origin in a protest against the inquisitorial and manifestly unjust methods of interrogating accused persons which had long obtained in the Continental system and . . . was not uncommon even in England." It has been remarked as singular that this provision should not have been put in the body of the Constitution, as it was already in the constitutions of several States at the time of the Convention.

Officers of the army placed a man in the establishment of one suspected of disloyalty, and he purloined papers which were used in evidence against the owner of them. Pointing out once more that the Fourth and Fifth Amendments cooperate to protect a man from being made a witness against himself, either orally or by his papers, the Supreme Court of the United States reversed (1921) the trial court for permitting the papers to be used, and said:

"It has been repeatedly decided that these Amendments should receive a liberal construction, so as to prevent stealthy encroachments or 'gradual depreciation' of the rights secured by them, by imperceptible practice of courts, or by well-intentioned but mistakenly over-zealous executive officers."

In 1893 Congress enacted that no person should be excused from producing books and papers in response to a *subpoena duces tecum* (a formal writ demanding the production of specified records) of the Interstate Commerce Commission; but it kept the statute within the purpose of this clause by adding that no prosecution should follow any disclosure made. The prosecution being made impossible, the basis of the constitutional right to refuse to answer the Interstate Commerce Commission no longer exists. This special legislation was considered necessary to aid the Commission in its investigations of railway operation and management.

Of course a person may waive the privilege. And if the statute of limitation bars prosecution for the crime, he will be compelled to answer. So he cannot claim privilege if he has been pardoned, for that prevents prosecution.

Compulsory self-incrimination existed for four hundred years after Magna Charta, and it gained some recognition among the early colonists, for the record of the trial of Mrs. Anne Hutchinson in 1673 shows that Governor Winthrop, who presided, was not aware of any privilege against self-incrimination.

nor be deprived of life, liberty, or property, without due process of law; [151]

[151] This prohibition as to National power is repeated (Note 173) in the Fourteenth Amendment respecting the conduct of the States.

Due process of law means substantially the same as "the law of the land," as used in the English Petition of Right in 1628. Indeed, both expressions were linked in that celebrated Petition, which said that no man should be "in any manner destroyed but by the lawful judgment of his peers or by the law of the land"; and that no man should be "put out of his land or tenements, nor taken nor imprisoned, nor disinherited, nor put to death, without being brought to answer by due process of law."

In 1855 the Supreme Court of the United States answered the question, What is due process of law? A trial or other legal proceeding must, in order to give due process, conform (1) to the guaranties contained in the Constitution, and (2) to all other guaranties that have come to the American through the adoption in this country of any part of the

laws of England.   This clause preserves to the citizen against
action by Congress, against action by the President, and
against action by the courts, not only the rights enumerated
in the Constitution itself, but also those privileges and immunities to which he became entitled through the early adoption and application in America of English law.

"The Constitution contains," said the Court, "no de-
scription of those processes which it was intended to allow
or forbid.   It does not even declare what principles are to
be applied to ascertain whether it be due process.   It is
manifest that it was not left to the legislative power to enact any process which might be devised.   The article is a
restraint on the legislative as well as on the executive and
judicial powers of the government, and cannot be so construed as to leave Congress free to make any process 'due
process of law,' by its mere will.   To what principles, then,
are we to resort to ascertain whether this process, enacted
by Congress, is due process?   To this the answer must be
twofold.   We must examine the Constitution itself, to see
whether this process be in conflict with any of its provisions.
If not found to be so, we must look to those settled usages
and modes of proceeding existing in the common and
statute law of England, before the emigration of our ancestors, and which are shown not to have been unsuited to
their civil and political condition by having been acted on
by them after the settlement of this country."

In the foregoing case the property of a revenue collector
of the Government, who had failed to turn over more than
a million dollars, was summarily seized under an act of
Congress (1820) authorizing such procedure.   The warrant
of seizure issued by the Treasury was legal process, but was
it due process?   The Constitution requires (Note 110) that
charges of crime be tried by a jury, while the Seventh
Amendment (Note 157) guarantees a jury trial in all civil
cases involving over twenty dollars.   Had the delinquent
collector been denied a constitutional right?   The Supreme

Court said No. In protecting its revenue or itself the Government is not obliged to sue or be sued like an individual; and as under English law, repeated substantially in the laws of Massachusetts (1786) and most of the other young States, like procedure had been established for safeguarding the public funds, the act of Congress complained of merely stated what was due process of law on both sides of the Atlantic when the Constitution was adopted.

Due process of law is another name for legal, judicial, and governmental fair play. But a trial in court is not always essential to due process. When a man has had a full hearing before the Secretary of the Interior, for example, on some question concerning public lands, the decision of the Secretary may be final and he cannot be heard in court. So of questions of fact before the Interstate Commerce Commission, which is not a court. And a tax-payer who has been permitted to produce evidence before a taxing board, in accordance with settled procedure, cannot complain that due process has been denied.

nor shall private property be taken for public use, without just compensation.[152]

[152] It was a rule of Roman law that private property could be taken for public use upon the owner's being paid an estimated value made by good men. Magna Charta provided that no one should be deprived of his property except by the law of the land or by a judgment of his peers. The Code Napoleon of France (1807) required "a just and previous indemnity" for the taking of property for public use.

A celebrated case under this article arose respecting the estate left by the widow of General Robert E. Lee, the military chieftain of the Southern Confederacy in the Civil War, which had been sold under an act of Congress for collecting taxes "in the insurrectionary districts" and upon one part of which military officers, acting under orders of the President, had, after seizing the estate, erected a military fort and upon another made **Arlington** Cemetery.   In the trial court a jury, acting under definite instructions as to the law, returned a verdict that **the sale** for taxes had been illegal.   The United States Government carried the case to the Supreme Court of the United States and that court said, in 1882 : "It is not pretended, as the case now stands, that the President had any lawful authority to do this, or that the legis ative body could give him any such authority except upon payment of just compensation.   The defense stands here solely upon the absolute immunity from judicial inquiry of every one who asserts authority from the executive branch of the government, however clear it may be made that the executive possessed no such power.   Not only no such power is given, but it is absolutely prohibited, both to the executive and the legislative, to deprive any one of life, liberty, or property without due process of law, or to take private property without just compensation. . . .   No man in this country is so high that he is above the law."

Owing to an equal division in opinion of the justices of the Supreme Court of the United States the decision of a State Supreme Court (1917), declaring valid the State's minimum wage law, stood. But an act of Congress requiring employers to pay minimum wages to women and children, regardless of their earning capability, was held (1923) to take private property for the public welfare in violation of this clause.   This decision was later reversed (1937) and the Women's Minimum Wage Act upheld (Note 173).

ARTICLE VI.

In all criminal prosecutions, the accused shall enjoy the right to a speedy and public trial, by an impartial jury of the State and district wherein the crime shall have been committed, which district shall have been previously ascertained by law,[153]

[153] This is the second time (Note 110) that provision is made for the trial by jury in criminal cases. When the Constitution was written, several of the States had such constitutional declarations.

It was charged in the Petition of Right to Charles I (1628) that when accused persons illegally held were released by judges in *habeas corpus* proceedings "they were detained by your Majesty's special command" and "were returned back to several prisons without being charged with anything to which they might make answer according. to the law." That is, they had no "speedy and public trial", or trial of any kind; they were left languishing in prison at the will of the king. It was pointed out that Magna Charta provided that no freeman should be taken or imprisoned " but by the lawful judgment of his peers [jury trial] or by the law of the land." Our forefathers were well learned in English history.

The speedy trial is one without unreasonable delay. A trial may not be demanded by the accused before the prosecuting attorney has had time to make preparation. But it was decided by the Supreme Court of the United States (1909) that a man might be held by the governor of a State without any trial at all when his imprisonment as the leader of persons in insurrection was deemed necessary to preserve the peace. The Court said that as in suppressing insurrection by force the governor might kill, the milder method of preserving the peace was not obnoxious to this clause guaranteeing speedy trial. The public trial is for the benefit of the accused and not the public, that publicity may prevent the doing of injustice to him. Therefore in proper cases the court may exclude those of the public who should not hear objectionable testimony. It is enough if a few of the public remain.

A complaint in the Declaration of Independence was "for transporting us beyond seas to be tried for pretended offenses." Hence the provision requiring that the accused be tried in the district wherein the crime was committed. This is the second time that this safeguard is stated. It was clearly declared in the Constitution (Note 111) and it was repeated in an Amendment. Nevertheless, many unsuccessful attempts have been made to break over this barrier.

and to be informed of the nature and cause of the accusation; [154]

[154] This is done in criminal cases by serving upon the accused, as required by an act of Congress, a copy of the indictment by the grand jury. He then has adequate time to prepare to meet in court before a petit or trial jury the charges set forth in the indictment. A demand in the Petition of Right was "that freemen be imprisoned or detained only by the law of the land or by due process of law, and not by the king's special command, *without any charge.*"

This clause and the Fifth Amendment were held by the Supreme Court (1921) to have been disregarded by Congress in framing the Food Control Act (1917), a war measure to restrict the enhancing of prices and to prevent the monopolizing of necessaries. A mercantile company was indicted in the language of the Act for making "an unjust and unreasonable rate and charge" for sugar; and it contended in defense that the law fixed "no immutable standard of guilt", but left the criminal act to be determined by "the variant views of the different courts and juries which may be called on to enforce it." Referring to "the conflicting results which have arisen from the painstaking attempts of enlightened judges in seeking to carry out the statute" Chief Justice White said that the section of the Act in question "was void for repugnancy to the Constitution." It has long been settled that a criminal law must be so clear and specific that a citizen will know whether the act which he intends to do will violate it. "It would certainly be dangerous," said the Supreme Court in an earlier case (1875), if the legislature could set a net large enough to catch all possible offenders, and leave it to the courts to step inside and say who could be rightfully detained and who should be set at large. This would, to some extent, substitute the Judicial for the Legislative Department of the government."

to be confronted with the witnesses against him; [155]

[155] This clause was framed against the odious practice which had prevailed in England of taking the depositions (written testimony) of witnesses and reading them in court. Not only was the accused not confronted by the witnesses against him, but he was necessarily in the circumstances prevented also from cross-examining them. The illustrious Sir Walter Raleigh was condemned to death in the reign of James I on the written testimony of a single witness who had in the meanwhile recanted his accusation. "On how precarious a thread the life of every man is suspended," wrote Hallam of the trial of the Duke of Somerset in the reign of Henry VIII, whose demand for confrontation by witnesses was denied, "when the private deposition of one suborned witness, unconfronted with the prisoner, could suffice to obtain a conviction in the case of treason."

The rule of the law of Imperial Rome regarding formal accusations and the confrontation by witnesses is illustrated in the case of St. Paul. Festus, the Roman procurator of Judea, answered Paul's accusers (Acts XXV, 16) at Jerusalem, "It is not the manner of the Romans to deliver any man to die before that he which is accused have the accusers face to face, and have licence to answer for himself concerning the crime laid against him." When Paul was sent before Felix, the Roman Governor of Cæsarea (Acts XXIII, 35), and the governor had read the letter of accusation, "I will hear thee, said he, when thine accusers are also come."

In the reign of Edward VI (1547-1553) it was enacted that no one should be convicted of treason except on the testimony of two lawful witnesses (Note 114) who should be brought in person before the accused at the time of his trial to avow and maintain what they had to say against him. Violations of this right cannot come to pass in the United States, where the Constitution is a law — "the supreme law of the land" — and where it is enforced by the courts like every other law.

As it was well established in law at the time the Constitution was drafted that the dying declaration (because the solemnity of the circumstances in which it is made impels belief) of a witness may be read against the accused at the trial, it has been stated by the Supreme Court (1897) that the rule is therefore contained in this clause.

But the Supreme Court held (1894), following a like decision in Massachusetts, that the protection of this Amendment was not violated by the reading on the second trial of the defendant of the testimony of a witness who had since died and who had at the first trial confronted the defendant and been thoroughly cross-examined by defendant's counsel. The Court said that the defendant had received the substance of the constitutional protection and could ask no more.

to have compulsory process for obtaining witnesses in his favor, and to have the Assistance of Counsel for his defence.[156]

[156] It was not until the reign of William IV (1836) that an act of the English Parliament gave to the accused the right to the assistance and protection of counsel in all cases of felony, that is, in which the offense is punishable by imprisonment or death. But in 1696 a bill was passed by Parliament allowing counsel to persons on trial for high treason, that is, offenses against the royal family or the government. In this country the man without means may have witnesses produced to testify in his behalf. The court appoints counsel to guard his legal rights, who (being an

Thomas Jefferson, then Minister to France, had no part in Constitution making, but favored strict interpretation

Benjamin Franklin, then 81, was influential in working out vital compromises, often saving the Convention by his humor

officer of the court) must serve when directed to do so and without compensation. Two lawyers of high repute were thus appointed to see that the case against the assassin of President McKinley should be made at the trial in conformity with the settled rules of law.

ARTICLE VII.

In suits at common law, where the value in controversy shall exceed twenty dollars, the right of trial by jury shall be preserved,[157]

[157] Although the Constitutional Convention very carefully safeguarded the jury trial for those accused of crime (Note 110), it defeated a proposal for a jury trial in civil cases. Suits at common law do not include suits in chancery or equity, such as suits for injunction, for divorce, for enforcing a trust, for cancelling naturalization papers, for accounting, for specific enforcement of a contract, and for several other kinds of relief, in which the right to a jury does not exist. It is a rather common practice for parties to waive a jury in common law suits or actions and leave the questions of fact to the trial judge along with the questions of law. Under the Workmen's Compensation Acts which many States have passed an injured workman is not entitled to a jury to determine what he should receive. This Amendment does not limit State power. It is therefore within the police power of a State to establish a system of compensation to supersede lawsuits in courts by employees seeking from employers money damages for personal injuries suffered in the course of employment.

and no fact tried by a jury, shall be otherwise reexamined in any Court of the United States, than according to the rules of the common law.[158]

[158] That is, these rules are (1) the granting of a new trial by the trial court and a hearing before another jury, or (2) a

new jury trial ordered by an appellate court for some error of law committed by the trial court. In brief, no judge of a trial court can substitute his opinion of the facts for that of the jury, nor can an appellate court set aside the jury's findings and make a final order on its own.

ARTICLE VIII.

Excessive bail shall not be required,[159]

[159] Long imprisonments which had been made possible by excessive bail and the prevention of trials had so offended the English people that when William III and Mary ascended the throne they were required in the Declaration of Rights to assent to a provision substantially like this clause in our Constitution. As far back as the reign of Henry VI (1444) there was an act of Parliament requiring sheriffs and other officers to "let out of prison all manner of persons upon reasonable sureties of sufficient persons." A reasonable bail is one large enough to prevent evasion of law by flight and still not beyond the means of the prisoner. In 1835 bail of $1,000 was fixed by a court for a man who had shot at President Andrew Jackson, but missed him. The court thought the amount sufficient because the offense did not call for imprisonment, no battery had been done, and the defendant had no property. The court said that to require a greater bail than the prisoner could give in such a case would be excessive within the meaning of the Constitution.

nor excessive fines imposed,[160]

[160] The excessive fine under Magna Charta was the penalty or forfeiture which deprived a man of his "contenement" — of his living or ability to pursue his calling or his business. In Magna Charta it was declared that "a free man shall not be amerced for a small offense, but only to the degree of the offense; and for a great delinquency, ac-

cording to the magnitude of the delinquency, saving his contenement." Construing a similar provision in a State constitution, the Supreme Court held void an act of the legislature levying a penalty of not less than $100 nor more than $500 upon any druggist selling liquors contrary to law, and imprisonment of not less than ninety days nor more than one year, or both, with debarring from business for five years for a repeated offense. As the druggist would be cut off from his livelihood for five years, the punishment was excessive. The Supreme Court of the United States held void (1907) an act of the legislature of a State imposing such heavy and cumulative fines upon railway companies and their agents for failure to observe the freight rates and and passenger fares prescribed by the State that the persons convicted were by fear prevented from resorting to the courts to determine their rights or to test the validity of the law. The heavy fines imposed by the State (which could not be condemned as fines under this limitation upon National power) resulted in a denial of due process of law, which by the Fourteenth Amendment (Note 173) the State is forbidden to deny.

In 1909 the Supreme Court sustained a judgment for fines and penalties rendered under State law aggregating $1,623,500, and the cancellation of the defendant's permit to participate in commerce within the State. The company, incorporated in another State, was convicted of violating the anti-trust laws of the complaining State. Fines under one law were permitted as high as $5,000 a day for each day of violation. The Supreme Court said that the Eighth Amendment, forbidding excessive fines, is not a prohibition upon the State.

nor cruel and unusual punishments inflicted.[161]

[161] As late as Blackstone's time (1758) "the punishment of high treason in general is very solemn and terrible." He says that the guilty person was hanged by the neck and

then cut down alive, when he was disemboweled while yet
living. His head was cut off and his body divided into four
parts for disposition by the king. By an act of Parliament in 1814, a quarter of a century after our Constitution,
that punishment was mitigated.

Hallam gives many instances of cutting off of the ears,
of whipping, of standing in the pillory, of slitting the nose,
of branding the cheek. And many of those punishments
were followed by "perpetual imprisonment." But he says
that punishments on the Continent were even more severe.

The protection of this clause is needed now, perhaps not
so much as formerly, but it is needed. In February, 1910,
the Supreme Court of Oregon held void an act of the legislature for conflict with a provision of the State's constitution
similar to this of the Eighth Amendment. An officer of the
State who was unable to pay a fine of over $577,000, which
was imposed upon him for misapplying State funds, was
therefore sentenced under a State law to five years in the
penitentiary, and the fine was to be discharged by an additional imprisonment in jail at $2 for each day. The act
was upheld as to the sentence to the penitentiary, but it
was declared void as to the jail sentence for "not exceeding 288,426 days", a term of nearly 800 years. In 1891
the Supreme Court of the United States held that, as the
Eighth Amendment does not apply to States, it could give
no relief to a man who had been sentenced to the house of
correction in Vermont for 19,914 days or fifty-four years,
for shipping liquor from New York into the first-named
State. And as late as 1916 the flogging of a convict in North
Carolina was held by the Supreme Court of that State to
be illegal under the State Constitution, the Chief Justice
saying that the record contained "unprintable evidence
of brutality almost beyond conception."

The Bill of Rights of the Philippine Islands forbids the
infliction of cruel and unusual punishment, adopting this
provision from our Constitution. The Supreme Court of

the United States held (1910) that this safeguard of the citizen was violated where an officer of the government who had been convicted of making false entries in the public records was subjected to a heavy fine, sentenced to imprisonment for fifteen years, and condemned to carry a chain attached at the ankle and hanging from the wrist. Answering the contention that the cruel and unusual punishments referred to in this clause of our Constitution and in the Bill of Rights of the Philippines are those which were known in the time of the Stuart kings when the American Colonies were being planted, the Supreme Court said that the language, while used in the light of "an experience of evils", is nevertheless general and is intended to apply to new conditions. "Therefore," said the Court, "a principle to be vital must be capable of wider application than the mischief which gave it birth. This is peculiarly true of constitutions."

The Supreme Court has steadily refused to apply this Amendment as a prohibition upon State action; and it, therefore, held that punishment by electrocution is within the State power and cannot be considered cruel or unusual under this clause.

ARTICLE IX.

The enumeration in the Constitution, of certain rights, shall not be construed to deny or disparage others retained by the people.[162]

[162] This is a statement of the rule of construction that an affirmation in particular cases implies a negation in all others. The Amendment indicates that the National Government is one of delegated and enumerated powers and that the powers named (with the necessarily implied powers) are all that the United States possesses or may presume to exercise. A step beyond the enumeration is unconstitutional and void.

ARTICLE X.

The powers not delegated to the United States **by** **the Constitution, nor prohibited by it to the States,** **are reserved to the States respectively, or to the peo-** **ple.**[163]

[163] "The reservation to the States respectively," says the Supreme Court, "can only mean the reservation of the rights of sovereignty which they respectively possessed before the adoption of the Constitution of the United States and which they had not parted from by that instrument. And any legislation by Congress beyond the limits of the power delegated would be trespassing upon the rights of the States or the people and would not be the supreme law of the land, but null and void."

Thus if North Carolina and Rhode Island, which did not ratify the Constitution until after the new government had become operative, had chosen not to enter the Union, they would have had the powers inhering in independent governments, such as the power to declare war, to coin money, to raise armies, to make treaties, to regulate commerce, to impose duties on imports and exports, and so on, — all of which were, under the Constitution, for the general welfare, yielded up to the National Government.

This Amendment and the preceding one "disclosed widespread fear that the National Government might, under the pressure of the supposed general welfare, attempt to exercise powers which had not been granted."

"I ask for no straining of words against the General Government," wrote Jefferson in 1823, "nor yet against the States. I believe the States can best govern over home concerns and the General Government over foreign ones. I wish, therefore, to see maintained that wholesome distribution of powers established by the Constitution for the limitation of both, and never to see all offices transferred to Washington."

In the "Federalist" (No. XVIII) Madison had expressed the view of the other party. He reviewed fully the Amphictyonic Council of ancient Greece to show that "it emphatically illustrates the tendency of federal bodies rather to anarchy among the members than to tyranny in the head."

In 1911, discussing also the unsurrendered powers of the States, the Supreme Court used this language:

"Among the powers of the State not surrendered — which power therefore remains with the State — is the power to so regulate the relative rights and duties of all within its jurisdiction as to guard the public morals, the public safety, and the public health, as well as to promote the public convenience and the common good."

In Canada, on the contrary, the State (province) has no powers except those which are specified as belonging to it, all other powers being in the Dominion (or National) Government. But thirty-three years later (1900) the Australians followed our plan rather than that of Canada and declared in their constitution that powers not given to the Commonwealth (or Nation) remain in the States.

The Migratory Bird Act of July 3, 1918, passed by Congress in pursuance of a treaty (1916) with Great Britain for the protection of birds in their annual migrations between Canada and this country, did not violate, the Supreme Court held (1920), the reservation in the Tenth Amendment of power to the States. The claim was made that the State had property in the wild birds, but the Court answered that "the subject-matter is only transitorily within the State." An act of 1913 had been held by some of the Federal courts invalid, and it was contended that "such an act cannot be made valid by a treaty." The Supreme Court of course held the treaty to be the supreme law of the land (See Note 133).

This is the last of the Ten Amendments, written in restraint of National power against the people and the States, in addition to like curbs in the body of the Constitution.

ARTICLE XI.

Proposed by Congress September 5, 1794; proclaimed adopted January 8, 1798.

The Judicial power of the United States shall not be construed to extend to any suit in law or equity, commenced or prosecuted against one of the United States by Citizens of another State, or by Citizens or Subjects of any Foreign State.[164]

[164] This Amendment was proclaimed as adopted on January 8, 1798, following suit by a claimant in South Carolina against the State of Georgia, decided in 1793. Many of the States were under heavy financial embarrassment when the Union was formed and the case of Chisholm against Georgia excited much alarm. Although a resolution proposing an Amendment was offered in Congress two days after the decision was announced, the Eleventh Amendment did not become a part of the Constitution for almost five years. The Australian constitution expressly grants jurisdiction to the High Court where a citizen desires to sue a State.

ARTICLE XII.[165]

Proposed by Congress December 12, 1803; proclaimed adopted September 25, 1804.

[165] See Notes 76, 77, 78, and 79. The chief difference between this Amendment and the language which it superseded is that the elector votes for a named individual for President and another for Vice President. Under the old provision the elector voted "for two persons", without designating either for either office. "The person having the greatest number of votes" became President and the one receiving next to the highest number became Vice President, notwithstanding that, as in the case of Jefferson, he might be an intense disbeliever in the President's

(Adams's) political opinions. When, at the next election, Jefferson and Burr received the same number of electoral votes and the election therefore was thrown into the House of Representatives, where thirty-five ballots were taken before the choice of first place fell to Jefferson, the second place thereby going to Burr, the people became convinced that a change in the electoral machinery was necessary. Now, under this Amendment, the electors "name in their ballots the *person* voted for as President, and in distinct ballots the person voted for as Vice President." When the election of a President is now thrown into the House of Representatives, that body makes choice "from the persons having the highest numbers, not exceeding *three* on the list of those voted for"; before the choice was made "from the *five* highest on the list."

The Electors shall meet in their respective states and vote by ballot for President and Vice-President, one of whom, at least, shall not be an inhabitant of the same state with themselves; they shall name in their ballots the person voted for as President, and in distinct ballots the person voted for as Vice-President, and they shall make distinct lists of all persons voted for as President, and of all persons voted for as Vice-President, and of the number of votes for each, which lists they shall sign and certify, and transmit sealed to the seat of the government of the United States, directed to the President of the Senate; [166]

[166] Since the passage of the Twentieth Amendment (Note 188) it is required that the electors meet on the first Monday after the second Wednesday in December following elections to cast their votes.

— the President of the Senate shall, in the presence of the Senate and House of Representatives, open all the certificates and the votes shall then be counted; [167]

[167] A controversy which threatened the peace of the country arose in 1876 respecting the electoral vote for Rutherford B. Hayes. the Republican candidate for the presidency, and that cast for Samuel J. Tilden, the nominee of the Democratic party. In Louisiana two electoral returns were made under rivals claiming to be governor. The legality of the returns made in some other States to the president of the Senate also was questioned. The claim was made that the president of the Senate (who was then a Republican) should, under this clause, do the counting. On many points the disagreement between the partisans was so wide and apparently so hopeless that it was finally determined to leave all questions to an Electoral Commission to be created by act of Congress and to consist of five members of the Senate. five members of the House. and five justices of the Supreme Court. That Commission, after an extended hearing of evidence and argument, found, by a strictly partisan vote, that 185 electoral votes belonged to Hayes and 184 to Tilden. To prevent the recurrence of some of the questions, Congress passed the Electoral Count Act of February 3, 1887, providing (1) that if there has been in a State a final determination of any electoral controversy, the Governor shall certify the decision to the Secretary of State, who shall transmit the information to the first meeting of Congress; (2) that if more than one return of vote should be made by a State to the president of the Senate, that one shall be counted which was delivered by the regular electors; (3) that when the question is which of two election boards in a State is regular, that one will be recognized which the Senate and the House decide to be the one authorized by law, (4) but if the Houses disagree, then the electors certified by the Governor of the State shall be accepted; (5) that Congress shall sit in joint session in the House of Representatives at one o'clock in the afternoon of the second Wednesday in February following the meeting of electors; (6) that there shall be two tellers for the Senate and two for

the House, who shall receive from the president of the Senate the election returns from each State as he opens them in alphabetical order and who shall read the returns in the hearing of the joint session and make lists of the results and give them to the president of the Senate for announcement; (7) and that the president of the Senate shall call for objections in writing of any State for consideration by each House.

Since the passage of the Twentieth Amendment (Note 188) Congress meets on January 6 after the presidential election, to receive the votes of the electoral college.

—The person having the greatest number of votes for President shall be the President, if such number be a majority of the whole number of Electors appointed; and if no person have such majority, then from the persons having the highest numbers not exceeding three on the list of those voted for as President, the House of Representatives shall choose immediately, by ballot, the President. But in choosing the President the votes shall be taken by states, the representation from each state having one vote; a quorum for this purpose shall consist of a member or members from two-thirds of the states, and a majority of all the states shall be necessary to a choice. And if the House of Representatives shall not choose a President whenever the right of choice shall devolve upon them, before the fourth day of March next following, then the Vice-President shall act as President, as in the case of the death or other constitutional disability of the President. The person having the greatest number of votes as Vice-President, shall be the Vice-President, if such number be a majority of the whole number of Electors appointed, and if no per-

son have a majority, then from the two highest numbers on the list, the Senate shall choose the Vice-President; a quorum for the purpose shall consist of two-thirds of the whole number of Senators, and a majority of the whole number shall be necessary to a choice. But no person constitutionally ineligible to the office of President shall be eligible to that of Vice-President of the United States.

ARTICLE XIII. [168]

Proposed by Congress February 1, 1865, proclaimed adopted December 18, 1865.

[168] It has been pointed out that the first ten Amendments sprang from the fear of National power which many of the States possessed. Those Amendments were designed to stay the National hand. But the Civil War taught that the Nation may be in even greater peril from the States than they ever were from the Nation. And so, after more than seventy years, the people, by this Amendment and the two Amendments following, laid upon the States restrictions which a few years before would have been impossible. The country had gone sixty-one years (1804–1865) without an Amendment.

Section 1. Neither slavery nor involuntary servitude, except as a punishment for crime whereof the party shall have been duly convicted, shall exist within the United States, or any place subject to their jurisdiction.[169]

[169] The language of this Amendment is older than the Constitution itself. On July 13, 1787, the Congress under the Articles of Confederation passed the ordinance creating the Northwest Territory (Ohio, Illinois, Indiana, Michigan, and Wisconsin), which provided: "There shall ox neither

slavery nor involuntary servitude in the said territory otherwise than in punishment of crimes, whereof the party shall have been duly convicted." But a proviso required the return from the territory of fugitive slaves.

When, on January 13, 1865, a two-thirds vote was taken in the House of Representatives for proposing the Thirteenth Amendment "in honor of the immortal and sublime event" the House adjourned.

Congress had previously abolished slavery in the District of Columbia and in the Territories, had repealed the Fugitive Slave Law, and had given freedom to the Negroes who had served in the Union armies.

The Emancipation Proclamation freed the slaves only in the seceded States, excepting some parishes (counties) in Louisiana, a few counties in Virginia, and the whole of Tennessee. Besides, the validity of the proclamation under the war power of the President was questioned. To remove the legal doubt and to liberate slaves everywhere the Amendment was adopted.

Of the Thirteenth Amendment a Federal court said:

"It trenches directly upon the power of the States and of the people of the States. It is the first and only instance of a change of this character in the organic law. It destroyed the most important relation between capital and labor in all the States where slavery existed. It affected deeply the fortunes of a large portion of their people. It struck out of existence millions of property. The measure was the consequence of a strife of opinions, and a conflict of interests, real or imaginary, as old as the Constitution itself. These elements of discord grew in intensity. Their violence was increased by the throes and convulsions of a civil war. The impetuous vortex finally swallowed up the evil, and with it forever the power to restore it."

A law of a State under which one fined for a misdemeanor confessed judgment and agreed to work out the fine for the surety who paid it for him was held by the Supreme Court

(1914) to be unconstitutional as creating "involuntary servitude" in violation of this Amendment.

A person who hired another under a contract by which the hirer had the right to imprison the worker or keep him under guard until the contract should be performed was held (1903) by a Federal court to violate the Peonage Act of Congress (1867) passed under this Amendment. And so it was held (1907) of a State law making it a misdemeanor punishable by imprisonment for one to agree to perform service and then, after receiving a part of the consideration in advance, refuse to perform.

Thus it is seen from very late cases that this provision is still vital and active.

But in many cases it has been held that city ordinances requiring persons committed to the city prison to work out their fines in the streets or elsewhere do not violate this Amendment.

Section 2. Congress shall have power to enforce this article by appropriate legislation.[170]

[170] Congress passed under this constitutional authority the Civil Rights Act of March 1, 1875, another act prohibiting peonage, and some other statutes. The first and second sections of the Civil Rights Act of Congress were held (1888) by the Supreme Court in contravention of this Amendment, which is a regulation of the *States* with regard to slavery, and which does not authorize Congress to regulate the conduct of *individuals* who prevent Negroes from having the full and equal enjoyment of hotels, theatres, and other public places. Legislation of this kind comes within the police power of the State. In many of the States there has been legislation requiring the providing of separate but equal accommodations for white persons and Negroes. Such regulations have been held valid as essential to public order.

The Supreme Court has said that while the object of this Amendment was undoubtedly to enforce the absolute equality of the two races before the law, "in the nature of things it could not have been intended to abolish distinctions based upon color, or to enforce social, as distinguished from political equality, or a commingling of the two races upon terms unsatisfactory to either." The Court said that laws permitting and even requiring separation did not imply the inferiority of either race to the other, and such laws had been generally, if not universally, recognized as within the competency of State legislatures in the exercise of their police powers.

ARTICLE XIV.

Proposed by Congress June 16, 1866; proclaimed adopted July 21, 1868.

Section 1. All persons born or naturalized in the United States, and subject to the jurisdiction thereof, are citizens of the United States and of the State wherein they reside.[171]

[171] The Thirteenth Amendment was found to be not enough. Reviewing the history of the times, the Supreme Court pointed out that in some States the former slaves were "forbidden to appear in the towns in any other character than menial servants" that they were required to reside upon and cultivate the land "without the right to purchase or own it"; that they were excluded from many occupations of gain and were "not permitted to give testimony in the courts in any case where a white man was a party"; that laws were passed imposing heavy fines on vagrants and loiterers, who, if unable to pay the fines, were sold to the highest bidder. "These circumstances, said the Supreme Court, "whatever of falsehood or misconcep-

tion may have been mingled with their presentation, forced upon the statesmen who had conducted the Federal Government in safety through the crisis of the rebellion and who supposed that by the Thirteenth Article of Amendment they had secured the result of their labors, the conviction that something more was necessary in the way of constitutional protection to the unfortunate race who had suffered so much."

Hence the Fourteenth Amendment.

This Amendment made the Negro not only a citizen of the United States but also of the State of his residence. It struck the word "white" from the constitutions of northern States which had limited citizenship to white males. In North and South the Negro became possessed in law of all the rights of citizenship.

The citizen was not, under the theory of States' rights, in contact with the National Government. He owed allegiance to his State, and the State dealt with the Nation. That theory was definitely set aside by this Amendment, which made all persons born or naturalized in the United States and subject to the jurisdiction thereof citizens of both the Nation and the State, owing allegiance to both authorities. James Wilson of Pennsylvania stated (Note 19) this doctrine clearly in the Constitutional Convention.

The contention was made in the first great case to arise under this Amendment, which did not involve the Negro at all, the controversy being between rival business houses, that the Amendment *originated* a new citizenship for all, which supplanted former State citizenship and changed the rights attending it. That would mean that the National Government would now be the source of all those rights of a fundamental character which belong to the citizens of all free governments by virtue of their manhood, and for the protection (not creation) of which all just governments are formed. The Supreme Court rejected (1873) the contention and said that the Amendment did not disclose "any purpose to destroy the main features of the general system." It held that the command that "no State shall . . . abridge the privileges or immunities of citizens of the United States" does not prevent a State from abridging privileges of State citizenship as distinguished from privileges of National citizenship. This momentous decision, involving the preservation of State citizenship and State rights, was, like that upholding the power of the President in the Civil War to blockade ports and take any steps necessary to preserve the life of the Nation, rendered by a majority of one vote.

In the Dred Scott case (1856), brought by a negro servant of a surgeon in the United States army, who had been taken into Illinois and other free territory and who claimed for that reason the right to liberty, as the negro slave Somerset had by the decision of Lord Mansfield been liberated when he was taken from Virginia to England, the Supreme Court held that the Negro was "not intended to be included under the word 'citizen' in the Constitution". for which reason he had no standing in court. By this Amendment he became a citizen of the Nation and a citizen of his State, and possessed of the benefits of all State and National constitutions and laws. The fugitive slave provision (Note 121) was inserted in the Constitution to prevent the application in this country of the rule announced in the Somerset case.

"While the Fourteenth Amendment was intended primarily for the benefit of the negro race," said a Federal court, "it also confers the right of citizenship upon persons of all other races, . . . born or naturalized in the United States." But a person born in the United States and not "subject to the jurisdiction thereof" does not become a citizen, such as the child of a foreign minister or consul.

The refusal of Congress to permit the naturalization of Chinese was held by the Supreme Court (1898) not to ex-

clude from the benefit of this Amendment a Chinese "born
. . . in the United States and subject to the jurisdiction
thereof." While the parents were subjects of the Emperor
of China, they were permanently domiciled in the United
States and carrying on business. The definition of " citizen" in this Amendment is only an affirmation of the ancient rule of citizenship by birth within the territory of
allegiance. The alien owes allegiance to the country of
his residence — he is "subject to the jurisdiction thereof"
— and therefore his children become citizens by birth.

An act of 1907 expatriating an American woman marrying a foreigner, even though remaining in the United States,
sustained by the Supreme Court as constitutional, was
amended in 1922 so that expatriation results only from
her residing two years continuously in her husband's country or five years outside of the United States.

After the Fourteenth Amendment was adopted a woman
in Missouri, where the right to vote was limited to males,
sued the registrar because he refused (1872) to put her name
on the list of voters. She contended that as she was a "citizen of the United States" under the Amendment, the State
could not "abridge" her right as such citizen to vote for
the presidential electors. The Supreme Court, denying
her claim (1874), said that as she was a citizen born of citizen parents before the Amendment, her status with respect
to voting was not changed by it, because the right to vote
before the Amendment was not necessarily one of the privileges or immunities of citizenship. That was demonstrated by the necessity for the Fifteenth Amendment, which
protected the Negro from being excluded from voting because of color. That Amendment did not affect the Negro's
wife, who remained debarred on account of sex. But she
became entitled to vote when the Nineteenth Amendment
removed that bar.

No State shall make or enforce any law which shall

abridge the privileges or immunities of citizens of the United States; [172]

[172] This was held by the Supreme Court to mean, as the language imports, the privileges and immunities of National citizenship and not to include those belonging to the citizen of the State. It is a prohibition, not respecting action by an individual or by a group of individuals, but only action by the legislative, the executive, or the judicial department of a State government. The Supreme Court held (1897) that the State acted, and not the individual, where the law empowered the county judge to select jurors and he rejected Negroes. But not so where in another State white jurors only were selected, there being no State law on the subject; that action was by individuals. This command is not violated by State laws fairly regulating the qualifications of jurors.

The fundamental rights protected by the first ten Amendments against *National* invasion were not, the Supreme Court has said (1900), by this clause converted into or superseded by rights or immunities which the *State* cannot touch. State action is no further restrained than it was before, except in the particulars clearly within the purpose of this Amendment. Accordingly a State law limiting the length of a day's work in mines and smelters was held (1896) by the Supreme Court to deny no National immunity or privilege of the employer under this clause. The subject involved in that case was one affecting the citizen of the State and not the citizen of the United States. The relation between employer and employe is one to be supervised by the police power of the State, except that the Nation, under the commerce clause, has dealt with the safety, the hours, and the wages of employes of railways in interstate commerce.

The laws enacted by the States for the benefit of the working classes have been generally held by the Supreme

Courts of the States not to deny to the employer any constitutional privilege, and the Supreme Court of the United States has sustained such decisions when cases have been carried to it. The Supreme Court held (1917) that no privilege or immunity of National citizenship was abridged by a State law limiting the length of the day of workers, or by another for paying wages in cash. While the right to labor and the privilege of organizing are fundamental, under State citizenship, they are secured by State law and not by this Amendment. The Supreme Court upheld (1915) the law of a State, which was challenged as abridging the privilege of citizens of the United States under this clause, requiring that only citizens of the United States be employed on public works and that citizens of the State be preferred. But while the State as an employer may thus select its employes, it cannot control other employers; and a State constitutional provision requiring that eighty per cent of the employes in mines and smelters be natives of the United States was held by the Supreme Court (1915) to "abridge the privileges" of naturalized citizens of the United States in violation of this clause.

The privilege of a child to attend the public schools is one springing from the State and not the Nation, and therefore the child cannot assert a constitutional right to admission under this clause. Nor is it the denial of a privilege of National citizenship, the Supreme Court held (1915), for a State to enact that a student entering its university must renounce his allegiance to any Greek-letter or like fraternity. And so the right to bear arms guaranteed by the Second Amendment against National interference, is not (1886) one of the "privileges or immunities" belonging to citizens of the United States, as distinguished from citizens of a State. Should the State restrict the bearing of arms, it would not interfere with a National privilege.

State laws forbidding litigants to remove cases to the Federal courts have been uniformly held to abridge the privileges and immunities of citizens of the United States. In 1914 the Supreme Court said that a State cannot penalize the assertion by a citizen of a Federal or National right.

While a corporation is a "person" within this Amendment, it is not a "citizen" of the United States whose "privileges or immunities" a State is forbidden to abridge. A State may therefore impose upon a corporation created by another State restrictive conditions respecting its doing business (but not interstate commerce) within the first-named State.

Many forms of regulation by States have been held by State supreme courts and by the Supreme Court of the United States not to be abridgments under this clause of the rights or privileges of the citizens of the United States, such as the regulation of professions and occupations, of the manufacture of foods, of jury trials and criminal prosecutions, and so on.

nor shall any State deprive any person of life, liberty, or property, without due process of law; [173]

[173] In the Fifth Amendment the Nation is forbidden (Note 151) to deprive any one "of life, liberty or property without due process of law"; and here the like command is issued by the people to the State. In the beginning it was National power that was feared. Experience later taught that the power of the State also may be tyrannical. Due process of law means, said the Supreme Court in a late case (1908), that 'no change in ancient procedure can be made which disregards those fundamental principles . . . which . . . protect the citizen in his private right and guard him against the arbitrary action of the government."

Private property is taken for public use in opening streets in cities, in constructing railways and canals, in erecting public buildings, in laying out public parks, and for kindred purposes. The owner cannot be deprived of his property for such purposes by the State without due process of law, that is, without a full hearing and adequate compensation.

In 1884 it was held by the Supreme Court of the United States that a law of California under which a person accused of crime was brought to trial, convicted, and sentenced to death under an "information" or written charge by the prosecuting attorney instead of under an indictment by a grand jury (Note 148) did not violate the due-process clause. The grand jury guaranteed by the Fifth Amendment is granted against National power and not against the State.

And it was later held (1900) by the Supreme Court that due process of law was not denied to the accused by a statute of Utah under which he was convicted by eight of the twelve jurors, as the "impartial jury" (twelve men agreeing unanimously) guaranteed by the Sixth Amendment (Note 153) must be provided only in Federal courts.

The "liberty" which this clause safeguards is not merely the freedom of the person from unjust or unlawful imprisonment. It embraces also the free use of his faculties in all lawful ways.

The liberty of the citizen to make contracts is not denied by a State law limiting the hours of the day of labor and fixing a fine for each violation, the Supreme Court held (1908), because liberty is not absolute when the welfare of society is involved. And so the Supreme Court upheld (1914) as constitutional under this clause the law of a State forbidding under penalty that women be employed longer than a designated day.

In 1930 the Supreme Court upheld a law (1913) of the State of Washington establishing wages and working conditions for women and children, overruling in principle a decision (p. 216) in 1923, and others following it, that a law requiring minimum wages to women and children regardless of their earning capability took private property for public welfare in violation of this Clause.

The Supreme Court held (1905) that personal liberty under this clause was not infringed by a law for compulsory vaccination when smallpox was prevalent and increasing.

This clause was held (1911) contravened by a State law forbidding the employing of any foreign-born person who was not naturalized or who had not declared his intention to become a citizen, as the alien has the like right to liberty and property and the "equal protection of the laws" that a native enjoys.

State laws prohibiting the employing of children under specified ages and in employments named have been upheld as denying no right to the employer, the parent, or the child. This clause was not violated by a State law imposing upon manufacturers, under heavy penalty, the absolute duty of making expenditures for safeguarding their machinery to prevent injury to employes. Laws prohibiting the payment of wages in scrip or orders on stores, laws requiring semi-monthly payment of wages in some employments, laws prohibiting the assignment of wages not yet earned without the written consent of the wife of the employe, and many other kinds of laws for the help of the working classes have been upheld by the Supreme Courts of the States and the Supreme Court of the United States.

The Supreme Court of Colorado held (1921) an amendment to the Constitution of that State (1913) a denial of due process of law because it prohibited the courts of the State (except the Supreme Court) from passing upon certain State and Federal constitutional questions and left it for the people to determine at the polls whether a decision of the Supreme Court should become effective at all. As the National Constitution is the supreme law of the land (Note 133), and as "the judges in every State shall be bound thereby, anything in the Constitution or laws of any State to the contrary notwithstanding" (Note 134), the duty thus placed upon the judges of State courts to uphold the Constitution of the United States could not be stripped of them by any act of either the legislature or the people.

nor deny to any person within its jurisdiction the equal protection of the laws.[174]

[174] By Section 2 of Article IV (Note 119) "the citizens of each State shall be entitled to all the privileges and immunities of citizens in the several States." That is, a citizen of one State doing business in another State cannot be denied the privileges and immunities of the citizens of that State. But the clause in this Amendment was designed to prevent a State from making discriminations between its own citizens. While it was written primarily for the liberated Negro (who is not mentioned in the Amendment), the language is without limitation, extending to "any person", and it has been applied in upwards of a thousand cases in State and National courts to every conceivable form of inequality arising or alleged to arise out of the laws of States.

An Act of Congress fixing punishment for three or more *persons* conspiring to deprive another of the equal protection of the laws was held invalid by the Supreme Court (1883) because the Fourteenth Amendment is a limitation upon the State and not upon persons. The word "persons" includes a resident alien or a corporation.

But this language does not prevent reasonable classification as long as all within a class are treated alike. The design of this clause was "to prevent any person or class of persons from being singled out as a special subject for discriminating and hostile legislation." This does not prevent, for example, the imposition of different species of taxes. Thus while houses and lands are taxed upon their actual value, railroad companies may be required to pay taxes upon their gross income, and neither owner has a ground of complaint that he has been denied the equal protection of the laws. So taxes on inheritances, which the Supreme Court held to be by permission of law, contrary to the decisions of supreme courts of several States, may be graduated according to the size of the estate one receives upon the death of another, and the one inheriting a large estate cannot complain that the scale of rates applied in his case is higher than that used for a smaller inheritance. The provision of a State homestead law excluding Negroes from the benefits of the act denied equal protection and was therefore held (1885) unconstitutional. Because a State law requiring voters to read excludes a greater number of Negroes than others, it does not therefore deny equal protection. The Supreme Court upheld (1896) a State law requiring railway companies to provide separate accommodations for white and colored passengers; with equal accommodations equal protection was preserved. And so where schools for Chinese offered the advantages of other schools it was held (1902) that equal protection was not denied. A law putting in effect the Australian system of balloting was held (1874) not to deny equal protection to the blind or to others physically or educationally unable to vote. A city ordinance requiring that the hair of prisoners be clipped was held (1879) invalid as directed against Chinese and imposing a degrading and cruel punishment. A privilege tax of $25 on business men resident in the State and a tax of $100 on non-residents was held (1919) to deny equal protection.

The Supreme Court held (1920) it within the police power of a State to enact that natural gas coming from wells within ten miles of an incorporated town or an industrial plant should not be burned for its products (such as carbon black) unless the remainder of the heat contained in the gas should be fully and actually applied for other manufacturing purposes or for domestic uses. A company which was burning gas in making carbon black for printer's ink claimed that the legislation discriminated respecting owners of wells and producers of carbon black within ten miles of a town and those beyond that radius, and that it was therefore a denial of that "equal protection" which a State is forbidden to withhold.   The court said that the classification of users, appearing to have been made for the conservation of natural resources and not arbitrarily, was valid.

A city ordinance prohibiting Negroes from residing in blocks in which the majority of the houses were occupied by white persons, and in like manner prohibiting white persons from residing in blocks largely occupied by Negroes, was by the Supreme Court held (1917) unconstitutional, where a Negro purchased property and could not occupy it under the ordinance.

But the Supreme Court of California held (1920) that a condition subsequent in a deed to land, that the premises would revert to the grantor or seller if occupation of them should ever be permitted to any but a Caucasian, did not conflict with the Fourteenth Amendment, as that prohibits action, not by an individual, but by a State.

Equal protection was held (1892) denied by a State law forbidding mining companies to keep general stores for the patronage of the employes, because no such limitation was placed upon other employers.

The foregoing examples are sufficient to show the meaning of the equality-of-treatment clause and to illustrate that the Constitution remains a much-used and very serviceable instrument.

Section 2. Representatives shall be apportioned among the several States according to their respective numbers, counting the whole number of persons in each State, excluding Indians not taxed.[175]

[175] Up to this time members of the House of Representatives were allowed to each State in proportion to the white population and three fifths of the slaves (Note 11), but this provision made each Negro count one.

But when the right to vote at any election for the choice of Electors for President and Vice-President

of the United States, Representatives in Congress, the Executive and Judicial officers of a State, or the members of the Legislature thereof, is denied to any of the male inhabitants of such State, being twenty-one years of age, and citizens of the United States, or in any way abridged, except for participation in rebellion, or other crime, the basis of representation therein shall be reduced in the proportion which the number of such male citizens shall bear to the whole number of male citizens twenty-one years of age in such State.[176]

[176] This enables the Nation to inflict punishment upon the State for preventing citizens from voting — from voting for National officers not only, but also some officers of the State, as the executive who calls elections to fill vacancies in Congress, the judges who may pass upon questions of election, and the members of the legislature who in 1866 (but not since the Seventeenth Amendment, 1913) elected the Senators of the United States. A State law or constitution requiring of voters ability to read and write does not contravene this provision. Congress never has exerted its power under this Amendment to reduce the number of a State's representatives in the National House.

Section 3. No person shall be a Senator or Representative in Congress, or elector of President and Vice-President, or hold any office, civil or military, under the United States, or under any State, who, having previously taken an oath, as a member of Congress, or as an officer of the United States, or as a member of any State legislature, or as an executive or judicial officer of any State, to support the Constitution of the United States, shall have engaged in insurrection or rebellion against the same, or given aid or comfort to the enemies thereof. But Congress may by a vote of two-thirds of each House, remove such disability. [177]

[177] It was claimed by Jefferson Davis, who had been President of the Confederate States of America (1861–1865), and who had in 1845 been a member of the National Congress, that the punishment specified in this Section, which prevented him from ever holding any office, National or State, superseded in his case the punishment for treason which Congress had fixed (Note 115) and that therefore the indictment charging him with treason must be quashed. The point was argued, but before it was decided by the court a proclamation of general amnesty was issued by the President, and later the indictment was dismissed. On Christmas day, 1868, President Johnson issued a general proclamation of amnesty, granting "unconditionally and without reservation" to all who had been engaged in the Southern cause, "a full pardon."

Not until June 6, 1898, did Congress remove the last vestige of this disability. On March 31, 1896, Congress repealed an earlier act forbidding that any one who had left the army or navy of the United States to aid the Confederacy should ever hold place in the army or navy again. But the Act of Oblivion came two years later, when the disability imposed by the Fourteenth Amendment was removed as to all. War with Spain had begun in April of that year.

Among the most eager volunteers were "elderly Southerners" who had served as soldiers or officers in the Confederate army. General Joseph Wheeler, a noted cavalry leader of the South, and a son of Robert E. Lee were among those to receive military commissions from President McKinley, the Commander in Chief, who had served in the Union army in the Civil War.

Section 4. The validity of the public debt of the United States, authorized by law, including debts in-

curred for payment of pensions and bounties for services in suppressing insurrection or rebellion, shall not
be questioned. But neither the United States nor
any State shall assume or pay any debt or obligation
incurred in aid of insurrection or rebellion against the
United States, or any claim for the loss or emancipation of any slave; but all such debts, obligations and
claims shall be held illegal and void.[178]

[178] The debt incurred for the Union during the Civil War,
including bounties and pensions, was by the adoption of
this Amendment acknowledged and proportionately assumed by the southern States; and at the same time they
were rendered incapable of paying any part of the debt (over
$1,400,000,000) which they owed to their own citizens and
to England, France, and other countries. The southern
States lost also the value of the emancipated slaves.

This section deals only with what the Nation and the
State shall do. An individual was held bound by the Supreme Court to pay after emancipation the price which he
had agreed before the Civil War to give for a slave, when
such a contract was legal, for it was out of the power of a
State to impair (Note 71), as it undertook to do, the obligation of such a contract.

Section 5. The Congress shall have power to enforce, by appropriate legislation, the provisions of this
article.[179]

[179] Appropriate legislation by Congress means such as is
"adapted to the mischief and wrong which the Amendment
was intended to provide against" — that is, to prevent
oppressive action, not by individuals, but by State governments. Therefore the Civil Rights Act of March 1, 1875,
which declared that all persons (meaning the emancipated
Negroes) should be "entitled to the full and equal enjoyment
of the accommodations, advantages, facilities and privi-

leges of inns, public conveyances on land or water, theatres, and other places of public amusement", was held (1883) by the Supreme Court to be unconstitutional as to the sections which provided punishment for *persons* who should interfere with the rights mentioned, for the prohibition of the Amendment is directed only against action by States. "Until some State law has been passed," said the Supreme Court, "or some State action through its officers or agents has been taken adverse to the rights of the citizens sought to be protected by the Fourteenth Amendment, no legislation of the United States under said Amendment, nor any proceeding under such legislation, can be called into activity."

ARTICLE XV.

Proposed by Congress February 27, 1869; proclaimed adopted March 30, 1870.

Section 1. The right of citizens of the United States to vote shall not be denied or abridged by the United States or by any State on account of race, color, or previous condition of servitude.[180]

[180] This is the last of the three Amendments arising from the Civil War. By these "the chains of the Constitution", as Jefferson called its limitations, were placed upon the States, as by the first ten Amendments they had been put upon the Nation.

"The Fifteenth Amendment," said the Supreme Court (1875), "does not confer the right of suffrage upon any one. It prevents the States, or the United States, however, from giving preference in this particular to one citizen of the United States over another on account of race, color, or previous condition of servitude. Before its adoption this could be done. It was as much within the power of a State to exclude citizens of the United States from voting on account of race, etc., as it was on account of age, property, or education. Now it is not."

A State which voted against the adoption of this Amendment left the word "white" in its constitution as descriptive of those entitled to vote. The Supreme Court said (1880) that the Amendment struck the word from the constitution of the State.

The "Grandfather's Clause" cases, as they were called, were decided by the Supreme Court in 1915. In 1908 a law was passed in Maryland giving the right to vote to all persons who, prior to January 1, 1868, were entitled to vote in that State "and to the lawful male descendants of any person" who was at that time entitled to vote. As the Negro was not at that time entitled to vote in the State, and as the Fifteenth Amendment forbidding restrictions upon him had not been adopted, the State law operated to exclude all his descendants from the polls. In 1910 a constitutional amendment in Oklahoma presented a literacy test (which may be legal if fair) and at the same time limited the right to vote to a person who was a voter on January 1, 1866, or a lineal descendant of such a person. In both of these instances the "previous condition of servitude" actually determined that a class could not vote. The Supreme Court held that the State law and the State constitutional provision were both violative of the Fifteenth Amendment, because they were based on standards which became illegal by the self-operating force of the Amendment.

Section 2. The Congress shall have power to enforce this article by appropriate legislation.

ARTICLE XVI.

Proposed by Congress July 31, 1909; proclaimed adopted February 25, 1913.

The Congress shall have power to lay and collect taxes on incomes,[181]

[181] The purpose of the Amendment, said the Supreme Court (1916), was, not to extend the taxing power of the government, but only to exclude the source from which a taxed income is derived from being used as the criterion in determining whether it should be apportioned by Congress among the States on the basis of population in obedience to the clause explained by Note 10.

from whatever source derived,[182] without apportionment among the several States, and without regard to any census or enumeration.

[182] But this does not authorize the taxing of the salaries of the justices of the Supreme Court of the United States and of the judges of the inferior Federal courts, for it is forbidden (Note 98) that they be diminished. Therefore the Supreme Court held (1920) unconstitutional that clause of the Income Tax Act of 1919 which named such salaries as subject to taxation. The command that the salaries of judges be not reduced was given, not in any sense to favor the individuals who receive the salaries, but solely to protect the judicial officers of the Nation from being intimidated by the Legislative and Executive departments out of a state of independence into a condition of fear. But in 1939, the majority of the Supreme Court having been changed by new appointments, it was held that, following the act of 1932 taxing the salaries of judges "taking office after" the enactment, the imposition of an income tax on salaries would not operate to diminish them contrary to the prohibition (Note 98) in Article III.

ARTICLE XVII.

Proposed by Congress May 15, 1912; proclaimed adopted May 31, 1913.

The Senate of the United States shall be composed of two Senators from each State, elected by the peo-

ple thereof, for six years; [183] and each Senator shall have one vote.

[183] This Amendment changes the clause explained by Note 19. Senators are now elected by the people (as members of the House of Representatives always have been) instead of by the legislatures of the States. More than thirty States had declared for the direct election of senators. During the preceding twenty years so many protracted election contests had been conducted in State legislatures that legislation for the benefit of the States could not be carried on. In some instances no senator was elected and thus the State was deprived of its full vote in the Senate. The first resolution to amend the Constitution in this respect was introduced in Congress in 1826. Many others were introduced from time to time.

In 1869 President Johnson suggested to Congress an amendment for the direct election of senators.

Before this Amendment public opinion often affected or controlled the choice of a senator. Thus the famous debates throughout Illinois between Lincoln and Douglas (1858) were in quest of a senatorship.

The electors in each State shall have the qualifications requisite for electors of the most numerous branch of the State legislatures.

When vacancies happen in the representation of any State in the Senate, the executive authority of such State shall issue writs of election to fill such vacancies; Provided, that the legislature of any State may empower the executive thereof to make temporary appointment until the people fill the vacancies by election as the legislature may direct.

This Amendment shall not be so construed as to affect the election or term of any Senator chosen before it becomes valid as part of the Constitution.

ARTICLE XVIII.

Proposed by Congress December 19, 1917; proclaimed adopted
January 29, 1919.

Section 1. **After one year from the ratification of
this article the manufacture, sale, or transportation
of intoxicating liquors within, the importation thereof
into, or the exportation thereof from the United
States and all territory subject to the jurisdiction
thereof for beverage purposes is hereby prohibited.**[184]

[184] On June 7, 1920, the Supreme Court of the United
States, disposing in one opinion of seven cases arising in
New Jersey, Rhode Island, Massachusetts, Kentucky, Wisconsin, and Missouri, held that by Article V of the Constitution (Note 129) the power to make this Amendment was
reserved by the people. As the source of all power is in
the people, it is difficult to conceive of an invalid amendment if it has been carried through by regular proceedings.
While originally the people may not have believed a subject one for consideration in the Constitution, they may
change their opinion, and their will is the supreme law.
The Supreme Court said that the first section (the one
declaring the prohibition) "is operative throughout the
entire territorial limits of the United States, binds all
legislative bodies, courts, public officers and individuals
within those limits, and of its own force invalidates
every legislative act — whether by Congress, by a State
legislature, or by a territorial assembly — which authorizes
or sanctions what the section prohibits."

That gives a remarkably striking illustration of the practical operation of that marvelous invention of American
statesmanship, — the Constitution as the supreme law of
the land, before which all conflicting constitutions and laws
are nullities, as ineffectual as if they never existed. In like
manner the Fourteenth Amendment, as has been seen, struck

racial limitations out of northern as well as southern State constitutions, wiped away volumes of enactments by the Congress and by the legislatures of the States, and rendered useless except as history a great number of judicial decisions upon the status of the slave.

It was contended that "two-thirds of both Houses" in Article V means two thirds of the membership of each House, and that as such a vote did not propose this Amendment, it was invalid. But the Supreme Court repeated what it had held in an earlier case, that two thirds of the members present, assuming the presence of a quorum (majority), may propose an Amendment.

A score of proposals to amend the Constitution in this way had been made in Congress, beginning with a resolution of Senator Blair of New Hampshire in 1876.

Section 2. The Congress and the several States shall have concurrent power to enforce this article by appropriate legislation.[185]

[185] The meaning of this language provoked a great deal of discussion while the Amendment was pending. Where State and Federal courts have "concurrent jurisdiction" of a subject, for example, the one whose jurisdiction is first invoked retains the case to the exclusion of the other. Did Congress mean anything like that when it wrote "concurrent power" in the Amendment? Would the inadequate legislation of an unsympathetic State prevent Congress from legislating? Would early legislation by Congress exclude a State from the field? The Supreme Court said that the words do not mean joint power, or require that legislation by Congress must be sanctioned by a State, or that the power is divided along lines which distinguish State commerce from interstate.

It was evidently the purpose to make use of the experience of many of the States in enforcing prohibitory laws and to put with that experience the power of the

Nation, the National power to be employed more vigorously where a State might be indifferent.

Section 3. This article shall be inoperative unless it shall have been ratified as an amendment to the Constitution by the Legislatures of the several States, as provided in the Constitution, within seven years [186] **from the date of the submission hereof to the States by the Congress.**

[186] No other Amendment contains such a limitation as to time. This was introduced upon a showing that many old proposals are still pending, one against the extension of slavery. In 1873, in the days of the "salary grab", the Senate of Ohio took up and approved by resolution, after it had been pending for eighty-four years without ratification by three fourths of the States, what had been originally proposed as the Second Amendment, prohibiting a change of the pay of Congressmen until an election had intervened.

ARTICLE XIX.

Proposed by Congress June 5, 1919; proclaimed August 26, 1920.

Section 1. The right of citizens of the United States to vote shall not be denied or abridged by the United States or by any State on account of sex. [187]

[187] The resolution of proposal was first introduced in Congress by Senator A. A. Sargent of California at the request of Miss Susan B. Anthony, on June 10, 1878, nearly forty-one years before it was passed by both Houses.

Eleven years before that, when the Reform Bill of 1867 was pending in the English Parliament, which made manhood suffrage almost general by extending it beyond the upper and middle classes to which it had been limited by the Reform Bill of 1832, John Stuart Mill proposed an amendment that the Bill include suffrage by women. The proposal was first taken as "something droll" (McCarthy's "History of Our Own Times"), but it finally produced "a very interesting, grave, and able discussion in the House of Commons." The amendment received 73 votes; there were 196 against it. In 1884 the third Reform Bill extended suffrage to all males except paupers, lunatics, and criminals. The franchise was given to women in 1919, and the first woman to take a seat in the House of Commons, elected in November and admitted in December of that year, Lady Nancy Astor of Plymouth, was born in Virginia of the Langhorne family. The first woman entered the Australian Parliament in 1921, and in the same year Miss Agnes McPhail was elected to the Canadian Parliament. In March, 1922, the Committee for Privileges of the House of Lords approved the petition of Viscountess Rhondda for the seat which her father had occupied, but the House denied it.

In many States in the Union women enjoyed suffrage in State affairs before this Amendment. Wyoming enfranchised women in 1869, Colorado in 1893, Utah and Idaho in 1896, and Washington in 1910. In some other States they enjoyed suffrage with respect to minor offices. As the qualifications stated in the Constitution entitling one to a seat in the House of Representatives (Notes 8 and 9) are applicable to a woman, a female member of the House was elected by Montana in 1916, nearly four years before this Amendment was proclaimed. The first woman thus to be distinguished by a seat in the Congress of the United States was Miss Jeannette Rankin.

This Amendment, being the Supreme law of the land, rendered ineffectual forever the provisions in many Acts of Congress, in many State constitutions and in the enactments of many State legislatures containing the word "male" with respect to suffrage.

Section 2. Congress shall have power to enforce this Article by appropriate legislation.

ARTICLE XX

Proposed by Congress March 3, 1932; proclaimed February 6, 1933.

Section 1. The terms of the President and Vice President shall end at noon on the 20th day of January, and the terms of Senators and Representatives at noon on the third day of January, of the years in which such terms would have ended if this Article had not been ratified; and the terms of their successors shall then begin.[188]

[188] This provided a Congress organized and in readiness to cooperate with the new President when he should come in seventeen days later. Formerly, when Congress expired on March 4 and a President took office on that date, there was no organized legislative body to do business, nor would there be until the first Monday in December next unless the President should call in special session the Representatives and Senators elected in the preceding November with those in both Houses holding over. It was the practice of the outgoing President to call a special session of the Senate for March 4 so that it would be in readiness to confirm the appointments of the new President to the Cabinet and to other posts.

When terms began on March 4 following the election in November a member of the House of Representatives elected in November, 1930, for illustration, would serve a term from March 4, 1931, to March 4, 1933. But he might be defeated for re-election in November, 1932. Yet he would serve out the second or short session, from the first Monday in December, 1932, to March 4, 1933. During that time he was known as a "lame duck," still serving though rejected by his constituents. Thus this was called the "lame duck Amendment."

Terms of Representatives elected in 1932 and of Senators chosen in 1928, which would have expired in March, 1934,

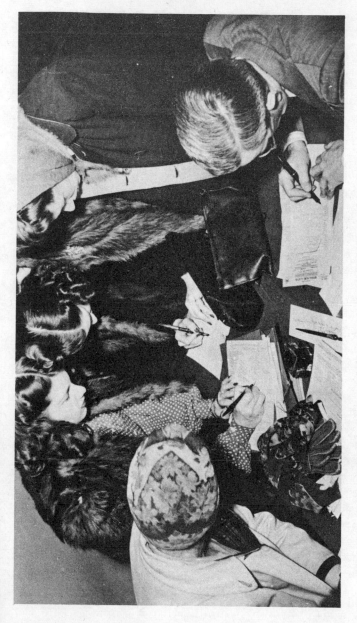

"The Congress shall have power to lay and collect taxes on incomes from whatever source derived"

The Archives Building in Washington, where the original signed copy of the Constitution is on view

were by this Amendment cut short on January 3. So was the term of the President elected in 1932.

Acting under authority given by Article I, section 4 (Note 26a), Congress in 1872 fixed the time for national elections as the first Tuesday after the first Monday in November.

Increased speed in travel had made unnecessary a long lapse of time between the election of public servants and their taking office.

Section 2. The Congress shall assemble at least once in every year, and such meeting shall begin at noon on the third day of January, unless they shall by law appoint a different day.[189]

[189] This section altered the provision of the original Constitution (Note 27) fixing "the first Monday in December" for the assembling of Congress.

Section 3. If, at the time fixed for the beginning of the term of the President, the President Elect shall have died, the Vice President Elect shall become President. If a President shall not have been chosen before the time fixed for the beginning of his term, or if the President Elect shall have failed to qualify, then the Vice President Elect shall act as President until a President shall have qualified; and the Congress may by law provide for the case wherein neither a President Elect nor a Vice President Elect shall have qualified, declaring who shall then act as President, or the manner in which one who is to act shall be selected, and such person shall act accordingly until a President or Vice President shall have qualified.[190]

[190] The Twelfth Amendment (page 231) did not cover the failure of both a President elect and a Vice President elect

to qualify. The latter half of the final sentence in the foregoing empowers Congress to meet such a contingency.

Section 4. The Congress may by law provide for the case of the death of any of the persons from whom the House of Representatives may choose a President, whenever the right of choice shall have devolved upon them, and for the case of the death of any of the persons from whom the Senate may choose a Vice President whenever the right of choice shall have devolved upon them.[191]

[191] This section further strengthens the Twelfth Amendment by empowering Congress to meet the possibility of the death of any of the three persons (page 231) from whom the House of Representatives might choose a President upon the failure of the electors to do so; and the death of either of the two persons (page 232) eligible in a like contingency to election by the Senate to the Vice Presidency.

Section 5. Sections 1 and 2 shall take effect on the fifteenth day of October following the ratification of this Article.[192]

[192] As the Amendment was proclaimed ratified on February 6, 1933, it went into effect in October of that year and affected elections thereafter.

Section 6. This Article shall be inoperative unless it shall have been ratified as an Amendment to the Constitution by the Legislatures of three-fourths of the several States within seven years from the date of its submission.[193]

[193] The first limitation on the time for the legislatures of the States to ratify a proposal by Congress to amend the Constitution was inserted in the Eighteenth or Prohibitory Amendment (Note 186).

ARTICLE XXI

Proposed by Congress February 20, 1933; proclaimed adopted December 5, 1933.

Section 1. **The Eighteenth Article of Amendment to the Constitution of the United States is hereby repealed.**[194]

[194] At the time of this proposal the Eighteenth or Prohibitory Amendment (Note 184) had been in effect for over thirteen years and ten months. It was the first grant of police power to the Nation. The police power over "the health, safety, morals, and general well-being of the people" resides inherently in the States. It was not the intention of the writers of the Constitution that the Nation should have any police power beyond that necessarily attending each special grant to it, as, for illustration, the implied power under the Money Clause to punish counterfeiting. Therefore, when the Nation took over the vast police duties imposed by the Eighteenth Amendment it found itself structurally unfitted to carry them. While "concurrent power" was left with the States to enforce prohibition along with the Nation (Note 185), they generally lost interest, especially as the aggressive government at Washington seemed desirous of going alone. The Amendment not only failed to meet the expectations of its proponents, but its operation was found hospitable to organized criminality. The proposal to revoke the Amendment was ratified within the short time of nine months and fifteen days.

Section 2. **The transportation or importation into any State, Territory, or Possession of the United States for delivery therein of Intoxicating Liquors, in violation of the laws thereof, is hereby prohibited.**[195]

[195] As far back as 1913 Congress exerted its power under the Commerce Clause to forbid the shipment of liquors (page 53) into States having prohibitory laws.

The Supreme Court of the United States held in 1936 that a law of California imposing a license on the privilege of bringing beer into the State was not, since this Amendment, an unreasonable burden on interstate commerce in violation of the Commerce Clause, as it would have been before the Amendment, which abrogated the right to import liquors. Other decisions springing from this Amendment have sustained similar regulations by States through license and taxation.

Section 3. This Article shall be inoperative unless it shall have been ratified as an Amendment to the Constitution by Conventions in the several States, as provided in the Constitution, within seven years from the date of the submission hereof to the States by the Congress.[196]

[196] The Constitution itself was by the Congress under the Articles of Confederation submitted to "conventions in the several States", as fear was held that three-fourths of the legislatures would not ratify it. But down to this proposal Congress never had submitted an amendment to conventions of delegates chosen by the people in the States to pass upon the particular proposition. While Article V (Note 129) authorizes Congress to submit a proposal either way, that discretion should be regardful of whether the proposition is to alter the constitutional structure, or only to extend the application of principles long in working effect.

This is the third proposal (Notes 186 and 192) to contain a time limit for ratification. A proposal in 1924 for a Child-Labor Amendment has been pending for sixteen years. It was rejected in 1925 by enough legislative bodies to defeat it, but in 1933 the national administration revived interest in it so as to cause some legislatures to change their rejections to ratifications. Yet it remains outside the Constitution.

ARTICLE XXII

Automatically effective February 26, 1951 when it was approved by 36th State Legislature.

No person shall be elected to the office of the President more than twice, and no person who has held the office of President, or acted as President, for more than two years of a term to which some other person was elected President shall be elected to the office of the President more than once.

But this Article shall not apply to any person holding the office of President when this Article was proposed by the Congress, and shall not prevent any person who may be holding the office of President, or acting as President, during the term within which this Article becomes operative from holding the office of President or acting as President during the remainder of such term.

As for more than a century and a half of unexampled social, civil, and material advancement, in which it has been the controlling force, the Constitution has applied itself, adapted itself, developed itself, amended itself, and, through stress and shock of civil war the like of which no other constitution ever felt, maintained its equilibrium, the American has reason to believe that his fundamental law contains inherently what the Scriptures call "the power of an endless life."

> "Love thou thy land, with love far-brought
> From out the storied Past, and used
> Within the Present, but transfused
> Through future time by power of thought.
>
> .   .   .   .
>
> "A land of settled government,
> A land of just and old renown,
> Where Freedom slowly broadens down
> From precedent to precedent "

APPENDIX A

DECLARATION OF INDEPENDENCE

The Declaration of Independence was adopted by the Continental Congress, in Philadelphia, on July 4, 1776, and was signed by John Hancock as President and by Charles Thomson as Secretary. It was published first on July 6 in the Pennsylvania Evening Post. A copy of the Declaration, engrossed on parchment, was signed by members of Congress on and after Aug. 2, 1776.

When, in the Course of human events, it becomes necessary for one people to dissolve the political bands which have connected them with another, and to assume among the powers of the earth, the separate and equal station to which the Laws of Nature and of Nature's God entitle them, a decent respect to the opinions of mankind requires that they should declare the causes which impel them to the separation.

We hold these truths to be self-evident, that all men are created equal, that they are endowed by their Creator with certain unalienable Rights, that among these are Life, Liberty and the pursuit of Happiness. That to secure these rights, Governments are instituted among Men, deriving their just powers from the consent of the governed. That whenever any Form of Government becomes destructive of these ends, it is the Right of the People to alter or to abolish it, and to institute new Government, laying its foundation on such principles and organizing its powers in such form, as to them shall seem most likely to effect their Safety and Happiness. Prudence, indeed, will dictate that Governments long established should not be changed for light and transient causes; and accordingly all experience hath shewn, that mankind are more disposed to suffer, while evils are sufferable, than to right themselves by abolishing the forms to which they are accustomed. But when a long train of abuses and usurpations, pursuing invariably the same object, evidence a design to reduce them under absolute Despotism, it is their right, it is their duty, to throw off such Government, and to provide new Guards for their future security. Such has been the patient sufferance of these Colonies; and such is now the necessity which constrains them to alter their former Systems of Government. The history of the present King of Great Britain is a history of repeated injuries and usurpations, all having in direct object the establishment of an absolute Tyranny over these States. To prove this, let Facts be submitted to a candid world.

He has refused his Assent to Laws, the most wholesome and necessary for the public good.

He has forbidden his Governors to pass Laws of immediate and pressing importance, unless suspended in their operation till his Assent should be obtained, and when so suspended, he has utterly neglected to attend to them.

He has refused to pass other Laws for the accommodation of large districts of people, unless those people would relinquish the right of Representation in the Legislature, a right inestimable to them and formidable to tyrants only.

He has called together legislative bodies at places, unusual, uncomfortable, and distant from the depository of their public Records, for the sole purpose of fatiguing them into compliance with his measures.

He has dissolved Representative Houses repeatedly, for opposing with manly firmness his invasions on the rights of the people.

He has refused for a long time, after such dissolutions, to cause others to be elected; whereby the Legislative powers, incapable of Annihilation, have returned to the People at large for their exercise; the State remaining in the meantime exposed to all the dangers of invasion from without, and convulsions within.

He has endeavored to prevent the population of these States; for that purpose obstructing the Laws for Naturalization of Foreigners; refusing to pass others to encourage their migrations hither, and raising the conditions of new Appropriations of Lands.

He has obstructed the Administration of Justice, by refusing his Assent to Laws for establishing Judiciary powers.

He has made Judges dependent on his Will alone, for the tenure of their offices, and the amount and payment of their salaries.

He has erected a multitude of New Offices, and sent hither swarms of Officers to harass our people, and eat out their substance.

He has kept among us, in times of peace, Standing Armies, without the Consent of our legislatures.

He has affected to render the Military independent of and superior to the Civil power.

He has combined with others to subject us to a jurisdiction foreign to our constitution and unacknowledged by our laws; giving his Assent to their Acts of pretended Legislation: For quartering large bodies of armed troops among us: For protecting them by a mock Trial from punishment for any Murders which they should commit on the Inhabitants of these States: For cutting off our Trade with all parts of the world: For imposing Taxes on us without our Consent: For depriving us in many cases of the benefits of Trial by Jury: For transporting us beyond Seas to be tried for pretended offenses: For abolishing the free System of English Laws in a neighbouring Province, establishing therein an Arbitrary government, and enlarging its Boundaries so as to render it at once an example and fit instrument for introducing the same absolute rule into these Colonies: For taking away our Charters, abolishing our most valuable Laws and altering fundamentally the Forms of our Governments: For suspending our own Legislatures and declaring themselves invested with power to legislate for us in all cases whatsoever.

He has abdicated Government here by declaring us out of his Protection and waging War against us.

He has plundered our seas, ravished our Coasts, burnt our towns, and destroyed the lives of our people.

He is at this time transporting large Armies of foreign Mercenaries to complete the works of death, desolation and tyranny, already begun with circumstances of cruelty and perfidy scarcely paralleled in the most barbarous ages, and totally unworthy the Head of a civilized nation.

He has constrained our fellow Citizens taken Captive on the high Seas to bear Arms against their Country, to become the executioners of their friends and Brethren, or to fall themselves by their Hands.

He has excited domestic insurrections amongst us, and has endeavoured to bring on the inhabitants of our frontiers, the merciless Indian Savages, whose known rule of warfare is an undistinguished destruction of all ages, sexes and conditions. In every stage of these Oppressions We have Petitioned for Redress in the most humble terms. Our repeated Petitions have been answered only by repeated injury. A Prince, whose character is thus marked by every act which may define a Tyrant, is unfit to be the ruler of a free people. Nor have We been wanting in attention to our British brethren. We have warned them from time to time of attempts by their legislature to extend an unwarrantable jurisdiction over us. We have reminded them of the circumstances of our emigration and settlement here. We have appealed to their native justice and magnanimity, and we have conjured them by the ties of our common kindred to disavow these usurpations, which would inevitably interrupt our connections and correspondence. They too have been deaf to the voice of justice and of consanguinity. We must, therefore, acquiesce in the necessity, which denounces our Separation, and hold them, as we hold the rest of mankind, Enemies in War, in Peace Friends.

WE, THEREFORE, the Representatives of the United States of America, in General Congress, Assembled, appealing to the Supreme Judge of the world for the rectitude of our intentions do, in the Name, and by authority of the good People of these Colonies, solemnly publish and declare, That these United Colonies are, and of Right ought to be, Free and Independent States: that they are Absolved from all Allegiance to the British Crown, and that all political connection between them and the State of Great Britain is and ought to be totally dissolved: and that as Free and Independent States, they have full Power to levy War, conclude Peace, contract Alliances, establish Commerce, and to do all other Acts and Things which Independent States may of right do. And for the support of this Declaration, with a firm reliance on the protection of Divine Providence, we mutually pledge to each other our Lives, our Fortunes, and our sacred Honor.

APPENDIX B

CONSTITUTION OF THE UNITED STATES OF AMERICA

THE PREAMBLE

WE, the people of the United States, in Order to form a more perfect Union, establish Justice, insure domestic Tranquillity, provide for the common defence, promote the general Welfare, and secure the Blessings of Liberty to ourselves and our Posterity, do ordain and establish this Constitution for the United States of America.

ARTICLE I

Section 1. All legislative Powers herein granted shall be vested in a Congress of the United States, which shall consist of a Senate and House of Representatives.

Section 2. The House of Representatives shall be composed of Members chosen every second Year by the People of the several States and the Electors in each State shall have the Qualifications requisite for Electors of the most numerous Branch of the State Legislature.

No Person shall be a Representative who shall not have attained to the Age of twenty-five Years, and been seven Years a Citizen of the United States, and who shall not, when elected, be an Inhabitant of that State in which he shall be chosen.

Representatives and direct Taxes shall be apportioned among the several States which may be included within this Union, according to their respective Numbers, which shall be determined by adding to the whole Number of free Persons, including those bound to Service for a Term of Years. and excluding Indians not taxed, three fifths of all other Persons. The actual Enumeration shall be made within three Years after the first Meeting of the Congress of the United States, and within every subsequent Term of ten Years, in such Manner as they shall by Law direct. The Number of Representatives shall not exceed one for every thirty Thousand, but each State shall have at Least one Representative; and until such enumeration shall be made. the State of New Hampshire shall be entitled to chuse three, Massachusetts eight, Rhode-Island and Providence Plantations one, Connecticut five, New-York six, New Jersey four, Pennsylvania eight, Delaware one, Maryland six, Virginia ten, North Carolina five. South Carolina five, and Georgia three.

When vacancies happen in the Representation from any State, the Executive Authority thereof shall issue Writs of Election to fill such Vacancies.

The House of Representatives shall chuse their Speaker and other Officers; and shall have the sole Power of Impeachment.

Section 3. The Senate of the United States shall be composed of two Senators from each State, chosen by the Legislature thereof, for six Years; and each Senator shall have one Vote.

Immediately after they shall be assembled in Consequence of the first Election, they shall be divided as equally as may be into three Classes. The Seats of the Senators of the first Class shall be vacated at the Expiration of the second Year, of the second Class at the Expiration of the fourth Year, and of the third Class at the Expiration of the sixth Year, so that one-third may be chosen every second Year; and if Vacancies happen by Resignation, or otherwise, during the Recess of the Legislature of any State, the Executive thereof may make temporary Appointments until the next Meeting of the Legislature, which shall then fill such Vacancies.

No Person shall be a Senator who shall not have attained to the Age of thirty Years, and be nine Years a Citizen of the United States, and who shall not, when elected, be an Inhabitant of that State for which he shall be chosen.

The Vice-President of the United States shall be President of the Senate, but shall have no Vote, unless they be equally divided.

The Senate shall chuse their other Officers, and also a President pro tempore, in the absence of the Vice-President, or when he shall exercise the Office of President of the United States.

The Senate shall have the sole Power to try all Impeachments. When sitting for that Purpose, they shall be on Oath or Affirmation. When the President of the United States is tried, the Chief Justice shall preside: And no Person shall be convicted without the Concurrence of two thirds of the Members present.

Judgment in Cases of Impeachment shall not extend further than to removal from office, and disqualification to hold and enjoy any Office of honor, Trust, or Profit under the United States: but the Party convicted shall nevertheless be liable and subject to Indictment, Trial, Judgment and Punishment, according to Law.

Section 4. The Times, Places, and Manner of holding Elections for Senators and Representatives, shall be prescribed in each State by the Legislature thereof; but the Congress may at any time by Law make or alter such Regulations, except as to the Places of chusing Senators.

The Congress shall assemble at least once in every Year, and such Meeting shall be on the first Monday in December, unless they shall by Law appoint a different Day.

Section 5. Each House shall be the Judge of the Elections, Returns and Qualifications of its own Members, and a Majority of each shall constitute a Quorum to do Business; but a smaller Number may adjourn from day to day, and may be authorized to compel the Attendance of absent Members, in such Manner, and under such Penalties as each House may provide.

Each House may determine the Rules of its Proceedings, punish its Members for disorderly Behavior and, with the Concurrence of two thirds, expel a Member.

Each House shall keep a Journal of its Proceedings, and from time to time publish the same, excepting such Parts as may in their Judgment require Secrecy; and the Yeas and Nays of the Members of either House on any question shall, at the Desire of one fifth of those Present, be entered on the Journal.

Neither House, during the Session of Congress, shall without the Consent of the other, adjourn for more than three days, nor to any other Place than that in which the two Houses shall be sitting.

Section 6. The Senators and Representatives shall receive a Compensation for their Services, to be ascertained by Law, and paid out of the Treasury of the United States. They shall in all Cases, except Treason, Felony, and Breach of the Peace, be privileged from Arrest during their Attendance at the Session of their respective Houses, and in going to and returning from the same; and for any Speech or Debate in either House, they shall not be questioned in any other Place.

No Senator or Representative shall, during the Time for which he was elected, be appointed to any civil Office under the Authority of the United States, which shall have been created, or the Emoluments whereof shall have been encreased during such time; and no Person holding any Office under the United States, shall be a Member of either House during his Continuance in Office.

Section 7. All bills for raising Revenue shall originate in the House of Representatives; but the Senate may propose or concur with Amendments as on other bills.

Every Bill which shall have passed the House of Representatives and the Senate, shall, before it become a Law, be presented to the President of the United States; If he approve he shall sign it, but if not he shall return it, with his Objections to that House in which it shall have originated, who shall enter the Objections at large on their Journal, and proceed to reconsider it. If after such Reconsideration two thirds of that House shall agree to pass the Bill, it shall be sent, together with the Objections, to the other House, by which it shall likewise be reconsidered, and if approved by two thirds of that House, it shall become a Law. But in all such Cases the Votes of both Houses shall be determined by Yeas and Nays and the Names of the Persons voting for and against the Bill shall be entered on the Journal of each House respectively. If any Bill shall not be returned by the President within ten Days (Sundays excepted) after it shall have been presented to him, the Same shall be a Law, in like Manner as if he had signed it, unless the Congress by their Adjournment prevent its Return, in which Case it shall not be a Law.

Every Order, Resolution, or Vote to which the Concurrence of the Senate and House of Representatives may be necessary (except on a question of Adjournment) shall be presented to the President of the United States; and, before the Same shall take Effect, shall be approved by him, or, being disapproved by him, shall be repassed by two thirds of the Senate and House of Representatives, according to the Rules and Limitations prescribed in the Case of a Bill.

Section 8. The Congress shall have Power to lay and collect Taxes, Duties, Imposts and Excises, to pay the Debts and provide for the common Defence and general Welfare of the United States; but all Duties, Imposts and Excises shall be uniform throughout the United States;

To borrow Money on the credit of the United States;

To regulate Commerce with foreign Nations, and among the several States, and with the Indian tribes;

To establish an uniform Rule of Naturalization, and uniform Laws on the subject of Bankruptcies throughout the United States;

To coin Money, regulate the Value thereof, and of foreign Coin, and fix the Standard of Weights and Measures;

To provide for the Punishment of counterfeiting the Securities and current Coin of the United States;

To establish Post Offices and post Roads;

To promote the Progress of Science and useful Arts, by securing for limited Times to Authors and Inventors the exclusive Right to their respective Writings and Discoveries;

To constitute Tribunals inferior to the supreme Court;

To define and punish Piracies and Felonies committed on the high Seas, and Offenses against the Law of Nations;

To declare War, grant Letters of Marque and Reprisal and make Rules concerning Captures on Land and Water;

To raise and support Armies, but no Appropriation of Money to that Use shall be for a longer Term than two Years;

To provide and maintain a Navy;

To make Rules for the Government and Regulation of the land and naval Forces;

To provide for calling forth the Militia to execute the Laws of the Union, suppress Insurrections and repel Invasions;

To provide for organizing, arming, and disciplining the Militia, and for governing such Part of them as may be employed in the Service of the United States, reserving to the States respectively, the Appointment of the Officers, and the Authority of training the Militia according to the discipline prescribed by Congress;

To exercise exclusive Legislation in all Cases whatsoever, over such District (not exceeding ten Miles square) as may, by Cession of particular States, and the Acceptance of Congress, become the Seat of the Government of the United States, and to exercise like Authority over all Places purchased by the Consent of the Legislature of the State in which the Same shall be, for the Erection of Forts, Magazines, Arsenals, dock-Yards, and other needful Buildings;—And

To make all Laws which shall be necessary and proper for carrying into Execution the foregoing Powers, and all other Powers vested by this Constitution in the Government of the United States, or in any Department or Officer thereof.

Section 9. The Migration or Importation of such Persons as any of the States now existing shall think proper to admit, shall not be prohibited by the Congress prior to the Year one thousand eight hundred and eight, but a Tax or duty may be imposed on such Importation, not exceeding ten dollars for each Person.

The privilege of the Writ of Habeas Corpus shall not be suspended, unless when in Cases of Rebellion or Invasion the public Safety may require it.

No Bill of Attainder or ex post facto Law shall be passed.

No Capitation, or other direct, Tax shall be laid unless in Proportion to the Census or Enumeration herein before directed to be taken.

No Tax or Duty shall be laid on Articles exported from any State.

No Preference shall be given by any Regulation of Commerce or Revenue to the Ports of one State over those of another: nor shall Vessels bound to, or from, one State, be obliged to enter, clear, or pay Duties in another.

No Money shall be drawn from the Treasury, but in Consequence of Appropriations made by Law; and a regular Statement and Account of the Receipts and Expenditures of all public Money shall be published from time to time.

No Title of Nobility shall be granted by the United States: And no Person holding any Office of Profit or Trust under them, shall, without the Consent of the Congress, accept of any present, Emolument, Office, or Title, of any kind whatever, from any King, Prince, or foreign State.

Section 10. No State shall enter into any Treaty, Alliance, or Confederation; grant Letters of Marque and Reprisal; coin Money; emit Bills of Credit; make any Thing but gold and silver Coin a Tender in Payment of Debts; pass any Bill of Attainder, ex post facto Law, or Law impairing the Obligation of Contracts, or grant any Title of Nobility.

No State shall, without the Consent of the Congress, lay any Imposts or Duties on Imports or Exports, except what may be absolutely necessary for executing its inspection Laws: and the net Produce of all Duties and Imposts, laid by any State on Imports or Exports, shall be for the Use of the Treasury of the United States; and all such Laws shall be subject to the Revision and controul of the Congress.

No State shall, without the Consent of Congress, lay any duty of Tonnage, keep Troops, or Ships of War in time of Peace, enter into any Agreement or Compact with another State, or with a foreign Power, or engage in War, unless actually invaded, or in such imminent Danger as will not admit of delay.

ARTICLE II

Section 1. The executive Power shall be vested in a President of the United States of America. He shall hold his Office during the Term of four Years, and, together with the Vice President, chosen for the same Term, be elected, as follows:

Each State shall appoint, in such Manner as the Legislature thereof may direct, a Number of Electors, equal to the whole Number of Senators and Representatives to which the State may be entitled in the Congress: but no Senator or Representative, or Person holding an Office of Trust or Profit under the United States, shall be appointed an Elector.

[The Electors shall meet in their respective States, and vote by Ballot for two persons, of whom one at least shall not be an inhabitant of the same State with themselves. And they shall make a List of all the Persons voted for, and of the Number of Votes for each; which List they shall sign and certify, and transmit sealed to the Seat of the Government of the United States, directed to the President of the Senate. The President of the Senate shall, in the Presence of the Senate and House of Representatives, open all the Certificates, and the Votes shall then be counted. The Person having the greatest Number of Votes shall be the President, if such Number be a Majority of the whole Number of Electors appointed; and if there be more than one who have such Majority, and have an equal Number of Votes, then the House of Representatives shall immediately chuse by Ballot one of them for President; and if no Person have a Majority, then from the five highest on the List the said House shall in like manner chuse the President. But in chusing the President, the Votes shall be taken by States, the Representation from each State having one Vote; A quorum for this Purpose shall consist of a Member or Members from two-thirds of the States, and a Majority of all the States shall be necessary to a Choice. In every Case, after the Choice of the President, the Person having the greatest Number of Votes of the Electors shall be the Vice President. But if there should remain two or more who have equal Votes, the Senate shall chuse from them by Ballot the Vice President.] This paragraph in brackets was superseded on September 25, 1804.

The Congress may determine the Time of chusing the Electors, and the Day on which they shall give their Votes; which Day shall be the same throughout the United States.

No person except a natural born Citizen, or a Citizen of the United States, at the time of the Adoption of this Constitution, shall be eligible to the Office of President; neither shall any Person be eligible to that Office who shall not have attained to the Age of thirty-five Years, and been fourteen Years a Resident within the United States.

In Case of the Removal of the President from Office, or of his Death, Resignation, or Inability to discharge the Powers and Duties of the said Office, the same shall devolve on the Vice President, and the Congress may by Law provide for the Case of Removal, Death, Resignation or Inability, both of the President and Vice President, declaring what Officer shall then act as President, and such Officer shall act accordingly, until the Disability be removed, or a President shall be elected.

The President shall, at stated Times, receive for his Services, a Compensation, which shall neither be encreased nor diminished during the Period for which he shall have been elected, and he shall not receive within that Period any other Emolument from the United States, or any of them.

Before he enter on the Execution of his Office, he shall take the following Oath or Affirmation:—"I do solemnly swear (or affirm) that I will faithfully execute the Office of President of the United States, and will to the best of my Ability, preserve, protect and defend the Constitution of the United States."

Section 2. The President shall be Commander in Chief of the Army and Navy of the United States, and of the Militia of the several States, when called into the actual Service of the United States; he may require the Opinion, in writing of the principal Officer in each of the executive Departments, upon any subject relating to the Duties of their respective Offices. and he shall have Power to grant Reprieves and Pardons for Offences against the United States, except in Cases of Impeachment.

He shall have Power, by and with the Advice and Consent of the Senate, to make Treaties, provided two-thirds of the Senators present concur; and he shall nominate, and by and with the Advice and Consent of the Senate, shall appoint Ambassadors, other public Ministers and Consuls, Judges of the supreme Court, and all other Officers of the United States, whose Appointments are not herein otherwise provided for, and which shall be established by Law: but the Congress may by Law vest the Appointment of such inferior Officers, as they think proper, in the President alone, in the Courts of Law, or in the Heads of Departments.

The President shall have the Power to fill up all Vacancies that may happen during the Recess of the Senate, by granting Commissions which shall expire at the End of their next Session.

Section 3. He shall from time to time give to the Congress Information of the State of the Union, and recommend to their Consideration such Measures as he shall judge necessary and expedient; he may, on extraordinary Occasions, convene both Houses, or either of them, and in Case of Disagreement between them, with Respect to the Time of Adjournment, he may adjourn them to such Time as he shall think proper; he shall receive Ambassadors and other public Ministers; he shall take Care that the Laws be faithfully executed, and shall Commission all the Officers of the United States.

Section 4. The President, Vice President and all civil Officers of the United States, shall be removed from Office on Impeachment for, and Conviction of, Treason, Bribery, or other high Crimes and Misdemeanors.

ARTICLE III

Section 1. The judicial Power of the United States, shall be vested in one supreme Court, and in such inferior Courts as the Congress may from time to time ordain and establish.

The Judges, both of the supreme and inferior Courts, shall hold their Offices during good Behaviour, and shall, at stated Times, receive for their Services a Compensation which shall not be diminished during their Continuance in Office.

Section 2. The judicial Power shall extend to all Cases, in Law and Equity, arising under this Constitution, the Laws of the United States, and Treaties made, or which shall be made, under their Authority;—to all cases Affecting Ambassadors, other public Ministers, and Consuls;—to all Cases of admiralty and maritime Jurisdiction;—to Controversies to which the United States shall be a Party;—to Controversies between two or more States;—between a State and Citizens of another State;—between Citizens of different States,—between Citizens of the same State claiming Lands under Grants of different States, and between a State, or the Citizens thereof, and foreign States, Citizens or Subjects.

In all Cases affecting Ambassadors, other public Ministers and Consuls, and those in which a State shall be Party, the supreme Court shall have original Jurisdiction. In all the other Cases before mentioned, the supreme Court shall have appellate Jurisdiction, both as to Law and Fact, with such Exceptions, and under such Regulations as the Congress shall make.

The Trial of all Crimes, except in Cases of Impeachment, shall be by Jury; and such Trial shall be held in the State where the said Crimes shall have been committed; but when not committed within any State, the Trial shall be at such Place or Places as the Congress may by Law have directed.

Section 3. Treason against the United States, shall consist only in levying War against them, or in adhering to their Enemies, giving them Aid and Comfort.

No Person shall be convicted of Treason unless on the Testimony of two Witnesses to the same overt Act, or on Confession in open Court.

The Congress shall have Power to declare the Punishment of Treason, but no Attainder of Treason shall work Corruption of Blood, or Forfeiture except during the Life of the Person attainted.

ARTICLE IV

Section 1. Full Faith and Credit shall be given in each State to the public Acts, Records, and judicial Proceedings of every other State. And the Congress may by general Laws prescribe the Manner in which such Acts, Records and Proceedings shall be proved, and the Effect thereof.

Section 2. The Citizens of each State shall be entitled to all Privileges and Immunities of Citizens in the several States.

A Person charged in any State with Treason, Felony, or other Crime, who shall flee from Justice, and be found in another State, shall on demand of the executive Authority of the State from which he fled, be delivered up, to be removed to the State having Jurisdiction of the Crime.

No Person held to Service or Labor in one State, under the Laws thereof, escaping into another, shall, in Consequence of any Law or Regulation therein, be discharged from such Service or Labor, but shall be delivered up on Claim of the Party to whom such Service or labor may be due.

Section 3. New States may be admitted by the Congress into this Union; but no new State shall be formed or erected within the Jurisdiction of any other State; nor any State be formed by the Junction of two or more States, or parts of States, without the Consent of the Legislatures of the States concerned as well as of the Congress.

The Congress shall have Power to dispose of and make all needful Rules and Regulations respecting the Territory or other Property belonging to the United States; and nothing in this Constitution shall be so construed as to Prejudice any Claims of the United States, or of any particular State.

Section 4. The United States shall guarantee to every State in this Union a Republican Form of Government, and shall protect each of them against Invasion; and on Application of the Legislature, or of the Executive (when the Legislature cannot be convened) against domestic Violence.

ARTICLE V

The Congress, whenever two-thirds of both Houses shall deem it necessary, shall propose Amendments to this Constitution, or, on the Application of the Legislatures of two-thirds of the several States, shall call a Convention for proposing Amendments, which, in either Case, shall be valid to all Intents and Purposes, as part of this Constitution, when ratified by the Legislatures of three-fourths of the several States, or by Conventions in three-fourths thereof, as the one or the other Mode of Ratification may be proposed by the Congress; Provided that no Amendment which may be made prior to the Year One thousand eight hundred and eight shall in any Manner affect the first and fourth Clauses in the Ninth Section of the first Article; and that no State, without its Consent, shall be deprived of its equal Suffrage in the Senate.

ARTICLE VI

All Debts contracted and Engagements entered into, before the Adoption of this Constitution, shall be as valid against the United States under this Constitution as the Confederation.

This Constitution, and the Laws of the United States which shall be made in Pursuance thereof; and all Treaties made, or which shall be made, under the Authority of the United States, shall be the supreme Law of the Land; and the Judges in every State shall be bound thereby, any Thing in the Constitution or Laws of any State to the Contrary notwithstanding.

The Senators and Representatives before mentioned, and the Members of the several State Legislatures, and all executive and judicial Officers, both of the United States and of the several States, shall be bound by Oath or Affirmation, to support this Constitution; but no religious Test shall ever be required as a Qualification to any Office or public Trust under the United States.

ARTICLE VII

The Ratification of the Conventions of nine States shall be sufficient for the Establishment of this Constitution between the States so ratifying the Same.

ARTICLES

IN ADDITION TO, AND AMENDMENT OF,
THE CONSTITUTION OF THE UNITED STATES OF AMERICA

ARTICLE I

Congress shall make no law respecting an establishment of religion, or prohibiting the free exercise thereof; or abridging the freedom of speech, or of the press; or the right of the people peaceably to assemble, and to petition the Government for a redress of grievances.

ARTICLE II

A well regulated Militia, being necessary to the security of a free State, the right of the people to keep and bear Arms shall not be infringed.

ARTICLE III

No Soldier shall, in time of peace be quartered in any house, without the consent of the Owner, nor in time of war, but in a manner to be prescribed by law.

ARTICLE IV

The right of the people to be secure in their persons, houses, papers, and effects, against unreasonable searches and seizures, shall not be violated, and no Warrants shall issue, but upon probable cause, supported by Oath or affirmation, and particularly describing the place to be searched, and the persons or things to be seized.

ARTICLE V

No person shall be held to answer for a capital, or otherwise infamous crime, unless on a presentment or indictment of a Grand Jury, except in cases arising in the land or naval forces, or in the Militia, when in actual service in time of War or public danger; nor shall any person be subject for the same offence to be twice put in jeopardy of life or limb; nor shall be compelled in any criminal case to be a witness against himself, nor be deprived of life, liberty, or property, without due process of law; nor shall private property be taken for public use, without just compensation

ARTICLE VI

In all criminal prosecutions, the accused shall enjoy the right to a speedy and public trial, by an impartial jury of the State and district wherein the crime shall have been committed, which district shall have been previously ascertained by law, and to be informed of the nature and cause of the accusation; to be confronted with the witnesses against him; to have compulsory process for obtaining witnesses in his favor, and to have the Assistance of Counsel for his defence.

ARTICLE VII

In suits at common law, where the value in controversy shall exceed twenty dollars, the right of trial by jury shall be preserved, and no fact tried by a jury, shall be otherwise re-examined in any Court of the United States, than according to the rules of the common law.

ARTICLE VIII

Excessive bail shall not be required, nor excessive fines imposed, nor cruel and unusual punishments inflicted.

ARTICLE IX

The enumeration in the Constitution, of certain rights, shall not be construed to deny or disparage others retained by the people.

ARTICLE X

The powers not delegated to the United States by the Constitution, nor prohibited by it to the States, are reserved to the States respectively, or to the people.

ARTICLE XI

The Judicial power of the United States shall not be construed to extend to any suit in law or equity, commenced or prosecuted against one of the

United States by Citizens of another State, or by Citizens or Subjects of any Foreign State. ·

ARTICLE XII

The Electors shall meet in their respective states and vote by ballot for President and Vice-President, one of whom, at least, shall not be an inhabitant of the same state with themselves; they shall name in their ballots the person voted for as President, and in distinct ballots the person voted for as Vice-President, and they shall make distinct lists of all persons voted for as President and of all persons voted for as Vice-President, and of the number of votes for each, which lists they shall sign and certify, and transmit sealed to the seat of the government of the United States, directed to the President of the Senate;—

The President of the Senate shall, in the presence of the Senate and House of Representatives, open all the certificates and the votes shall then be counted;—

The person having the greatest number of votes for President shall be the President, if such number be a majority of the whole number of Electors appointed; and if no person have such majority, then from the persons having the highest numbers not exceeding three on the list of those voted for as President, the House of Representatives shall choose immediately, by ballot, the President. But in choosing the President the votes shall be taken by states, the representation from each state having one vote; a quorum for this purpose shall consist of a member or members from two-thirds of the states, and a majority of all the states shall be necessary to a choice. And if the House of Representatives shall not choose a President whenever the right of choice shall devolve upon them, before the fourth day of March next following, then the Vice-President shall act as President, as in the case of the death or other constitutional disability of the President. The person having the greatest number of votes as Vice-President, shall be the Vice-President, if such number be a majority of the whole number of Electors appointed, and if no person have a majority, then from the two highest numbers on the list, the Senate shall choose the Vice-President; a quorum for the purpose shall consist of two-thirds of the whole number of Senators, and a majority of the whole number shall be necessary to a choice. But no person constitutionally ineligible to the office of President shall be eligible to that of Vice-President of the United States.

ARTICLE XIII

Section 1. Neither slavery nor involuntary servitude, except as a punishment for crime whereof the party shall have been duly convicted, shall exist within the United States, or any place subject to their jurisdication.

Section 2. Congress shall have power to enforce this article by appropriate legislation.

ARTICLE XIV

Section 1. All persons born or naturalized in the United States, and subject to the jurisdiction thereof, are citizens of the United States and of the State wherein they reside. No State shall make or enforce any law which shall abridge the privileges or immunities of citizens of the United States; nor shall any State deprive any person of life, liberty, or property, without due process of law; nor deny to any person within its jurisdiction the equal protection of the laws.

Section 2. Representatives shall be apportioned among the several States according to their respective numbers, counting the whole number of persons in each State, excluding Indians not taxed. But when the right to vote at any election for the choice of Electors for President and Vice-President of the United States, Representatives in Congress, the Executive and Judicial officers of a State, or the members of the Legislature thereof, is denied to any of the male inhabitants of such State, being twenty-one years of age, and citizens of the United States, or in any way abridged, except for participation in rebellion, or other crime, the basis of representation therein shall be reduced in the proportion which the number of such male citizens shall bear to the whole number of male citizens twenty-one years of age in such State.

Section 3. No person shall be a Senator or Representative in Congress, or elector of President and Vice-President, or hold any office, civil or military, under the United States, or under any State, who, having previously taken an oath, as a member of Congress, or as an officer of the United States, or as a member of any State legislature, or as an executive or judicial officer of any State, to support the Constitution of the United States, shall have engaged in insurrection or rebellion against the same, or given aid or comfort to the enemies thereof. But Congress may by a vote of two-thirds of each House, remove such disability.

Section 4. The validitv of the public debt of the United States, authorized by law, including debts incurred for payment of pensions and bounties for services in suppressing insurrection or rebellion, shall not be questioned. But neither the United States nor any State shall assume or pay any debt or obligation incurred in aid of insurrection or rebellion against the United States, or any claim for the loss or emancipation of any slave; but all such debts, obligations and claims shall be held illegal and void.

Section 5. The Congress shall have power to enforce, by appropriate legislation, the provisions of this article.

ARTICLE XV

Section 1. The right of citizens of the United States to vote shall not be denied or abridged by the United States or by any State on account of race, color, or previous condition of servitude.

Section 2. The Congress shall have power to enforce this article by appropriate legislation.

ARTICLE XVI

The Congress shall have power to lay and collect taxes on incomes, from whatever source derived, without apportionment among the several States, and without regard to any census or enumeration.

ARTICLE XVII

The Senate of the United States shall be composed of two Senators from each State, elected by the people thereof, for six years; and each Senator shall have one vote.

The electors in each State shall have the qualifications requisite for electors of the most numerous branch of the State legislatures.

When vacancies happen in the representation of any State in the Senate, the executive authority of such State shall issue writs of election to fill such vacancies; Provided, that the legislature of any State may empower the executive thereof to make temporary appointment until the people fill the vacancies by election as the legislature may direct.

This Amendment shall not be so construed as to affect the election or term of any Senator chosen before it becomes valid as part of the Constitution.

Article XVIII

Section 1. After one year from the ratification of this article the manufacture, sale, or transportation of intoxicating liquors within, the importation thereof into, or the exportation thereof from the United States and all territory subject to the jurisdiction thereof for beverage purposes is hereby prohibited.

Section 2. The Congress and the several States shall have concurrent power to enforce this article by appropriate legislation.

Section 3. This article shall be inoperative unless it shall have been ratified as an amendment to the Constitution by the Legislatures of the several States, as provided in the Constitution, within seven years from the date of the submission hereof to the States by the Congress.

Article XIX

Section 1. The right of citizens of the United States to vote shall not be denied or abridged by the United States or by any State on account of sex.

Section 2. Congress shall have power to enforce this Article by appropriate legislation.

Article XX

Section 1. The terms of the President and Vice-President shall end at noon on the 20th day of January, and the terms of Senators and Representatives at noon on the third day of January, of the years in which such terms would have ended if this Article had not been ratified; and the terms of their successors shall then begin.

Section 2. The Congress shall assemble at least once in every year, and such meeting shall begin at noon on the third day of January, unless they shall by law appoint a different day.

Section 3. If, at the time fixed for the beginning of the term of the President, the President Elect shall have died, the Vice-President Elect shall become President. If a President shall not have been chosen before the time fixed for the beginning of his term, or if the President Elect shall have failed to qualify, then the Vice-President Elect shall act as President until a President shall have qualified; and the Congress may by law provide for the case wherein neither a President Elect nor a Vice-President Elect shall have qualified, declaring who shall then act as President, or the manner in which one who is to act shall be selected, and such person shall act accordingly until a President or Vice-President shall have qualified.

Section 4. The Congress may by law provide for the case of the death of any of the persons from whom the House of Representatives may choose a President, whenever the right of choice shall have devolved upon them, and for the case of the death of any of the persons from whom the Senate may choose a Vice-President whenever the right of choice shall have devolved upon them.

Section 5. Sections 1 and 2 shall take effect on the fifteenth day of October following the ratification of this Article.

Section 6. This Article shall be inoperative unless it shall have been ratified as an Amendment to the Constitution by the Legislatures of three-fourths of the several States within seven years from the date of its submission.

ARTICLE XXI

Section 1. The Eighteenth Article of Amendment to the Constitution of the United States is hereby repealed.

Section 2. The transportation or importation into any State, Territory, or Possession of the United States for delivery therein of Intoxicating Liquors, in violation of the laws thereof, is hereby prohibited.

Section 3. This Article shall be inoperative unless it shall have been ratified as an Amendment to the Constitution by Conventions in the several States, as provided in the Constitution, within seven years from the date of the submission hereof to the States by the Congress.

ARTICLE XXII

No person shall be elected to the office of the President more than twice, and no person who has held the office of President, or acted as President, for more than two years of a term to which some other person was elected President shall be elected to the office of the President more than once.

But this Article shall not apply to any person holding the office of President when this Article was proposed by the Congress, and shall not prevent any person who may be holding the office of President, or acting as President, during the term within which this Article becomes operative from holding the office of President or acting as President during the remainder of such term.

APPENDIX C

A LIST OF THE LEADING CASES EXPOUND-ING THE CONSTITUTION, WITH NOTES INDICATING THE TENOR OF EACH CASE

Table of Cases

COURTS,
CRIMINAL PROCEDURE,

DARTMOUTH COLLEGE CASE,
DUE PROCESS OF LAW,

EDITOR. *See* MAIL; NEWSPAPER; TRIAL.
EIGHTEENTH AMENDMENT,
ELECTIONS, CORRUPT PRACTICES IN,
EMANCIPATION PROCLAMATION,
EQUAL PROTECTION,

INDEX

ADAMS, JOHN. Vote as Vice-President saved neutrality, 20; oral messages to Congress, 122; strife over appointment of judges by, 132; Sedition Law in term of, 200.

Adams, John Quincy, on Jefferson's purchase of Louisiana, 81.

Alien, Act of Congress restricts ownership of land in Territories by, 57; regulations various as to owning of land by, 56; privileged to vote in some States, 57; American woman marrying, forfeits citizenship, 238; State constitutional provision excluding, labor void, 243. *See* also NATURALIZATION.

Alien Contract Labor Law of 1885, 6.

Amendment, resolution for, need not be signed by President, 42; respecting title of nobility failed, 90; Congress by two-thirds vote members present may propose, 170, 255; Congress may determine mode of ratification, 170; conventions in States ratified, 170, 262; legislatures have not yet proposed, 170; legislatures of two-thirds of States may call convention, 170; ratification of, 170; cannot be ratified by referendum, 171; State cannot withdraw ratification, 171, 255; in other countries, 172; Lecky praised plan of, 172; Washington for, not usurpation, 172; suggested by Presidents, 173; examples of late proposals for, 174; slavery not to be affected prior to 1808 by, 174; State cannot be deprived of equal suffrage in Senate by, without consent, 174; and Bill of Rights, 194; first resolution proposing, 194; long period without, 232.

Anti-Trust Laws, 52.

Appointment to Office, and Tenure of Office Act of 1867, 16, 120; Congress may direct, of inferior grades, 120; objection in Constitutional Convention to power of, 120; power of, in actual practice, 120; vacancies filled by President during recess of Senate, 121; with consent of Senate President has power of, 120.

Appropriation, Jackson on menace of Congressional, 45; other Presidents on abuse of, 46; no money drawn from treasury except by, 88. *See* also MONEY.

Arms, right to bear, shall not be infringed by Congress, 206; State law may limit, 206.

Army, Congress alone raises and supports, 73; no appropriation for, for more than two years, 73; English fear of standing, 73; Hamilton's views on, 74; opposition to, in Constitutional Convention, 74; raising and equipment of, in World War I, 75; not dangerous at home, 75; rules governing, made by Congress, 76; President commander in chief of, 110. *See* also QUARTERING TROOPS; WAR.

Arthur, Chester Alan, vetoed objectionable appropriations by Congress, 46.

251; Act of 1919 invalid as to Federal judges' salaries, 135, 252; Taney protested Civil War tax, 135; salary of President not subject to, 136.

Insular Cases, Congress prepares acquired territory for Union, 72.

Interstate Commerce Commission, 52, 133.

Iron-Clad Oath, 86, 182.

JACKSON, ANDREW, on menace of Congressional appropriations, 45; vetoed appropriation bills not for general welfare, 45; asked discharge from prison and liability of debtor, 59; asked Congress to exclude abolitionist newspapers from mail, 204; bail discussed for assailant of, 222.

James I, of England, Hallam's comment on execution of Raleigh by, 151.

Jefferson, Thomas, opinion on extent of veto power, 39; with Hamilton helped locate National capital, 78; believed amendment necessary for public improvements, 80; questioned constitutional power to purchase Louisiana, 80; Bill of Attainder in Parliament against, 85; favored one term for President but served two, 101; elected by House of Representatives, 106; introduced written messages to Congress, 122; his action in prosecution of Burr, 150; worked for religious freedom in Virginia, 198; opposed too much government at Washington, 226.

Jenks, Edward, on decline in value of English money, 37.

Jeopardy, explanation of the term, 211; accused not to be placed in, twice, 211.

Johnson, Andrew, controversy with Congress over Reconstruction, 15; impeached by House of Representatives, 15; immediate cause of impeachment, 16; failure to convict, 16; vetoed Tenure of Office Act, 16; humorous comment on his view of power, 17; Christmas-day pardon for those in Civil War, 113.

Judges (State), and treaty as supreme law, 178; bound by National Constitution, Laws and Treaties, 179; Dicey on effect of this obligation, 181; required to take oath to support Constitution, 182.

Judicial Department, Fiske on importance of American judiciary, 131; judicial power vested in Supreme and inferior courts, 131; compensation of judges not to be diminished, 133, 135; term of judges during good behavior, 133; American plan of, followed elsewhere, 134; Lecky on status of judges, 134; terms of judges in other countries, 134; income tax invalid as to salaries of judges, 135; court acts only when case is brought, 136; judicial powers of, 136, 138, 139, 140, 141, 142, 144; restrictions on judicial powers of, 137, 166-168, 228; designed to be free from local influence, 137; Hamilton on relative powers of three departments, 137; Articles of Confederation provided no judicial system, 137; United States makes general use of its courts, 139; Constitution makes justiciable questions formerly met by force, 140, 141; United States removes cases from State courts, 140; Dicey's opinion of working of, 180, 181. *See also* COURTS (Inferior); SUPREME COURT.

Jury, trial by, demanded in Colonial Declaration of Rights 1765 and 1774, 145; trial for crimes except impeachment by, 145; cannot be superseded by military court in time of peace, 146; defined, 146; in civil cases involving over twenty dollars, 146, 221; of State and district where crime committed, 147; provision for, in early State constitutions, 146. *See* also TRIAL.

LABOR, Contract Labor Law of 1885 referred to, 6; National Labor Relations Act upheld by Supreme Court, 53; hours of, may be limited, 239, 242; laws for benefit of, generally upheld, 239, 240; minimum wage law upheld, 240; State may employ only citizens of United States if desired, 240; length of working day for women may be fixed, 242; minimum wages and regulated working conditions for women and children held legal, 242; aliens cannot be excluded by State from employment, 243; employment of children may be prohibited, 243; safeguards on machinery and semi-monthly wage payments may be required, 243; payment in script may be forbidden, 243.

Lands, aliens may hold in some States, 57. *See* also PUBLIC LANDS; WESTERN LANDS.

Law, how enacted in United States, 38; resolution to amend Constitution not a law, 42; to be faithfully executed by President, 126; Woodrow Wilson on this power, 126.

Lecky, W. E. H., on bills of attainder in America, 85; on the status of judges, 134; praises plan of amending Constitution, 172.

Legal Tender, Act of Congress sustained, 48, 61, 132; the "Greenback" Cases, 48; paper money of Civil War made, 48; power to "emit bills" refused by Convention, 48; greenbacks redeemed, 49; issue of paper money after Civil War upheld, 49; State may make only gold and silver, 91. *See* also MONEY.

Legislative Department, all powers vested in a Congress, 7; consists of Senate and House of Representatives, 7; two branches indispensably necessary, 7; Monroe on fundamental importance of, 7; one house under Articles of Confederation, 7; Colonial Declaration of Rights 1774, for two houses, 195. *See* also CONGRESS.

Letters of Marque and Reprisal. Congress can grant, 70, 73.

Liberty, blessings of, one purpose of Constitution, 5; not to be deprived of, except by due process of law, 241; labor laws not denial of, 242; what is included in term, 242; laws prohibiting employment of children not denial of, 243; not infringed by compulsory vaccination, 243.

Life, not to be deprived of, by Nation or State except by due process of law, 241.

Liquors, intoxicating, Eighteenth Amendment sustained, 254; manufacture, sale and transportation of, prohibited, 254; Congress and States have concurrent power over, 255; Eighteenth Amendment repealed by Twenty-first, 261.

Lincoln, Abraham, declaration regarding the Union, 3; in reaper patent case, 66; held to be without power to suspend *habeas corpus*, 83; Congress granted power

Do You Know The Constitution?

Or think you ought to know it?

Or wish to know *more* about it?

Then you need this book.

Our Constitution is the best plan ever made to assure freedom and to release the creative powers of men. It guarantees all the freedoms. Its guarantees of life, liberty and property made possible the American way of life. They stimulated more new enterprise and invention and gave us in this country a higher standard of living, better housing, more food and greater freedom in our civil, religious and personal lives than any other people in history have enjoyed.

Our Constitution is a landmark in the age-long struggle for the liberty of the individual. In it are guaranteed all the freedoms. It is your shield and armor so long as its provisions prevail and so long as the majority of our people sustain them in their original strength and significance.

There is no more universally useful book on the Constitution than the one now before you. Phrase by phrase, the Constitution is examined and thoroughly and fascinatingly explained.

Has this book helped you and given you inspiration? You too may wish to do what you can to keep the Constitution alive in minds of your fellow citizens. Extra copies may be ordered from your bookstore or by mail direct.